THE SEASONAL FESTIVALS AS SOUL EXPERIENCE

Rudolf Steiner
(1923)

THE SEASONAL FESTIVALS AS SOUL EXPERIENCE

The Human Being in Relation to Individual Spiritual Beings

Eleven Lectures held in Bern, Dornach, Prague, Stuttgart, and Berlin from April 6 to July 11, 1923

TRANSLATION BY
AGNES SCHNEEBERG-DE STEUR

INTRODUCTION BY
CLIFFORD VENHO

RUDOLF STEINER

SteinerBooks

CW 224

SteinerBooks | Anthroposophic Press
834 Main Street, P.O. Box 358
Spencertown, New York 12165
www.steinerbooks.org

Original translation from German by Agnes Schneeberg-de Steur
Introduction by Clifford Venho

This book is volume 224 in the Collected Works (CW) of Rudolf Steiner, published by SteinerBooks, 2025. It is a translation of *Die menschliche Seele in ihrem Zusammenhang mit göttlich-geistigen Individualitäten. Die Verinnerlichung der Jahresfeste*, 4th edition, published by Rudolf Steiner Verlag, Dornach, Switzerland, 2015.

ISBN: 978-1-62148-181-2
eBook ISBN: 978-1-62148-182-9

Printed in the United States of America by Versa Press

CONTENTS

Our Thought Life in Sleeping and Waking and in the Existence after Death

STUTTGART, JUNE 21, 1923

In earthly life, the life of thought is the most valuable thing for human beings. The life of emotions and of will works from the unconscious, just as it also works unconsciously during sleep. Thoughts live in the physical and etheric bodies. After death, they melt away as these bodies dissolve. But what the I and the astral body unconsciously experienced during the nights—going over our earthly life in the light of the moral world order—now becomes conscious. From what is experienced spiritually the spiritual germ of our next earthly life is formed. Then we can no longer perceive the spirit world and develop an interest in our new earthly life and our ancestors before we descend again. We grow into our physical heredity from the spiritual world. Our spiritual origin becomes embedded in the nerves, the earthly side lives in the blood. Freedom exists only in the pivoting point of the two balance beams: offspring of heaven versus seed of the earth, spiritual determination versus natural causality.

The Hollowness of Words and the Shallowness of Contemporary Thinking

An Evaluation of Mauthner, Rubner, Schweitzer

STUTTGART, JULY 4, 1923

In his *Critique of Language*, Fritz Mauthner points to the unreality of our words with respect to the word "soul." Anthroposophy points to the reality—thinking as a reflection of the physical brain and as the sculpting quality of thought-force in the formation of the body; feeling as an earthly phenomenon and as a legacy from pre-earthly life, directed toward the spirit; willing as a conscious experience and as something eternal that is working on karma. Then there are realities behind the words thinking, feeling, and willing. The lack of clarity of contemporary thinking, illustrated in a speech of Max Rubner. The lack of wakefulness in thinking, illustrated in Albert Schweitzer's recent publication.

The Four Members of the Human Being Intellectual Thinking versus the Moral-Religious Experience

STUTTGART, JULY 11, 1923

The four members of the human being come from four different worlds: the physical body from the earth world containing earthly laws, the etheric body from the etheric world, which intensifies at the periphery of the world; the astral body from the astral realm where earthly law transitions to cosmic law; the I from yet another world. Each of these worlds has its own laws. Their working together gives rise to the human being. The possibility of freedom arises because of the separation of the etheric body and physical body from the astral body and the I during sleep. The nourishment of the soul is morality and religion, which today, with our bodies being permeated by electrical currents, can only be attained through increased strength. The Anthroposophical Society aims to develop this strength.

pages 83–102

Three Stages in the Awakening of the Human Soul

PRAGUE, APRIL 28, 1923

As the child develops, it learns to walk, speak, and think. Thinking can only develop from speaking. In our pre-earthly existence, we live in a living stream of thought with the Angeloi; from this, the forces of thinking develop in earthly life; from our association with the Archangeloi, we gain the ability to speak; from our association with the Archai, we gain the forces of standing upright and using our limbs. In our earthly life, we enter into a relationship with these higher beings each time we sleep, but in order to do this in the right way, we need idealism in thought, speech, and deeds. This leads us after death to a conscious relationship with the first hierarchy. In the next life, the consequences of our previous earthly life appear in the form of learning to walk in association with the Archai; learning to speak is made possible by the Archangeloi in conjunction with the second hierarchy; thinking is given to us by the Angeloi in association with the first hierarchy.

pages 103–114

Anthroposophy as a Path toward a Deeper Understanding of the Mystery of Easter

PRAGUE, APRIL 29, 1923

The soul life of humanity is transformed in the course of development. Until the fourth century AD, the pre-earthly living thinking continued in earthly life. Then humanity advanced toward dead thinking, which allows for an awareness of freedom. The appearance of Christ was still experienced through living thinking as the appearance of the only divine being who descended from the pre-earthly into the earthly realm through birth and death and who came from the sun to the earth to share humanity's fate of going through birth and death. Through Christ's overcoming of death, the fear of the finality of death was overcome. Gnosis still held on to these spiritual views. Augustine could no longer understand them. Today they have been completely lost. Christ is seen as the "simple man from Nazareth"; Ranke's historiography without the Christ-event. The connection with Christ must be spiritually rediscovered. Anthroposophy provides the tools.

pages 115–131

The Revelation of Ascension and the Mystery of Pentecost

DORNACH, MAY 7, 1923

The picture of Ascension seems to contradict the fact that Christ will remain with the earth forever. Since the midpoint of the evolution of the earth in the middle of Atlantis, the earth has been dying, along with plants, animals, and physical human beings. The geologist, Eduard Suess, confirms the dying of the mineral element. The etheric body of the human being tends to strive toward the sun, so that humanity would no longer be able to incarnate in the future. Christ gave the etheric body and the physical body new strength. The Mystery of Golgotha is an objective occurrence; it took place for all human beings, regardless of their creeds or affiliations. The disciples experienced this in the Ascension image. In the Pentecost experience, they felt the Christ-force entering the I and the astral body; to experience this, the individual human being must acquire an understanding of the Mystery of Golgotha. After death, every human being experiences both images.

pages 132–145

The Mood of Saint John's
The Heightened Awareness at Saint John's Tide

DORNACH, JUNE 24, 1923

The physical body lives in the daily cycle, the soul in the yearly cycle, the spirit in the passage of time. New tendencies in thinking and feeling among the younger generation point to a new era. It demands spiritual vision as a counterbalance to the narrow horizons of materialism. Example given: Attempts to make plant growth independent of cosmic influences were only successful because researchers made use of ahrimanic sunlight, electricity, which has its origin in the recapitulation of the Sun phase during the Earth phase of evolution. This kind of research needs a spirit-based counter pole through anthroposophy. The appropriate mood of St. John's tide can be achieved by sharpening our understanding of today's world-historical moment.

pages 146–161

Regaining the Living Source of Speech through the Christ-impulse
The Michael-thought as an Appeal to the Human Will

DORNACH, APRIL 13, 1923

The evolution of human language is a reflection of the development of the Archangeloi, the spirits of language. Until the later Atlantean period, language was an expression of will, because the Archangeloi received it as intuition from the second hierarchy; until the Greek period, language was an expression of feeling, because the Archangeloi received it as inspiration from the first hierarchy; since

INTRODUCTION

CLIFFORD VENHO

1923 WAS A year of trials for Rudolf Steiner and the anthroposophical movement. Having suffered the loss of the Goetheanum, that house of the Word into which he had poured his forces for ten years, Steiner was faced with the possible, and even likely, splintering of the anthroposophical movement and its Society. He expressed this in potent words in Dornach on January 14, 1923, shortly after the fire:

> The misfortune that has befallen us should first and foremost be a wake-up call to do something about the Anthroposophical Society to make it a reality. . . . The living stream from human being to human being within the Anthroposophical Society, this must be there. A certain lovelessness has so often taken the place of mutual trust in the most recent phase of the Anthroposophical Society, and if this lovelessness continues to gain prevalence, then the Anthroposophical Society must decay.
>
> . . . Today, in these times, when slander hails upon the window, some people long for all kinds of esotericism. Yes, my dear friends, esotericism is here. Take hold of it! But that which is esoteric above all else within the whole Anthroposophical Society, that is the will to awaken. This will to awaken must take hold in the first place within the Anthroposophical Society. Then, it will be a radiating point for the awakening of the whole present civilization.*

In January and February, 1923, these difficulties weighed upon Rudolf Steiner, requiring him to constantly travel to Stuttgart to deal with the disfunction in the Society and the initiatives there. The "Stuttgart System," as he called it, was characterized by a lack

* *1923: Year of Destiny in the History of the Anthroposophical Society* (CW 259), trans. Joshua Kelberman (forthcoming from SteinerBooks, 2025).

of communication between colleagues, a bureaucratization of institutions, a certain "lovelessness," and a splitting of the practical work from its source in anthroposophy. The daughter movements had started to forget the mother.

Rudolf Steiner emphasized that beginning in 1918, various practical initiatives were incorporated into the "ready-made" Anthroposophical Society. Anthroposophy itself started to get lost in the attempt to establish all kinds of organizations and institutions, often with a noticeable lack of follow-through. Convenience and comfort were sought in place of integrity and inner coherence. Steiner said at the time:

> Actual leadership is entirely missing. And that's why there had to be talk of the "Stuttgart System," which consists in the fact that everything possible is grafted onto the Anthroposophical Society, but no effort is made to work for anthroposophy. . . . Everywhere one is choosing the most comfortable paths and then leaving them again, concerning oneself with them no further. Sitting upon curule chairs without any activity! All this is typical of the "Stuttgart System."[†]

The Delegates Conference, during which Rudolf Steiner gave important lectures on anthroposophical community building,[‡] took place from February 25 to 28, 1923, in the large hall of the Siegle House in Stuttgart. It was the first of many important turning-points in the course of the year that culminated in the Christmas Conference 1923/24. Delegates from the Stuttgart organizations and the Branch gathered to determine the fate of the Society. As Steiner stated during the Delegates Conference:

> It is perhaps truly the case (although this has not been emphasized thoroughly enough) that the destiny of the Society depends on these three days. Should we not come to a result in these three days, there remains nothing left for me to do, but that I myself turn to each individual member of the Society so that what needs to be done will

---

[†] Ibid.

[‡] See *Awakening to Community* (CW 257).

> be carried out. So, should a reorganization take place from out of the Society itself, then it must occur in these three days.[§]

One of the most contentious elements at the time was the clash between the older and younger generations. The two groups had come to an impasse and further positive collaboration seemed impossible. The solution to this situation was proposed by Rudolf Steiner during the Delegates Conference, and initially it seemed radical to many: the creation of a separate Free Anthroposophical Society in Germany. As Marie Steiner, who was present during the deliberations, reports:

> Two groups of people in this hall cannot understand each other, but both want to stand up for anthroposophy: That is the reality of the present situation. Since there is now no possibility of bringing the two groups of people in the Anthroposophical Society to a mutual understanding, there is only one solution left: In separate organizations, each group could continue to work in its own way. They could then mutually accept each other, since they would no longer stand in each other's way, and would, through this merely organizational separation, be able to achieve the desired unity and fellowship.[¶]

Rudolf Steiner clarified that anyone could be a member of both Societies, regardless of age. This was not a matter of creating a decisive split but rather of allowing mutual respect and autonomy to arise between the two streams. Once it was understood in the assembly that this was a temporary measure to allow the two groups to work in harmony toward the common aim of serving anthroposophy, the proposal was gratefully accepted. Steiner then spoke the significant words: "For a few years, things [can] now go further! One will now, at least, be able to work again."[**] Having stabilized the work of the Society in Germany, Rudolf Steiner then began to travel abroad, helping to establish the individual national Societies, upon which the General Anthroposophical Society would be based.

---

§ *1923: Year of Destiny* (CW 259).

¶ Ibid.

** Ibid.

These important events allow the lectures in this volume to appear in their proper context. The lectures belong to the rebuilding phase after the burning of the Goetheanum, after the temporary solution to the Society issues established through the Stuttgart Delegates Conference, and before the final phase of rebuilding, leading to the founding of the General Anthroposophical Society at Christmas 1923/24.

*

All the lectures have, as a common thematic thread, the connection of the human being with the work of the hierarchies through the rhythms of human life and the cycles of time. A renewal of the festivals was among Steiner's foremost goals during this period, as evidenced by his lectures in Dornach at Easter and then in Vienna at Michaelmas 1923,[††] followed by the cycle of five lectures again in Dornach on the imaginations of the archangels and the seasons of the year.[‡‡]

The mysteries of the first years of life—the years in which we learn to walk, speak, and think (in that order)—are also a consistent theme throughout these lectures. By learning to stand upright and move through space, we orient ourselves in earthly life; we seek the balance we need to be earthly human beings:

> To those who have the ability to observe such things in the right way, the most remarkable, most magnificent riddles of life are expressed in this learning to walk. A whole world is expressed in the very manner in which the child progresses from crawling to standing upright, to moving its little feet, but also to other things—to raising its head, to making use of its arms and legs. (Berlin, May 23, 1923, p. 177)

This first attempt at finding balance in life, at orienting ourselves in space and time, forms the foundation for our entire destiny on earth,

---

[††] These are currently published separately in English, although they belong to the same volume in the German: *The Cycle of the Year as Breathing Process of the Earth* and *Michaelmas and the Soul-forces of Man* (CW 223).

[‡‡] *The Four Seasons and the Archangels* (CW 229).

revealing in an intimate language of movement our pre-birth experiences. *How* a child places his foot on the earth can disclose deep mysteries of human existence.

This activity, this rhythmic movement of arms and legs then leads quite naturally to the formation of speech sounds, which do not only convey conceptual content but also express a dynamic life of their own. The child learns language by forming the consonant and vowel sounds out of an inner sense for movement, not in order to express conceptual content but rather the immediate life of feeling and sensation. And a child's movements—how he takes hold of objects, whether dreamily or forcefully—plays into the forming of his words.

In relation to the transition from the second to the third stage (learning to think), Rudolf Steiner remarks:

> Here we see that the more delicate organs of the brain, which form the basis of thinking, develop in turn out of the speech organism. No one should suppose that, in the normal development of the child, thinking could develop before speaking. Anyone observing these things will find that for the child, speech is not initially an expression of "thinking." Not at all! It would be silly to believe that. For the child, speech is an expression of feelings, sensations, and the life of the soul. This is why you will find that what the child initially expresses through language are all the things connected with feelings, words related to feelings. When the child says "Mama" or "Papa," it wants to express its feelings for Mama or Papa, not any particular concepts or thoughts. Thinking only develops out of speaking. (Berlin, May 23, 1923, p. 177)

These three capacities of walking, speaking, and thinking do not, of course, come to an end once we have acquired them but take on an essential role in our further development in life. Rudolf Steiner describes how the effects of the actions we perform during the day work on at night during sleep and bring us into relationship with the Archai, while our life of speech connects us during sleep with the Archangels, and our life of thought with the Angels. It is an illusion to believe that our deeds, words, and thoughts only pertain to us as individuals or to our immediate community. No, they work on during sleep and become nourishment for the gods. The quality of this nourishment depends on whether we have imbued our deeds, words, and thoughts with idealism or cynicism, apathy, and materialism. Thus, we are intimately interwoven with the entire spiritual cosmos, and a seemingly insignificant action, word, or thought, if it is fired with idealism, with a will to serve the spirit in freedom, can have a powerful effect on the world.

*

This volume draws its title especially from the later lectures, which are centered around a renewal of the seasonal festivals. Rudolf Steiner speaks about Easter, Ascension and Pentecost, St. John's, and Michaelmas, illuminating new paths toward the celebration of true festivals in our time.

In the lecture on Ascension and Pentecost, we find a powerful account of the redemption of the physical-etheric nature of humanity. On Ascension Day, as they perceived Christ rising into the heights, the disciples realized that if Earth evolution had continued without the intervention of the Mystery of Golgotha, then the physical bodies of human beings would have disintegrated more and more, and the etheric bodies would have detached themselves from these decaying physical bodies and returned to the universal ether, to their home in the Sun sphere. They recognized that through the Mystery of Golgotha, Christ had redeemed the physical-etheric nature for all humanity and thus ensured that humanity would continue its life on Earth into the future. However, a burning question remained for them:

> Thus, the mighty picture arising in the Ascension image is that of *the rescue of the physical-etheric nature of the human being through Christ.* But, at the same time, this image also shows the disciples withdrawing, becoming absorbed in thought, becoming pensive and deep in contemplation. For in their souls lives the knowledge that everything that happened through the Mystery of Golgotha occurred in the first instance for the physical-etheric nature of human beings. But what is happening, they wonder, with the soul-

> spiritual? How, and from where, will human beings receive the power to absorb the Christ-impulse into their soul-spiritual nature, into the I and the astral body? (Dornach, May 7, 1923, p. 132)

It is through the event of Pentecost, the sending of the Holy Spirit to the disciples, that the redemption of the astral body and I through an active engagement with the Mystery of Golgotha becomes possible. This active engagement requires one to overcome sense-bound thinking and to develop the forces of spiritual cognition in order to grasp the Mystery of Golgotha in its essential nature. This development of spiritual cognition is connected with the festival of Pentecost:

> Thus, the image of the festival of Pentecost, of Whitsun, is the image of *the permeation of the soul-spiritual nature of the human being with the power to understand the Mystery of Golgotha*, that is, *the sending of the Holy Spirit.* Christ accomplished his deed for all of humanity. But it was to individual human beings, who are meant to understand this deed, to each human being individually, that Christ sent the Spirit—so that the soul-spiritual may find access to the deed that was fulfilled for all human beings in common. Through the Spirit, the human being must—inwardly, as a being of spirit and soul—acquire the Christ-Mystery. (Dornach, May 7, 1923, p. 132)

Finally, the Berlin lecture on the founding of a new Michael Festival is of particular significance. It was the last that Rudolf Steiner ever gave in Berlin, the city where he had lived and worked on behalf of anthroposophy for many years. In the lecture, Rudolf Steiner draws a parallel between the autumn and spring seasons. Just as we experience the death and resurrection through the spring festival of Easter, so, in the autumn, when outer nature dies away and the human being hears the inner call to awaken, he can, out of his inner forces of consciousness during earthly life, experience a resurrection in spirit before death, so that when he passes through the gate of death, he will have first accomplished this resurrection and will thereby find his rightful path in the spiritual worlds. Thus the death and resurrection at Easter is mirrored in the resurrection and death at Michaelmas.

This is a theme that Rudolf Steiner picks up again in his lectures at Michaelmas 1923 in Vienna.[§§]

Between Easter and Michaelmas lies the festival of St. John's, when the soul of the earth unites itself with the world of the stars, with the cosmic expanses. It then returns from the cosmos to the body of the earth toward Michaelmas time. But something is different today than in past ages. The Michael-power, the power connected with the rulership of the cosmic intelligence in all past ages of humanity,[¶¶] "is now coming down to earth through the forces of nature, meaning that we are now able to meet the approaching autumn, with its falling leaves, by perceiving in it the Michael-power as it comes down from the clouds to the earth" (Berlin, May 23, 1923, p. 177). Michael's relationship to humanity today is entirely different than in the past, and there are opportunities for uniting with this truly universal, all-encompassing power of Michael through inner activity of the soul, through a resurrection in our life of thought, feeling, and will.

This inner path of Michaelic self-transformation leads to the possibility of moving beyond mere talk about social change to an actual capacity to become socially creative, not merely to understand through the head the meaning of the old festivals, but rather to create festivals out of an inner sense for the course of the year, out of a will to awaken!

The sparks of fire that set the Goetheanum, that temple of the Word, ablaze flashed forth from the jealousy of man. The human world, in that moment, denied the spirit. But the spirit could not and cannot be irradicated. It flames up anew wherever human beings give it a dwelling place. This is the real story of the year 1923 in the life of Rudolf Steiner and his work on behalf of the spirit, of anthroposophy: the continuation of the spiritual fire in the hearts of those willing to freely work in service of the true spirit of humanity. His words from the final lecture in Berlin are a testament to this fact:

> The true value of the Anthroposophical Society can only be assessed by verifying whether it understands not only dead anthroposophy,

[§§] *Michaelmas and the Soul-forces of Man* (CW 223). He also spoke on this theme at Easter 1923, in *The Cycle of the Year as Breathing Process of the Earth* (CW 223).

[¶¶] See *Karmic Relationships*, vol. 3 (CW 237).

which concerns itself with what is past, but whether it also understands living anthroposophy. Living anthroposophy can also be a sum of flaming sparks! But these sparks of fire will be inside a temple that is not made of external material. Physical flames consume temples that consist of outer materials. The flames of genuine spiritual enthusiasm, of true spiritual life—which must permeate the temple because they must illuminate it with what lights up in the spirit—these flames cannot destroy the temple; they can only give an ever more glorious form to this temple. Let us think of what living anthroposophy is; let us think of it as the fiery flame that will lead us ever further, like the living spirit of anthroposophy itself—which shall lead us to the further evolution of humanity and to the rebuilding of what is now in such an evident decline. (Berlin, May 23, 1923, p. 204)

THE SEASONAL FESTIVALS AS SOUL EXPERIENCE

The Forming of Destiny in Sleeping and Waking

The Spirituality of Language and the Voice of Conscience

BERN, APRIL 6, 1923

Today, let us consider something that can perhaps, in a certain sense, become a continuation and an expansion of yesterday's public lecture.† What I would like to take a closer look at today is how human beings are placed within that part of the cosmic world order that is related to a person's own destiny, to what we usually call karma in our circles. How does this forming of destiny actually occur for a human being? In order to be able to answer this question in a way that is capable of fostering life, instead of theories, we shall have to consider the nature of the human being in more detail.

People often speak of human life in a way that can be expressed as follows: Human life is subdivided into two distinct states of human consciousness—waking and sleeping. But in saying this, people actually only view sleep in the sense of the concepts they have formed about sleep, that is to say, simply as a human being's state of rest. The scientific view also generally assumes that conscious activity ceases when we fall asleep and then resumes again—meaning that, even in terms of the organism, sleep is viewed as nothing more than a suspension of human activity for the sake of rest. But sleep is by no means merely a matter of rest; rather, we must be quite clear about the fact that from the moment of falling asleep to the time of waking up, initially what we call the astral body and then the I—as a real entity—are outside the physical and etheric bodies.

Now, at the current stage of evolution reached by human beings in earthly life, it is not possible to have a direct awareness of what this

I and this astral body are actually doing between falling asleep and waking up. However, what these two entities are engaged in during that time has at least as great a significance for human life as what happens during our waking state. The reason that the I and the astral body cannot develop any consciousness of all the complicated events in which they are immersed during sleep is simply that, in the present Earth-stage of evolution, this I and this astral body have no organs capable of perceiving the events in which they are involved. But these events are there. From the moment of falling asleep until the time of waking up, these events are experienced and they have an impact on the everyday life, on the conscious life of the human being.

The best way to form an accurate picture of how, and to what extent, the experiences of the I and the astral body are working into our waking life is by considering the beginning of the life of a human being. We have already done this several times on previous occasions. What happens during the earliest period of life is that the human being, as a very small child, "sleeps its way" into earthly life, as it were. When referring to this, one should not only think of the time when a child is fully asleep—that is, when it is actually sleeping—but one should really think of the whole period [in earliest childhood] that cannot be remembered at all in later life with our normal consciousness. To external observation, the child may of course appear to be awake during this period, but what is occurring in the child's consciousness does not take shape in such a way that it can be remembered in later life. And everything that is experienced by the child—without having a memory of it in later life—all this can be described by saying: We are referring here to the period during which the human being "sleeps his way" into earthly life.

But what is it specifically that develops from this sleeping state at the beginning of human life on earth? There are three things that should be considered in particular if one wants to understand the effects of what we bring with us from pre-earthly existence and then weave into our physical existence in a way which, for us as human beings, is obscured in darkness, obscured by sleep. There are three things, three faculties, which the human being has to acquire in a way that is different from the animals. Animals either do not acquire these faculties at all, or they already possess them to a greater or lesser extent when they are born on the earth.

These three faculties are generally defined in a way that indicates a one-sided interpretation. Very little of the whole process is actually being considered. The first faculty is *learning to walk*. The human being enters the earthly world as a being who cannot walk, who must first acquire the ability to walk. The second faculty that must be acquired is *speaking*, and the third is *thinking*. One can sometimes clearly distinguish one faculty developing sooner in a particular child; but if we consider humanity in general, we can say that, on the whole, the human being learns to walk, speak, and think—or in any case that thinking develops after learning to speak. For it is only through speaking that the ability emerges, gradually, to also retain in thoughts what is expressed in words. And it actually takes quite a long time before one can truly say that a child thinks.

Walking, in particular, is usually understood from one perspective only. But walking encompasses much more than learning to stand upright and being able to move one's legs in a pendular motion, so to speak. What it also entails for the child is acquiring balance, gaining complete mastery of the equilibrium that human beings have on the earth—in other words, the fact that we can stand upright anywhere without falling over; that we learn to position our body into the world; that we learn to control muscles and limbs in such a way that the body's center of gravity is positioned at the correct point, whether standing or walking. But even this is still a one-sided interpretation, for we must remember that something else of tremendous significance occurs during the process of learning to walk—namely, differentiating the functions of the legs and the arms.

Animals use their four limbs in a uniform way—at any rate, as a general rule, and deviations from this rule can be readily explained—whereas in the human being there is differentiation. We need our legs to walk and to maintain our balance while standing, whereas the arms and the hands become wonderful tools of expression for the life of the soul, vehicles for the work we undertake in the world. This differentiation between feet and hands, arms and legs, is precisely what is overlooked—but should be taken into account—in what is usually defined, inadequately, as the concept of "learning to walk." By indicating this differentiation, we have identified the very thing that human beings only acquire in the physical world during physical life on earth.

The second faculty is also acquired by imitation, by attempting to imitate—just as happens with walking and standing, with balancing oneself, and with differentiating the function of the hands from that of the feet. This second faculty, acquired in this way through imitation, is that of speech. And it can even be said that speaking is not entirely unconnected with walking—more specifically, with the use of the hands (as a differentiated function of walking). For we know that speech is connected with the development of a specific section of the brain, namely, the left temporal gyrus (Gyrus Temporalis Superior). This only applies, however, to those who are inclined to use the right hand for the most important tasks in life; in left-handed people the organ of speech lies at the other side of the brain—at the right side. From these facts we can already see that there is a connection between the finding of balance and what comes to expression in speaking.

And it is from speaking that thinking then develops. A person who is born mute can only be made to think through special, resourceful methods. But in all those people who are not born mute, thinking is something that develops exclusively from speaking.

However, one can really only come to a full understanding of the characteristic development that I have just described if one observes how, in later life, the human being transitions from the waking state to the sleeping state. What happens then is that the physical and etheric bodies are resting in bed, in a physical sense, and that the I and the astral body have separated in essence from the physical and etheric bodies. But if we now take a closer look at this astral body of the human being—with the methods of spiritual science—and observe it when it is separated from the physical and etheric bodies during sleep, then we find that this astral body contains within it the essential forces that are connected with learning to speak. It is extraordinarily interesting to observe the processes of falling asleep and of waking up in a human being who, as a child, is learning to speak—and this is even interesting in the case of someone who only learns to speak as an adult—to see the intensity with which the astral body is involved, particularly in this activity of learning to speak. For, in the period during which the human being is involved in the activity of learning to speak—and also later on, when he or she is using speech in everyday life—the astral body takes with it the soul-spiritual element that is inherently contained in our words and in our speaking, and carries it away from the physical and etheric bodies.

If one is able to perceive how a human being speaks, how the words are formed, how the words are given their own characteristic intonation, how the words are imbued with the strength of the soul's convictions, how the soul's experiences are incorporated into the words—then one can also pursue this further and perceive how, when the individual falls asleep, the astral body carries this soul-spiritual element out of the physical and etheric bodies. One can then perceive how the astral body, during sleep, holds within it the echoing effects of this soul-spiritual element of speech in the world of soul and spirit, how it holds this as an echoing, oscillating reverberation. The forming of the words, the tonal nuances in the voice, the persuasive force that a person can inject into the words—all this can be perceived in that person's astral body during sleep. Naturally, this does not involve anything like a vibrational force being transmitted by means of the physical air; consequently, no physical vocal sound is produced. But what proceeds as soul-spiritual quality from the human mouth in the waves of words and is then heard by human ears, what is communicated by the soul in the flow of speech—all this is carried as soul-spiritual content into the spiritual world by the astral body while the human being sleeps. And even though one can perceive this more clearly when a child, or even an adult, is actively engaged in learning to speak a language, it is nonetheless the case throughout the whole of life that what we convey in our speaking during the day is then, with respect to its soul-spiritual quality, carried over into the spiritual world by the astral body at night. Accordingly, one can say: It is especially the nuances of our feelings, conveyed in the spoken word, that are carried away from the human being by the astral body during the night. This is a characteristic function of the astral body.

And now let us observe what the I does from the time of falling asleep until waking up. To begin with, the I is similarly related—in what might be called a purely natural way—to the limb system. Just as the astral body is connected with the chest, and speech arises from the chest, so is the I, in quite a similar way, connected with all the things we accomplish with our limbs, with everything we do from the time of waking up to the time of falling asleep—inasmuch as we use our limbs in a certain way and accomplish certain things with our arms and hands. Just as the astral body flows into every word, and then takes the soul-aspect contained in the words with it during sleep, so the I is connected with every movement we make—inasmuch as we move about in the world from one place to another when we are awake. The I is connected with every hand movement, with every act of grasping things. When considering the astral body, it already happens—because speech contains so much of the soul—that people tend not to pay much attention to the actual soul-element, tend not to notice that something very special, something coming directly from the soul, is really flowing into speech. But when it comes to considering the connection between the I and the limbs, people are even less inclined to take any account of the fact that something soul-spiritual is connected with it. Walking, doing something with the hands, is simply viewed as something that functions purely like a physical mechanism; because this is how people view the human organism. But this is by no means the case.

In every movement we make with our fingers during the day, in every step we take as we move around, something soul-spiritual is involved as well—just as there is something soul-spiritual contained in our words. And what is connected with our limbs, what is connected with our movements—all of this is taken by the I and carried away from our physical and etheric bodies into the spiritual world when we fall asleep; but it is now also clearly tied to a very special soul-spiritual element. For, in every moment between falling asleep and waking up, the I is unconsciously satisfied or dissatisfied—and you will understand this better presently, when I have explained it more fully. The I—if I am to express this precisely, albeit somewhat trivially—the I is either satisfied or dissatisfied with the legs having moved toward one place or another, or with the arms having accomplished one thing or another. It is not only the lingering effect of the movements of the legs and the arms that is carried away from us in sleep but also this satisfaction or dissatisfaction.

From the time of falling asleep until waking up, the I is occupied with experiences like, "You really should not have gone there," or instead, "Actually, it was a good thing that you went there," or, "It was very good that you did this particular thing with your arms," or instead, "That particular action was not good." This is the soul-spiritual element that the I also brings along, in addition to what it carries from the limbs of the human being into sleep.

And what is the reason for the fact that these things occur as described? The reason is that the astral body, as it is carried into the spiritual world between falling asleep and waking up, is actually destined—in keeping with the world order as it relates to the human being—to come into intimate contact, between falling asleep and waking up, with those beings who in my *Outline of Esoteric Science*† are described as belonging to the hierarchy of the Archangeloi, the Archangels.† For, these archangelic beings feel a kinship with what we take with us into sleep as the echoing reverberation of speech. This is something they need, something they long to experience.

One could actually say: Just as we human beings in our physical life on earth are dependent on breathing, that is, on having oxygen around us and therefore experience oxygen as something beneficial, so do the Archangels, who are connected with the interior of the earth, experience it as an essential need that human souls, when they sleep, bring them the reverberating echo of what is contained in their speech.

It is a special characteristic of human speech that, through the mediating agency of the sleep state, it is connected with the hierarchy of the Archangeloi, the Archangels. You will remember, by recalling what I have said from a variety of perspectives in earlier lecture courses,† that the Archangels are actually the genii, the leading guides, the guiding spirits of the traditional folk-languages. The origin of this connection is the following. The Archangels are the leading guides of the folk-languages because—expressed figuratively, but true nonetheless—they practically breathe in what human beings bring to them from their speech when falling asleep. But a particular shortcoming will be revealed right away, when a human being does not, with his or her speech, carry the right quality into the sleeping state.

This is something that can be observed particularly within contemporary culture. Within this contemporary culture there is actually very little of what we refer to as idealism, and human words have gradually taken on the kind of denotations that relate strictly to external, physical, material things. Designating something as an ideal—which of course presupposes a belief in the spiritual, because an ideal is something spiritual—calling something an ideal is occurring less and less. People do not develop an inner impulse, an inner enthusiasm for idealism while they are awake. As a result, they actually mostly talk about things that exist in the physical world. Words are increasingly becoming mere designations for things in the physical world.

It is often the case in our time that even those people who, sometimes fanatically, want to believe in the spirit, in reality reject the spirit. They may then set up spiritualistic experiments with the objective of producing manifestations of the spirit; they do this because, essentially, they are only willing to believe in a spirit that can manifest in a material sense. But what appears in the physical shimmering of light and in similar manifestations is not spirit. Spiritualism is actually the most extreme form of materialism. By only accepting as spirit what takes form in the physical material world, such experiments are, in reality, attempts to deny the spirit.

We are living in an age when words do not arise[†] from the human soul in a way that would allow them to be infused with the stimulating impulse of idealism. And this will only become less so over time. But if this impulse is lacking, if, in other words, the human being is unable, while in the waking state, to speak of ideals too (besides speaking of physical things), to focus on what belongs in the realm of idealism, on what transcends the physical world, on what provides life with goals that go beyond physical existence, if the human being does not develop words in daily speech that express ideals, if speech itself is not moulded by ideals—then it will be exceedingly difficult, while in the state of sleep, to find the connection with the archangelic being, a connection that is of such fundamental importance for human beings. Then, there will be no ordered structure in what is supposed to take place, during sleep, between the human soul and the hierarchy of the Archangeloi. If this is the case, if the human being, having fallen prey to materialism, develops no idealism in his speech, and the words have gradually become such that they do not contain much about ideals anymore—then earthly life takes its course in such a way that, during sleep, the human being loses the opportunity, if I may express it like this, to establish a connection with the archangelic being. Then it becomes difficult to have the kind of intimate connection with the spiritual world that enables the human being to imbue life after death—from death to a new birth—with strong, vital forces. Then, because no idealism is contained in his speech, the human being's strength for life between death and a new birth is lessened.

Knowing how these things are interconnected already constitutes a real knowledge of life. Anyone who understands what significance it has when speech does *not* contain idealism, will in the end want to gain the strength to ensure that idealism will once again permeate human speech. Even during earthly life, it can already be observed that a person who—between the time of falling asleep and waking up—is not able to draw the necessary forces from the archangelic being, will then also not be able to develop the strength that should rightly be his or hers. Therefore, with respect to what speech should accomplish for us human beings during sleep, one can actually say the following: If we are to receive the right qualities for life from what happens during sleep, then we must make a real effort to develop idealism in such a way that our words do not merely express an understanding of everyday life, but are also imbued with spiritual qualities, in the form of idealism.

This becomes even more apparent, however, when we observe the sleeping state of the I. The I takes with it, into the sleeping state, satisfaction and dissatisfaction about the actions of the limbs. Just as the astral body, as a result of the reverberating after-effects of speech, is brought to the hierarchy of the Archangels, so the I is brought to the hierarchy of the Archai—the Primal Powers, or

Primal Beginnings—by virtue of what it carries into the state of sleep as a reverberating echo of the accomplishments of the arms and legs during the day. And it is from these Primal Beginnings that we initially receive the power to permeate the physical body in the right way, so that we not only desire what is good but also are able to have a measure of control over the urges and instincts of the physical body, at least to the extent that the physical body no longer acts as a hindrance, keeping us from accomplishing what we—in freedom of thought—have set ourselves as duty or goal. In our thinking we are free; but we can only acquire the power to make use of freedom in our life if we carry the basis for a right connection to the Primal Powers, to the Archai, out into sleep.

But how can we achieve this? Idealism brings our astral body into the right connection with the archangelic beings. But what enables the I to establish the right connection to the Primal Powers, the Archai? Even though *we* remain, to begin with, unconscious during sleep, the being from the hierarchy of the Archai is fully conscious of our condition, takes what we carry unconsciously within us, and develops it into a distinctly formed thought-concept of satisfaction or dissatisfaction about what we did during the day. But what is it that enables us to establish the right connection with these Primal Powers, a connection like the one we can establish to the Archangels through idealism in our speech?

There is only one quality that will enable the I to come into the right relationship with the Archai during sleep: real, genuine, true love of humanity, unbiased love of human beings, universal human love, sincere interest in every human being with whom life brings us into contact—*not* sympathy or antipathy, which merely arises from things we are not willing to overcome. True, genuine love for human beings, developed during the waking state, leads us, during the time from falling asleep to waking up, into the "bosom" of the Primal Powers in the right way. And there, while the I is resting in the bosom of the Archai, karma or destiny[†] is shaped. There, judgments are formed, such as: I am dissatisfied with what I have accomplished with my arms and legs. And from what then arises, either as satisfaction or dissatisfaction, something is generated which applies not only to the period immediately following death but particularly to the next life on earth; what is generated is the power to shape our destiny in the right way so that we will be able to bring true balance to all the things we have experienced in our I, in our life on earth—during the state of sleep—in connection with the Archai.

If you reflect on these things, then you will develop a precise insight into this remarkable connection between the I and destiny—that is, karma. For, just as we can see that, in the case of someone who is an idealist, the astral body presents speech as an offering to the Archangels—thus enabling the Archangels to guide the human being in the right way between death and a new birth—so we can observe that the I is involved in weaving destiny. In the case of the I, karma is worked on and expanded in conjunction with the Primal Powers, the Archai. And these Primal Powers, moreover, have the commanding power to bestow upon us what we need not only to pass through the period between death and a new birth, but also, upon our next descent into the earthly realm, to enter life with the kind of strength that enables us in earliest childhood—by implementing what we have brought with us from the previous life—to learn, in our own individual way, to walk, to find our balance, and to differentiate the functions of feet and hands, arms and legs.

It is quite extraordinary, in observing a child—as it transitions from crawling to walking, as it begins to find its balance—to notice how something is still actively at work in these efforts, something that reflects the way in which the I, in its previous life on earth, was able, through a universal love for humanity, to bring its sleep into the right connection with the Archai. This comes to expression in the process of learning to walk and can be observed down to the smallest detail. Suppose, for instance, a little child is continually stumbling and falling over. It can then be seen that, in a previous life, strong feelings of antipathy or even hatred were developed; that this individual had only come near to the Archai but had not been able to find the right connection with these beings; and that it is precisely in this process of learning to walk, and particularly in the constant stumbling, that these aftereffects find a reflection. Anyone aspiring to develop correct insights into these things and to become, let us say, an educator in the true sense, could do so by deciding to carefully observe how little children learn to walk. If one were to carry this through in the right way, then one could indeed learn to recognize, from the way the child learns to walk, the enormity of what one needs to karmically compensate for as a teacher, as an educator, because of what is carried over into the child's present life from a previous life when there had been insufficient—or sufficient but misdirected—love for humanity.

From this example we can see how the materialistic way of looking at things remains within the realm of the physical. The materialistic view describes how the human organism raises itself to the upright position, learns to walk, and so on—like a machine. However, everything physical has a connection with something spiritual, and someone who is able to have an overview of the whole process learns to recognize that a previous earthly life plays a role in the child's learning to walk. This means that learning to walk is, in fact, an expression of how the human being, at the beginning of a new earthly life, learns to master his or her physical body. And to those who understand this process in its entirety, learning to walk involves a great deal more than being able to straighten one's legs and raise up one's whole body; they know that this extends as far as the inner processes of the human being, even including the way in which one gains some inner control over, for example, the activity of the glands. For, when a child has learned to walk, and even before, it is not just the actual walking that is involved, but it is also a question of the extent to which the child—if it has, for example, a phlegmatic or a choleric character, or an overabundance of certain emotions—learns to rein in the glandular processes. And this, in turn, is connected with what arose from the kind of relationship that could be established—during sleep, in a previous earthly life—with the Archai because of a universal human love, or lack thereof, that had been developed [in that previous life].

The materialistic way of thinking holds the view that the human being rests during sleep. But there is more involved than merely rest. If a human being develops the right kind of idealism while awake, then he or she carries into sleep the possibility for the astral body to ascend to the hierarchy of the Archangeloi, that is to say, to enter into a relationship with the spiritual world during sleep in such a way that the period between death and a new birth can be experienced to the right extent. For, obviously, if we do not undergo this period in the right way, then we carry weaknesses from it into our earthly life. Moreover, the way in which we construct† our next life depends on the nature of our connection with the Primal Powers, the Archai—on whether, or to what extent, we were able to establish the right connection. From this we can see that universal love of humanity really has creative power. For, on what does it depend for someone to have the vitality and strength in the current life to place the physical body in the service of the soul, to have command over the physical body? This depends on whether that person developed a love of humanity—something that is purely a soul-quality—in his or her previous life.

You will remember what I have said in previous lectures†—namely, that the soul nature of one earthly life manifests in the physical body of the next life, and that the spiritual aspect of one life manifests in the soul nature of the next earthly life. This is also how these things, which I have just described, are connected.

It will not do to generalize, to simply say that there is such a thing as destiny, as karma. It is better to say that we should take a look at how human beings work on forming their karma; how they weave it while asleep, but gather what is needed for its weaving while awake. For, what the human being weaves is either those threads that are formed from universal love of humanity, or the threads that continually break and form bad karma for the next life—threads that are woven out of a hatred of humanity. For, as far as the forces that create and shape karma are concerned, it is especially love or hatred of humanity that should be considered as contributing factors.

Now, these things must be regarded in the right way. We have, in truth, a rather convenient concept of karma if we simply say: "I am sick; well, it is my karma," or, "a misfortune has befallen me; it is my karma." I am not saying that this kind of "life-wisdom" does not afford some peace of mind, only that it is merely a convenient theory to make karma responsible for everything in this rather defeatist way. But this is not the correct way of looking at it. For, let us suppose that you are contemplating not your present life, but a third-next life in the future, so that, if something occurred in that third-next earthly life, you would then be able to look back at the present life and simply say: "It is my karma," while in reality, your karma, as it would be then, actually had its origin in that [future] earthly life. All this means that karma is continually being created.

In regard to these things, we should not focus only on the past. Having the right approach to karma—we must be clear about this—would lead us to say: "An illness which befalls me now, need not necessarily be the consequence of earlier soul weaknesses because an illness can also develop for the very first time. In any case, karma holds sway. If an illness or a misfortune befalls me in this present earthly life, then compensation will follow in due course, or alternatively, this very illness, this misfortune, may well be the compensation."

This means that we should always take the future into account as well, when speaking about karma. Our attitude toward karma should be such that we develop an unshakable confidence in a universal world-justice, and know that everything will be balanced out in the end—but not in such a way that we let our present life break the flow-sequence of earthly lives by simply believing that all karma has its causes in past lives.

Someone who recognizes that everything will be balanced out in the end, will be able to place him- or herself into the karmic flow of life's events in a way that is full of vital forces. However, what matters most with respect to any conception of karma is the mood of soul that arises from this conception. And the mood of the soul that should arise from a true understanding of karma is the following. It should induce us—in a situation where something, for example, a misfortune, is compensation for an earlier weakness of the soul—to say to ourselves: "If you had not experienced this misfortune, your soul-weakness would have persisted." It should induce us, when looking into the depths of our souls, to say to ourselves: "It is right that this misfortune has come upon me, because as a result of it, a weakness has been eliminated, a weakness has been taken away."

Whoever chooses to "wish away" such a misfortune—a misfortune that is a rectification of a previous soul-weakness or transgression—is not actually taking a position commensurate with full human dignity. For, in a sense, that person says: "It is a matter of indifference to me whether I remain weak or gain a specific strength!" The only way to understand such a misfortune in the right way is by realizing: "If it happened because of an earlier weakness, then it is good that it has befallen me. For, through this misfortune, I will sense my earlier weakness—which likely manifested in the form of a transgression. As a result of it, I will now eliminate the weakness; I will be strong again." On the other hand, if a particular misfortune arises as a first step in karma, as a karmic beginning, then we can meet this with the correct mood of soul by saying to ourselves: "If we were to encounter only what we wish for ourselves, then—precisely because of how our life would unfold as a result—we would actually become weaker." Depending on circumstances, we might live comfortably and well in one or two lives on earth by virtue of the fact that we would only encounter the very things we had wished for, but in a third or fourth life on earth we would become as though paralyzed in soul and spirit because no effort would ever arise in us to overcome impediments. After all, obstacles would then not be there for us to overcome unless the unexpected, the unwanted, entered our life. But if the right kind of strength is developed in meeting the obstacles, if enough human love is carried over into sleep, then what is woven as karma by the I—in communion with the Primal Powers, the Archai—will be shaped in such a way that the right compensation can come to pass in the next earthly life.

Anthroposophical truths need not remain just theoretical truths that enable us to know something; all these truths, rather, are such that they merge with a person's disposition and mood of soul. And if these truths have not merged with a person's mental and emotional disposition, then they have not yet been fully understood; then they have only been grasped as theoretical truths. Understanding karma, destiny, in the right way actually leads, on the one hand, to developing a more refined sensitivity to happiness and misfortune in life than would normally be the case—that is, happiness and misfortune will be experienced with a greater intensity—and, on the other hand, to being able to develop a specific soul disposition. For, it will then become possible to develop a soul-mood toward the spiritual world that no longer arises from any belief or assumption but, rather, from an understanding of what the I and astral body are doing while they have withdrawn from everyday waking life. Recognition of these things creates an inner mood of unshakable confidence in world justice. Understanding karma means having a correct view of world justice. It does *not* mean becoming apathetic with respect to happiness or unhappiness, joy and pain, but it does mean assigning joy and pain, happiness and unhappiness, their proper place in life.

Now, one could say that in observing the human being in daily life, we really only see the I and the astral body to the extent that they are working in the physical body, and that we can therefore only know something about their activity in the physical body, but not about the soul-spiritual qualities in the I and the astral body. When I am speaking with another person, I listen to the words that are spoken to me and, if I were a materialist, I would then explain this process somewhat as follows: The lungs, the larynx, and other organs are activated; this causes the air to vibrate and these vibrations then reach my ear—and so on. But if I view this process as it really is, then I can see that person's astral body vibrating in what is being formed as words, in what is taking shape in language. Moreover, I can then perceive, merged with this astral body, the human being's kinship with the divine-spiritual world. And I can then recognize that, even though the astral body is in the physical body during the everyday waking state, it stays hidden in speech and similar activities; that, during the night, the astral body participates in the life of the higher hierarchies; and that, in a similar way, this is also the case for the I.

And so, we may say that when we are sleeping, we are not just resting for the sake of our daily life. We are then active in the spiritual world just as we work and speak by means of our physical body here in the physical world. And, just as materialism denies that the I and astral body exist as real beings during sleep, so materialism also ought to acknowledge that, consequently, it cannot understand the world in its entirety. For, what is the "moral world" to the materialistic view? Materialism sees the moral world as something that human beings have concocted in thought, *not* as something that has any relation to the world's creative powers. But to those who truly observe and develop insight into human life, the moral world order is the very realm in which human beings live just as fully while asleep, as they live in light and air while awake.

With respect to this, there is still something else, something essential, that must be considered. When we die, our speech accompanies us—and this, incidentally, applies to our karma as well. We die, and throughout our life we were connected to the world of the Archangeloi—either in a correct way or in a more or less deficient way—and this process recurred every time we slept. We carry with us through the portal of death and into the spiritual world what has been given to us by the archangelic beings during sleep. Accordingly, we can then find our orientation into the spiritual world in the right way—the spiritual world, which is the Logos,† and which consists of the cosmic elements that have their reflected images in the words of speech. Then, we can find the way into the spiritual world for our life between death and a new birth.

But it is not really that simple. When we have passed through death, we no longer have a physical body. After death, what the Archangels have given us, from all our periods of sleep, is sufficient to be effective and useful between death and a new birth. But when we wake up from sleep as physical, earthly human beings, we have to come down again into our physical body. This is something which, in point of fact, cannot be imparted to us by the Archangels. Here it becomes necessary that even higher hierarchies be involved—namely, the beings whom I have referred to in my *Esoteric Science* as the Exusiai and the Kyriotetes.† These higher beings must insert what we have initially gained in communion with the Archangels through the spirituality of speech, into the urges and desires of the physical body—which ordinarily offers resistance. That is where it then flashes up as the voice of conscience. But when this voice of conscience flashes up from what we carry out of sleep into the body, then there is something else at work in this voice of conscience as well—namely, the inherent inner quality of the hierarchy of the Exusiai and the Kyriotetes, as a higher hierarchy than the Archangels.

Accordingly, if we look around the physical world and find that someone is developing conscience to such a degree that the physical body begins to have better inclinations, better instincts—then [we realize that] the Kyriotetes and Exusiai have worked upon that human being in the right way because of the idealism in that individual's speech.

And, as described earlier, if we establish the right connection with the Archai, with the Primal Powers—through universal love of humanity—then we are working on our karma in such a way that its effects are incorporated in our body of the next life on earth; then, in the very first period of childhood, when we "sleep our way" into life on earth, these effects manifest in learning to walk, in finding one's balance, in becoming skilled in the use of one's arms, in reining in the glandular system, and so on. For, in that case, we would have acquired these qualities in our working-in-communion, as it were, with the Primal Powers, the Archai, between death and new birth. But in order for the human being here on earth to acquire a refined sensitivity, a heightened awareness of his or her own actions in the right way, it is necessary that the hierarchy which I have described for you in *An Outline of Esoteric Science* as the Dynamis—that is, once again, beings of a higher hierarchy—work in union with the Archai.

Now, if someone is lacking in universal love of humanity, fails to develop a real interest in other human beings, then that person will not find the right connection to the Archai. As a result, the individual spoils the opportunity to weave his or her karma in the right way for the next earthly life, and additional lives on earth will then be needed to compensate for this. But it creates a further disadvantage for the present earthly life as well, because the individual will have less and less strength to carry the judgments that are formed—of satisfaction or of dissatisfaction with what the legs and hands are doing—into the physical body. For, this is something that we cannot do ourselves; in order to achieve this, we must, through an intensified love of humanity, come together with the Dynamis in the right way. They will then provide our physical body with the kind of forces that can accomplish these things in the right way. Otherwise, we will crumble, despite the fact that we realize what is right.

In our thinking we can become free. But in order to be able to actually use this freedom in the right way in physical life, we must establish the right equilibrium in our waking and sleeping life, because we must meet in the right way not only with the Archai but also with the Dynamis.

The highest hierarchy—Seraphim, Cherubim, and Thrones—want to carry what we do, what we undertake, out into the universe. The Exusiai, Dynamis, and Kyriotetes carry what we think, what we grasp in thought, into our physical being; they carry this, as a moral force, out of our sleep state. The Seraphim, Cherubim, and Thrones, in turn, carry this out into the universe, so that our own moral forces become world-creating forces.

When the time comes for the earth to pass over into the Jupiter phase of evolution†—and our moral forces will be performing their proper functions in this transformation—then the Seraphim, Cherubim, and Thrones will of course only be able to participate in this process if we offer them the necessary support for it. If, instead, we offer them destructive forces by becoming weaker and weaker, then we would be contributing to the destruction of the earth, not to the building-up of Jupiter.

You see, when anthroposophy describes the structure of the spiritual world, this is by no means just done so that people have names for these various levels. Rather, this is done so that one can really enter, little by little, into all the interrelationships of the world, so that one can perceive the connection of the human being to the spiritual world in the same way as one would normally perceive the connection of the human being to the physical world. And human beings will acquire the right strength again for a well-formed life if, in the way described, they develop insight into their relationship to the spiritual world, if they do not simply believe that the purpose of sleep is to rest, but instead become convinced that the purpose of sleep is to establish the right relationship with the spiritual world, a relationship that is contingent upon the after-effects of physical life.

It is certainly possible for human beings to deny the spiritual-moral world because, initially, we are not aware of it at this present stage of Earth evolution; we "sleep through" it in a sense. But a true science must reveal what people are sleeping through—namely, the fact that certain elements of heavenly existence actually extend into earthly life; and that human beings have sleep for the very purpose of being able to derive the relevant strength from the spiritual world, particularly for their physical life.

With this perspective in mind, let us now consider the connection between what I attempted to sketch for you today and my *Philosophy of Freedom*.[†] There, I have distinctly emphasized—you will find it in the book—that in regard to this, it is not a matter of posing the theory that the will should be free but, rather, that thinking shall be free; that, in reality, thinking must govern the will if the human being is to be a free being. But I also described that, if the will is not to present an insurmountable hindrance to free thinking, then we must order our lives accordingly. As human beings living in the physical world today, we can make our thinking free. Feeling and will, however, can only become free if we, in the case of feeling, establish the right relationship with the Archangels and, in the case of our will, establish the right relationship with the Archai.

Accordingly, the following occurs: What lives in our speech withdraws from us, during sleep, together with the soul-spiritual; what lives in our limbs also leaves us. Astral body and I depart; the etheric body remains with the physical body. Our thinking, which is bound up with the etheric body, continues on in the etheric body. However, with our ordinary consciousness we do not know how the etheric body thinks from the time of falling asleep to that of waking up—because we are outside. It is actually not true that thinking ceases during sleep; we think from the moment of falling asleep until we wake up. Thoughts are constantly occurring in our etheric body; it is only that we know nothing about them. We only begin to know something again when we return [to our body]; then our thoughts come alive again for our consciousness. And it is because thoughts are connected with our physical earthly life through the etheric body in this way, that human beings can be free in their thinking. For we were put on the earth in order to become free. But we can acquire the power of freedom only from the spiritual world—the power that leads to freedom in feeling, the power that leads to freedom in will.

This also explains how these things are connected with the fact that the human being retains the actual foundation of thinking—the etheric body—throughout the entire life on earth. During earthly life, the etheric body does not withdraw from us into a cosmic world. The astral body and the I withdraw from us. Only when death occurs, does the etheric body also leave us. And then comes the review of life over the course of one, two, three days, during which the human being views his or her whole life—similarly to what I described yesterday† with respect to *imagination*, the first stage of suprasensory cognition.† It is indeed the case—under all circumstances—that, after death, human beings look back over their completed earthly life. But inasmuch as this whole sea of thoughts that has been experienced between birth and death—both in the sleeping and in the waking state—is present, inasmuch as it is present like a sea of inter-weaving thoughts during these three days after death, it is also a fact that, immediately thereafter, the cosmos avails itself of these thoughts. The thoughts dissolve, and after two or three days, the whole panoramic review of life has evaporated into the cosmos. We are accustomed to saying that the etheric body, too, has separated, has withdrawn. But in actual fact the cosmos has absorbed, "sucked up," the etheric body—which had grown larger and larger until it finally had completely merged into the cosmos. After that, we are again received—as an I and an astral entity—into the bosom of the higher hierarchies. And only when we acquire an etheric body once again, can we descend to earthly life and continue to work on becoming free human beings. For, the goal of life on earth is for the human being to become a free being. What lies in the activity of pure thinking as the foundation of freedom—this is what can be gifted to the human being on the earth. And it is also for this reason that the etheric body remains bound up with the physical body throughout life on earth, meaning that only at death does it dissolve into worlds where it is not possible to acquire freedom. Freedom is acquired during life on earth—in fact, as you know, only during certain epochs of life on earth.

Accordingly, we can understand that there is indeed a meaningful relationship between freedom and karma, because freedom is related to that which remains lying in bed [physical body and etheric body], which is bound to us even during sleep, which does not separate from us. Karma is woven by the I between the time of falling asleep and that of waking up. Karma is woven in another realm, away from those members of the human being in which freedom has its foundation. Karma also does not weave in the realm of free or unfree thoughts; it weaves, rather, in the realm of feeling and will. That is where karma emerges from the depths of human essential nature, from the "dreaming" feeling and the "sleeping" will. And into this we can pour the opposite—that is, what lives in the free activity of thoughts, in pure thinking, in the ethical and moral impulses, as I have described them in *The Philosophy of Freedom*; for these impulses must have their foundation in pure thinking.

This is, in reality, how everything is connected. And it is absolutely essential that we learn to recognize that the further we progress in anthroposophy, the more all the details come together and relate to each other. Obviously, it is quite possible for someone encountering certain details related to a particular field to discover one contradiction after another. This is inevitable, because in order to get any real insight into how something is presented in a particular field, one must examine how this one area is connected with the whole. Otherwise, one would be coming to judgments like someone who has an opinion about a particular planet but is unable to understand the reasons for its specific movements; for, in order to understand this, one must take into account the planetary system in its entirety. Similarly, if we want to know something about the world and about life, then we must try to get insight into all the connections, into all the realities and details of both the physical world and the worlds of soul and spirit.

This is what I wanted to present to you today, when the opportunity arose for us to be together again here in this branch. My aim was to offer something that would help you to perceive the kind of mood that can be developed with respect to karma—that is, to universal justice—when a human being becomes inwardly engaged in anthroposophy in the right way. For it really is a matter of the perceptions and experiences that we carry over into life, not of merely developing insights into theoretical aspects. May you succeed, to an ever-greater extent, in making the gifts of anthroposophy not merely the content of your thoughts, but the content of your soul, or—expressed more correctly—the content of your heart. The more it is possible for anthroposophy to fill the hearts of those who have the desire to understand it, the more it will become possible to introduce anthroposophy into the cultural and intellectual life of our age. This is what is urgently needed, for if humanity relies merely on old things, on the old traditions, it will not be able to move forward. Try to find the path of anthroposophy that leads from the head to the heart—for it is in your hearts that anthroposophy will have a secure home.

The Individualized Logos
and the Art of Extracting the Spirit from the Word

STUTTGART, MAY 2, 1923

The anthroposophical foundation of life in the present time must give rise to the cultivation of art again—the kind of art that was an inherent element of the ancient Mysteries. These Mystery centers were built upon a knowledge that was completely different from the human knowledge that we have today; and yet there was much in their customs—in what formed the foundation of all of their practices—that has been lost to humanity and must now be renewed again. The art that I am describing with these words can be characterized fully in the sense of the ancient Mysteries by saying: "Spirit must be brought out from the words." The situation in these old Mystery centers was such, however, that when people said "Word," or "Logos," they meant something far more significant than what is meant today when the word "Word" is used. But we must learn to find a deeper and ever deeper meaning again in the things and processes of the world—and therefore also in the sentence: "We must reach the stage once again where spirit is brought out from the words." Let us put these things before our souls today with the help of a very specific example.

It is actually something very abstract when we say that the human being essentially consists of physical body, etheric body, astral body, I, and so on. This is why the attempt was made on a number of different occasions to describe what is, in reality, meant by these individual members of the human being. But one can always develop such characterizations further and, in doing so, come closer to their spiritual reality. And it is in this sense that we shall consider the human etheric body today—grasping it through the soul's eye in such a way that we describe what presents itself to suprasensory observation about the essential nature of this human etheric body. We should get beyond the vague notions conveyed, for example, by characterizations of how this etheric body with its different substantiality compares or relates to the physical body, or something similar. Such descriptions are merely approximations of reality, and only by developing these approximate characterizations still further do we penetrate through to the real essence of the matter.

We know that when the human being, living under normal earthly conditions, passes into the sleeping state, the etheric body remains within the physical body as well, and that—as we have always described it—the astral body and the I leave this physical body and the etheric body. At the current stage of their cosmic evolution, the astral body and the I do not yet have the life-sustaining power that would enable them to have any conscious experiences between falling asleep and waking up. We have often discussed—albeit in a more general way—the nature of these unconscious experiences which the astral body and I undergo between falling asleep and waking up.

Today, however, we shall turn our attention to what remains behind in bed when a human being is asleep, and in particular to the etheric body. We shall, in a sense, treat the word "etheric body" in such a way that we lift the spirit out of it—by means of the kind of art which, as I mentioned earlier, had been cultivated in the ancient Mystery centers. What this involves, in reality, is that we look at this etheric body through the soul's eye, as it were, and then describe what really presents itself to suprasensory perception as the essence of this etheric body—when the human being is asleep.

As we fall asleep, it can be observed that the physical body grows still, that during sleep we lose the ability to move our limbs. But it can also be observed that we lose the possibility of sending our will through the inner bodily structure in such a way that our senses would have to be active. The relationship of the outer world to the senses does not change, but the relationship of the senses to the outer world does change, due to the fact that the human being becomes inwardly still—in the same sense as, outwardly, the arms and legs are at rest—meaning that the will is no longer active in the sense organs, so that these sense organs do not respond to the outer world through the kind of delicate movements that must be there if sense perceptions are to arise.

However, one would be altogether in error if one were to believe that the sense organs themselves—or, more precisely, the space encompassed by these sense organs—were not filled with some activity during sleep. The physical body does indeed remain still during this whole time of rest, but the human etheric body becomes all the more active, all the more internally mobile between the time of falling asleep and waking up. And it is especially characteristic of this process that, to the same degree that the functions of the physical body come to rest during and after the time of falling asleep, an ever-increasing lively activity of the etheric body begins with this state of sleep. And this activity, this liveliness of the etheric body radiates particularly from the senses. Accordingly, one can say: If suprasensory vision, suprasensory observation, focusses its attention on the sleeping human being—that is to say, on the part of the human being that is within the physical sheath—then it can be observed that from those places where the sense organs are located, a continual lively activity radiates inward. This activity, this liveliness, is the life of the etheric body—the "life" body—during sleep.

It can be seen, for example, that from the moment of falling asleep, a particular activity begins, originating from the region of the human eyes. What occurs with respect to the human eye is the following. It is as if the effects of the light during the waking state had filled the eye with forces for an activity that only unfolds when we fall asleep—and this activity is, in fact, an etheric one. To the same degree that the influence of light and color from outside darkens within the eyes, do the eyes themselves, like two phosphorescent suns, begin to radiate etherically throughout the inner being of the physical part of the sleeping person. A phosphorescent, glowing light shines through the inner space of the human being. You need not wonder why this phosphorescent glow radiating within the human being cannot be seen in the usual way. For, it is understandable that the eyes of another human being cannot see the light that is radiating inwardly during sleep, considering that most of the human organization is impenetrable to the physical eye, and that this light activity is part of this inaccessible realm. Whatever goes on within the inner human being cannot be seen with outer, physical eyes; nor is there, at first, an inner organ within the physical body that would be capable of directly perceiving this glimmering, phosphorescent light.

With this description we have characterized one of the inner activities and living processes of the etheric body within the human being during sleep. But there is another activity that flows into these living processes. In fact, what a person can still sense while falling asleep—a kind of humming and chirping, a flowing murmur of the human inner organism—continues during the sleeping state as a musical activity, extraordinarily rich in melody and harmony, which also suffuses the whole inner realm of the human being during sleep. This musical activity continues from the time of falling asleep to that of awakening. And the members of the human being that are outside the physical and etheric bodies—the I and the astral body—receive strong impressions from what they have left behind in bed as the resounding, ringing etheric body, which, moreover, also shines light within its resounding and ringing. However, what is received as an impression by the I and the astral body initially remains in the unconscious.

Likewise, there are also etheric warmth-currents radiating from the whole surface of the skin into the inner regions of the human being. All this—together with many other elements from realms that lie further away from what is perceptible in the outer world as warmth, light, and sounds (and are therefore difficult to describe)—all this results in an immensely beautiful, magnificent, powerful inner activity, an inner moving and flowing of the human etheric body. It is as if, with the etheric body of the human being, this extraordinary sounding, glowing, and flowing in the warmth-currents of the individual human etheric body had lifted itself out of the universe. It is as if—for inner reasons, which are rooted in the very existence and essence of the human being—this etheric activity had lifted itself, island-like, one could say, out of the universal etheric life of the cosmos. And this warming flowing, this phosphorescent glowing, this musical sounding are also the very things which, a few days after the death of a human being, withdraw, as the etheric body, from the astral body and the I, and then flow out, stream out into the universal ether of the cosmos, the universe.

Many of you may have noticed—after attending, let us say, a concert the previous evening, which had made a vivid impression—how you may have woken up in the morning perceiving that this waking-up was such that it felt as if the soul had lifted itself out of a recurring experience of the music heard during the concert; as if the soul had gone through the whole concert once again during sleep. But this process is actually more complex than it appears to ordinary consciousness. For, in reality, the soul lifts itself out of the impressions of the cosmic music that is resounding in an individualized form within the human etheric body. And when the human being returns again into the etheric body—and everything that I have described to you with respect to this etheric body is drowned out as a result of the physical body's way of handling impressions—then the human soul "translates" what is actually this individualized cosmic music into the recently heard earthly sounds. One could say that these sounds are the clothing with which this cosmic music covers itself at the moment of waking up, because this cosmic music has something in common with the flowing stream of musical sounds heard at the concert. Because human beings are incapable of perceiving the cosmic music while in their normal state of consciousness, this cosmic music clothes itself in that which in earthly life is most comparable to it—the musical sounds heard in the concert. This is the real experience underlying the phenomenon that most of you may well have had at one time or another.

So, you can see the true complexity of the processes unfolding in the human etheric body. And if one attempts to pursue this further—using the methods with which one can penetrate deeper into such realms—then one notices that this streaming warmth, this gentle phosphorescent glow, this living music is the outer revelation of mighty cosmic beings. Everything that I have described to you is actually, in turn, the external garment, the outer revelation, the radiant image of mighty cosmic beings; and then it becomes clear that these mighty cosmic beings are the beings we have come to know, from anthroposophical writings, as the Exusiai.[†] I have often called these Exusiai *Revelations* because they live, in accordance with their inner nature, in the radiance which during earthly sleep flows from the human sense organs toward the inner region of the human being; and it is in this streaming, radiating activity that the weaving life of these spiritual beings, whom we call the Exusiai, is revealed.

Moreover, using the same methods with which one observes these manifestations of the human senses—which become so lively in their etheric substance especially during sleep—one can follow the further course of this inward flowing radiance and observe how this stream continues its activity further inward. And just as, in our waking state, we can see an illuminated object, and then locate this illuminated object somewhere outside on the line of sight by tracing, as it were, this line from the eye to the object—a line created by the eye, that is, by a sense organ—so it is also possible to trace, but now inward, what flows, shines, and radiates etherically from the senses toward the inner human being. Here, however, the path to be traced is not a long one; it is only a short path, and very soon one will come across something different. The gentle, phosphorescent glow emanating from the eyes, the effects of the music coming from the region of the hearing organs, the streaming warmth flowing inward from the whole surface of the skin—all of this very quickly becomes an organically coherent etheric system.

When looking at a human being in the waking state, one observes the etheric body in its activity (and one sees the whole physical body too, of course); but this activity is somewhat different from how it is during sleep, as I have described it. One sees this activity expanding a little beyond the physical body of the human being. One can observe what flows inward from the senses and from the entire skin, what ripples and radiates inward, forming a certain trajectory that resembles a shell-like copy of the human being, which extends inward. One can observe a phosphorescent glow coming from the eyes and shining inward, and then changing into something else, which I will describe shortly. One can observe warmth currents streaming inward from the skin, resembling a kind of shell modeled after the human physical organism; one can observe that it attains a certain density, but that it is then transformed into a kind of ether organism which in its substance-content appears to be intermingled with, and composed of, musical activity, phosphorescent light, and streams of warmth.

All these, and many other things, flow into and through each other; they mutually influence each other and form a kind of organism—namely, the etheric organization of the human being. And if we then contemplate this etheric organism of the human being through spiritual vision, if we begin to understand it in view of all the ways in which it manifests, then we are bound to describe it as consisting entirely of thought forms, of streaming thoughts. What is streaming everywhere inside this etheric organism is *thought*. If we then were to trace this constantly fluctuating inner activity of the sleeping etheric body at any moment, and chart it at that particular moment, then we would of course paint lines or colored forms; but if we had to characterize the substance of these lines or colored forms, then we would be bound to say: It is just as if thoughts were starting to flow.

It is actually the same thing as what otherwise lives in thought activity, but now it becomes an ever-changing streaming and flowing. It is the thought-forming process of the cosmos, but individualized. This individualized thought-forming process of the cosmos manifests as the individualized Logos. Accordingly, one cannot even really say that what flows and weaves inside the human being as thought-forming process—and as an inner connector for these inwardly radiating and streaming movements coming from the senses—that this is just thought, streaming thought. For, it actually speaks, albeit in a silent language, but a language that is perceptible to the inner human being. It really speaks—as all things speak to us through the Logos—in an individual form, expressing the essential nature of the human being in inner words that can be perceived spiritually.

And so, if we follow this movement from the senses further inward, what then appears to us is human language turned inward, as it were. With respect to this process, one can really say: Although it is true that the I and the astral body of the human being—which are outside the physical and etheric bodies from the time of falling asleep until waking up—remain unconscious for our normal consciousness, they nonetheless experience what is happening. And, just as this I and this astral body experience the etheric activity of the senses during sleep as a streaming and flowing that is directed inward, so do they experience the etheric body during the human being's sleep state as individualized Logos—like speech turned inward. It is as if our speech, which otherwise streams out toward the ears of our fellow human beings, had turned inward, etherically transformed during sleep. It is as if we were once more speaking, but now toward our inner being, all the things we said during the day from the time of waking up until that of falling asleep, but now in reverse order, beginning with the evening and ending with the morning.

We speak once more—in a silent language toward our inner being—everything that we have spoken from morning to evening, but in such a way that we reveal the whole nature of our soul in this inwardly directed speech. Therefore, to the extent that the essential nature of the human being is experienced in what is spoken from morning to evening—to that extent does this speech-experience become realized inwardly, but now from evening to morning, in the resounding, speaking Logos. And this resounding, speaking, individualized Logos reveals at the same time—by "writing" it chronologically into the etheric, as it were—the spiritual script that describes, in the above-mentioned glimmering, mildly phosphorescent light, everything that flows inward during the night, as the other side of what is spoken during the day. (Incidentally, this appertains to sleep in general; it also applies to a daytime nap—although, in that case, these things unfold in a more fragmentary way.)

And if one then—using the same methods that brought to light the inner weaving of the individualized Logos—investigates what it really is that announces itself initially as a mere outer semblance, when compared to the actual essence of the world, if one searches further for its real, essential nature, then one discovers a profusion of hierarchical beings, those described in the anthroposophical literature as the Dynamis, who are ranked above the Exusiai.

And the third thing one finds—when attempting to develop the art of seeking the real essence contained in the words—the third thing one finds is the essential reality of what I once described as a kind of counter-spine. Perhaps some of you remember how I described the human etheric body many years ago. In the periodical *Lucifer-Gnosis*,† particularly in the articles dealing with the essential nature of the human being, it was already described how the streams belonging to the etheric body in general can also be found working in cooperation with a certain structure situated toward the front of the human being, just as in the physical body the bony structure of the vertebral column, with the spinal canal, are situated toward the back. In the physical body, we have this vertebral column and the spinal canal running vertically; in the etheric body, we have a confluence of streams, a confluence of rays in what I have just described as a kind of opposite spine, but one which, seen from the perspective of the physical body, lies toward the front of the human being. But whereas the nerve cords—and also, for example, the rib bones—originate from the physical spine, the above-mentioned rays and streams in the etheric body occur in such a way that they do not originate from this counter-spine. Rather, they are flowing together within this spine, as it were, with everything that is contained in them working together in the frontal region of the human etheric body.

This presents an extremely beautiful, magnificent, mighty etheric organ, which—more particularly—is a glittering, luminous, resounding entity, disseminating itself in diverse warmth-effects, but also speaking an inner language, an organ which manifests in this way notably while the human being is asleep. And if one beholds it more closely, then one can certainly get some insight into how this organ permeates what I once characterized (because these things must be described in their full pictorial quality) as the various lotus flowers; then, one can recognize how through this organ—which develops from the streams flowing through the etheric body and then forms the lotus flowers by uniting with the currents of the astral body—how through this organ the human being continually finds the connection to the external astral, cosmic world.

And this, again, is a kind of manifestation. Moreover, it is also again something that can be characterized as an external appearance, a semblance, whose true inner being will have to be discovered. And if we search for this inner essential being, then we will find it in the hierarchy designated as the Kyriotetes in my anthroposophical writings. And it is only at this point that we have extracted, from the term "etheric body," what in reality is the true essence of this human etheric body. It is an interactive, collaborative working, flowing, and weaving of the Exusiai, Dynamis, and Kyriotetes, who individualize their respective activities in this streaming, flowing, sounding, and speaking, and form the human etheric body. Moreover, if we consider what the Kyriotetes, Dynamis, and Exusiai are forming and individualizing in this way—so that it builds the etheric body by shining into the human physical body in this individualized way, by warming, sounding, and speaking into it—then we have actually already reached the realm of the human astral body. For within this engaged, active, intense involvement, within this individualizing activity of the second hierarchy—which streams from the cosmos, but becomes individualized in the human being—there is contained the essence of what constitutes the human astral body. In the etheric body, this activity *manifests*; in the astral body, it *is*.

And now, let us consider this combined activity in which the human being is interwoven during sleep. It is indeed so that we are interwoven, unconsciously, into this activity of the second hierarchy during sleep; that we need this whole activity once we have passed through the portal of death. For we must continue to live in this activity between death and a new birth, when the etheric body as such has been cast off, when—after a few days—this resounding, this musical movement, this mildly phosphorescent glowing, these streams of warmth, have flowed away. But in order to describe what one really perceives—when, a few days after death, all this has flowed out into the universal cosmos, when one notices that the glow is spreading out further and further but also growing fainter and fainter and that the music is becoming ever quieter—I would actually have to describe it differently. For, when speaking of these realms, it becomes natural to explain a particular thing through its polar opposite. It would therefore be better, because it corresponds more to what the dead person perceives, if I were to say: What is at first like a silent sounding—but a sounding that is perceptible to the inner human being—becomes louder and louder as it spreads; it is then as if one were to perceive this rise in sound-volume as a waning of the inner etheric music. The reason for this is that, as a soul-spiritual being—who is "dead" from the perspective of the earth—one can, precisely as a result of it becoming louder, no longer perceive this rise in sound-volume because one does not have physical ears, and physical ears would be needed.

Something similar applies with respect to the other experiences undergone by the human being in the first few days immediately after death. Then, however, these things are felt and experienced from within the astral body. And, once again, one speaks only of the outer side when using the words: The human being is in the soul-world, as I described it in my book *Theosophy*.[†] But what I described there—and this initially represents the perception of the soul-organ most immediately accessible to the human being—reveals itself to a universal, cosmic intelligence, which must be developed in the cosmic realm, as the intertwined, interlinked, interwoven activity of the beings of the second hierarchy.

And now, let us take note of what it really means to exist, soon after death, within the activity of these beings of the second hierarchy. Between birth and death, the human being lives on earth, alternating between waking and sleeping. While awake, we are interwoven with this activity, in which the human soul lives, we are interwoven in the Exusiai, Dynamis, and Kyriotetes; but we are obliged to descend again and again into the forms of the physical body. During sleep, we live with the etheric body; but the etheric body imposes an individual quality onto this combined activity [of the spiritual beings], in accordance with the forms of the human physical body. Consequently, the activity of the second hierarchy, in which the human being is interwoven, also has to absorb what one is morally—that is, to what extent one is good or evil, to what extent one is given over to error or truth. This means that the activities characteristic of the beings of the second hierarchy become individualized in accordance with what one is as an earthly human being who is good or bad, as an earthly human being who lives in truth or in error.

But we must first take our direction from the kind of activity that the beings of this second hierarchy intend to pursue, out of their own being, for the sake of the essential nature of the human being. We must, to some extent, take the following into account—and I will have to express it somewhat bluntly. Suppose one is interwoven with a particular being from the hierarchy of the Dynamis. Because of the fact that one has this connection—and also because an archangelic being is mediating this activity—one then develops the faculty of speech within the human organism. But as one develops this ability, the activities of the Dynamis become, in a sense, disarranged and distorted into trivialness. And when human beings use their words to say something evil, something filled with hatred, then these activities of the second hierarchy become seriously contorted. All of this must then be put in order again. All of this must become such that, as human beings, we do not continue to live in the forms that we had given, through our moral or our immoral nature, to all the things I have described. Rather, everything must become such that we strip away all these things and find our way into the work and the activities inherent to the beings of the second hierarchy. This stripping away of the contortions, the trivializations, of all the things that distort the work of the second hierarchy and turn it into its opposite, this stripping away is brought about by what I have described as "the passage of the human being through the soul world." And then we will have ascended to what I described in *Theosophy* as the spirit-land, where we can follow—with our own I-presence, with our innermost soul-spiritual presence—the activities that represent the essential being of the Dynamis and the Kyriotetes.

You see here—through the art of seeking to bring out the real essence from the words—how the true nature of the human being has been characterized once again. In doing so, we come closer and closer to a real insight into this essential nature. Just as one could give an initial indication of the distribution of the figures in a painting by Raphael[†]—say, the Sistine Madonna—by drawing only a few characteristic lines on the blackboard, so we must give only an initial sketch by using the terms physical body, etheric body, astral body, and I. We must first draw with a few lines what, in reality, is full of inner activity and liveliness; and it is precisely in this activity and liveliness that the beings of the cosmos reveal themselves—a cosmos that is both physical and soul-spiritual. In the end, one always comes to beings.

If we describe a particular phenomenon as something that is indeterminately spreading out in space, as something floating in time, if we describe it in this way and then call it the physical world or the etheric world—then what we are actually describing is a manifestation. It is like describing a swarm of insects seen in the distance as "a gray patch in the air" because, unable to distinguish the individual insects, all one can see and describe is a gray patch. Similarly, from the perspective of the real world, what we initially call the etheric body, or the astral body, is actually just such a gray patch. If we see gray patches forming in the physical air and we take a closer look at them, then we discover that, in reality, they are composed of individual insects; and if we take a closer look at the above-mentioned spiritual gray patches—the "etheric body," the "astral body"—then we will always discover beings.

In the end, what we must always come to, with respect to any explanation or understanding of the world, is beings. For the one and only thing that is real is the presence of beings. All things arise only through the interactive cooperation of beings; but, to an indistinct observation this is then seen as something that is not real. Just as the gray cloud, which is not real, is actually composed of real individual beings—the insects—so are individual beings actively at work everywhere in the world, and everything else is merely an illusion arising from the co-existence of these beings. Physical matter, too, is such an illusion. In truth, beings are at the root of everything. We must understand this again so that we do not speak of something that is not really there, whether it is about matter, or—and this is not much better—about spirit in general; so that we instead learn to speak of beings, of the individual beings of the universe.

Long ago, in the ancient Mysteries, people understood that one had to acknowledge the presence of cosmic beings in the universe. And it was already known at that time that one was not describing realities when speaking either of matter or of what is termed "spirit" in ordinary consciousness, which is merely a vague spirituality, supposed to be present in all things as a kind of pantheism. It was known that if one wanted to capture realities, then one must acknowledge the existence of individual beings. However, the awareness of these beings has gradually been lost—lost to the same extent as human beings were beginning to develop this being-like quality within themselves. It is unquestionably the case that in recent times, beginning with the first third of the fifteenth century—I have often mentioned this particular moment in time—human beings have become more and more intellectual, and their understanding of what a human being is has become more and more abstract. But behind this increasingly abstract existence, there is a being who is relying more and more on him- or herself, and becoming ever richer in inner spirituality. And it is precisely because human beings were developing an increasing awareness of their own essential beingness that humanity lost the dream-like consciousness, which it once had in regard to the beings in the cosmos. We must develop the insight again that we will only be able to capture realities if we identify and recognize individual beings in the cosmos.

The necessary course of human evolution was such that, in ancient times, people saw beingness (*Wesenhaftes*) everywhere, because they had a dream consciousness. Then came a time when people experienced these things in such a way that this beingness, all these beings living in the cosmos—Kyriotetes, Dynamis, Exusiai, Archai, Archangeloi, Angeloi, the 'I's of human beings, the group-souls of animals, the cosmic souls of the plants, and so on—were the true realities. They felt that even the animals, as they exist on earth, are not realities; that even they are only semblance, illusion. They felt that the group-souls were the realities; that it is not the earth's entire plant kingdom, but rather the earth's soul that is real; that plants are merely like the hair on the earth's organism, comparable to the hair on our own organism. Moreover, because it was known at one time that all these beings are present in the cosmos—raying out their being, manifesting their being, expressing themselves in speech—people also knew that these revelations, these expressions were emanating from the inner nature of these beings. And this universal resounding that resulted from the confluence of what arises when the individual beings are speaking—this is the Logos. But even the Logos was initially only semblance. And it is only because Christ took hold of this semblance and condensed it within his own being, that this semblance-Logos—through the Mystery of Golgotha—was born on the earth as the real Logos.

This is how we must develop our insight into these interconnections. Then the individual beings can be described spiritually; then one can describe how they shine and resound in a mild phosphorescence, how they disperse streams of warmth, how they speak and express their own essential being. Then a complete spiritual configuration can be found for each individual being. And these complete spiritual formations are the only reality in the universe. With their old dream consciousness, people knew a great deal about these individual realities in the universe. But this knowledge dwindled more and more; one could say that it shrank. At one time people knew: This is how a particular being, known to belong to the Kyriotetes, rays out its form; this is how a human I radiates its form, this is how the Angeloi shine their form, and so on. But people could see less and less of these realities; gradually, all of this shrunk away—as though vanishing into one collective point. Originally, people knew quite well how the manifestations of the Exusiai, for example, differed from the manifestations of the human I, or how these, in turn, differed from the manifestations of the group-souls of the animals or of the earth-soul of the plants. People had known these differences, but this knowledge had gradually descended into the realm of unconsciousness.

Then came a time when all that was left was the awareness: Yes, such realities exist; everything else is not real. Space is not real; time is not real; matter is not real; even spirit, as a general spirituality, is not real. But cosmic individualities are real. These could, however, no longer be distinguished. And so, these entities were described with a uniform term, with the uniform word *monad*. For example, Leibnitz and Giordano Bruno[†] used the term monads in this way. These "monads"—shrunk down to their smallest possible size—actually are the realities I have spoken of. And one monad was, at most, only distinguished from other ones through the addition of a qualitative designation to the word monad: the monads of the Exusiai, the monads of human beings, the monads of animals, and so on.

And finally, human beings also lost the possibility of speaking of monads—to which the great German thinker [Leibnitz] had initially ascribed an imaginative power, because he had an inkling that something spiritual did indeed exist in this idea that had been shrunk down to the "monad." But we should remember that the monad is something living. If human civilization is not to fall into decay but actually advance in its development, then we must do more than just remember the monad; rather, we must understand again—but now with an enhanced, clear consciousness—that all true realities are actually soul-spiritual living beings. But then we must also bring to life what initially is only sketched in a few lines—physical body, etheric body, astral body—in the way we have done today.

Then we begin to see the soul-spiritual nature of the human being interwoven, as it were, with the beings of the second hierarchy. Moreover, if we then pursue how the human being goes from earthly life to earthly life; how a compensating cosmic justice, karma, is working from earthly life to earthly life; how all this accords, at the same time, with certain powers working in the cosmos—then we will, in turn, not stay with the abstract notions "karma," or "universal justice," or even the abstraction "moral world order"; instead, we will come to the realities. If we begin by describing the etheric body, then we will also reach the realm of the second hierarchy; moreover, in doing so, we will then also have described the astral body of the human being. And in just the same way, we can begin by describing the astral body and will then be able to simultaneously get hold of thinking, feeling, and willing in the astral body—as they fade away at the moment of falling asleep and leave together with the astral body. If we begin there, and look for the realities with respect to these faculties, then we find the following. In our human thinking, there actually is the living activity of the Angeloi. In our human speech, which arises out of feeling, there is—as the human being sleeps—the living activity of the Archangeloi. And in what manifests in waking life through the movements of the limbs, through everything that is imbued with will (in which the astral body is involved as well) there is—as the human being sleeps and the astral body is outside—the living world of the Archai.

However, what is outside in this way—the suprasensory activities of Archai, Archangeloi, and Angeloi, which find a reflection in the waking human being in willing, feeling, and thinking—must be brought into harmony with the etheric body and the physical body. The physical body must therefore also be formed in such a way that it can become an organ of thought, an organ of speech, an organism of movement. And here we see how the activity of the Kyriotetes, Dynamis, Exusiai, in turn, transitions into an even higher activity—the activity of the Thrones, who bring the will-actions of human beings into accord with their physical organism, with the metabolic-limb organization of the human being. Then we come to the hierarchy of the Cherubim, who bring the human faculty of speech into accord with the organs that provide the physical basis of speech. In the organs of speaking and singing—in fact, in everything that serves as organs of speech or speech-like functions in the human being—the Cherubim bring the human life of feeling into accord with the speech organism. Now, everything related to the faculty of thinking must also have its physical organ in the human nerve-sense organism, and it is the Seraphim who bring thinking into accord with this nerve-sense organism of the human being, while speech, and everything connected with speaking, is brought into accord with both thinking and feeling by the Cherubim.

Accordingly, when we consider the threefold human being, we see the Seraphim and their creative power in the nerve-sense organization, which is the foundation for thinking; we see the Cherubim and their creative power in everything that comprises the human rhythmic organization—which, as a physical organism, must be brought into accord with the faculty of speech. And everything that comes to expression in the movements of the human limbs and in all activity of will—which requires the inner organization of the human metabolic-limb system—all of this is brought into concordance by the Thrones. From this we can also see what the physical human form actually is; how it dissolves into semblance; and that, behind it, stand the realities: the Seraphim, Cherubim, and Thrones. We are, therefore, always seeing into the activity of the Seraphim, Cherubim, and Thrones whenever the human I is interwoven with its inner actions, whenever the human being—in waking life—moves, speaks, feels, and thinks.

In this way, we can once again find a renewed Mystery wisdom for humanity, a Mystery wisdom which, one could say, again employs the art of freeing the spirit from the word, of uncovering the essence from what can initially only be sketched in a few lines as physical human being, etheric human being, astral human being, and I. This essence always consists of individual spiritual beings, who inwardly carry and actively experience anything of a soul nature, and who fashion what becomes outwardly manifest—the physical. The only true realities are the spirit-individualities who exist in the act of being (*seiende Geistindividualitäten*). The reason that they express themselves as something soul-like is that they have inner experiences both of themselves and of each other while mutually invigorating one another. The reason that there is a physical world is that these spiritual individualities—who were reduced to the abstraction "monads" and then disappeared altogether from human perception—reveal themselves in the process of creating, in accordance with their various stages of existence. At this point, we can step back from the created world—which is actually nothing other than the outer appearance of beings in the act of creating—and turn to the world that experiences itself, the world of soul, which is the creating, self-experiencing world of spirit-individualities. If, in this way, we turn to the actual reality, then we come to the individual spiritual beings themselves; for the world is their manifestation and their life.

While we stand on the earth as human beings, we invariably live among the manifestations of individual spiritual beings. Between death and a new birth, we must behold and pass through the full reality of the characteristic forms of these spiritual individualities. And in order to achieve a certain perfection in our overall development, we must try to find our way from a state of being in which we are able to behold the spiritual realities in their true form, to our earthly state of being, in which we do not behold the individual spiritual beings, in which they show themselves only from outside, as it were, only in their outer garments.

Moreover, if earthly life is not to fall into complete decay, we must learn again to behold, recognize, and understand—from these outer garments—the inner spirit-individuality of the higher world. Then we will see that our whole life consists in an ongoing effort within this outer garment of the divine; that it is a life within the essential being of the divine. But we can only find our right bearing within this being of the divine if we gradually educate our own being toward a true beholding—also of this outer garment. But we must also learn to penetrate through this garment in order to reach the beings. We must not stay with the outer depictions, but advance to the inner life.

And if, one day, a considerable number of people will be striving for this, then it will bring about the dawn of a future development of the Earth, of a transformation of Earth existence into the new forms of existence on Jupiter, Venus, and Vulcan. The Anthroposophical Society must unite human beings who sense that they are the nucleus of what must spread to ever wider circles in the civilization of humanity, so that progress in the evolution of humanity can come about and that earthly life will not degenerate.

Our Thought Life in Sleeping and Waking and in the Existence after Death

STUTTGART, JUNE 21, 1923

IF WE CONTEMPLATE the human being and human existence on the earth, then what must undoubtedly appear most important among the manifestations of this earthly life is the ability to think and form mental images, the ability to think about the world, about one's own actions and so on. We would be deceiving ourselves if we were to come to any other conclusions about how life on earth unfolds. Certainly, many things might lead us to conclude that our thinking cannot possibly be the most valuable aspect. For example, we may well perceive—just below the threshold of conscious thoughts, as it were—that our perceptions and feelings about our own tasks, about our conduct toward our fellow human beings, and even about the world, are of more value than our faculty of thinking. And, especially if we consider our moral existence, and become attentive to the voice of conscience, then we may well tell ourselves that this voice of conscience speaks to us from soul-depths that can never be reached by our faculty of thinking.

We may be particularly inclined to make such a comment if we wanted to point out that, even with the most well-developed faculty of thinking attainable through schooling in ordinary earthly life, we would not be able, in a moral sense, to match what the impulses of a purer—one may even be tempted to say, a simpler—conscience achieves. Nevertheless, we would be mistaken if we were to believe that, since all these things are true—and they are certainly true—our faculty of thinking is *not* the most essential element of human life on earth, because undoubtedly the voice of conscience, feelings of compassion, and so on, ring forth from inexpressibly deeper sources than our thoughts. However, these impulses welling up and sounding forth from deep levels of the soul only appear in the right light for human beings and only become something that is elevated to the human level, if they are permeated by thinking. The voice of conscience, too, only derives its value from the fact that it works its way up from the depths of the soul, but then comes to full expression in the realm of our thoughts, so that we can clothe in thoughts what this voice of conscience tells us. If we want to stay clear of illusions regarding our human consciousness, then we will have to acknowledge—without overestimating the faculty of thinking—that it is this ability to think that makes a human being into a human being. And, in a certain respect, the German philosopher Hegel[†] is right when he states that thinking is what distinguishes human beings from animals.

However, if we consider the total compass of the thoughts that fill us throughout our entire life from the time of waking up to the time of falling asleep, and if we are honest in contemplating and observing this, then we would have to say that most of our thoughts in this earthly life are in some way dependent on what comes from outside, on the sense impressions and experiences that are associated with the material circumstances of earthly existence; we would have to say that, since our thoughts are intimately connected with life on earth, the most valuable things in human life are associated with our earthly life as it exists between birth and death. But if we consider earthly human life in its entirety—as we did from certain points of view in previous lectures that I was privileged to give here—then we must note that at least a third of our existence on earth goes by without any thoughts at all. If, using the means available to ordinary consciousness, we look back on our earthly life, then we actually link daytime experiences to daytime experiences and, naturally, leave out the sleep experiences—which remain in the unconscious. But in doing so, in reviewing our life in the usual way, we leave out at least a third of our life from this contemplation. This is self-evident, of course, because this third of earthly life, the third that we spent sleeping, remains in the unconscious.

You know, however, from my earlier lectures, that the time we spend in unconscious sleep is not without experiences. Our I and our astral being undergo their own experiences between falling asleep and waking up; but these experiences do not light up within our consciousness. And if we look more closely, we will find that these unconscious forces that are active between falling asleep and waking up, continue to exist in the waking state. But one could say that, even there, they continue to live a sleep existence. These forces work in the whole realm of our will activity, which is no clearer to our ordinary consciousness than the state of sleep. And they also continue to work in a large portion of our feeling life, which constitutes a kind of dream existence.

It is specifically when we contemplate what rises up from our deepest being, from our fundamental nature, that we must look at this as something that is unconscious even during our waking state. Then we find, through spiritual-scientific observation, that what is active in the human being between falling asleep and waking up continues to work in the waking state, continues to work as an I and an astral being; then we find that these forces, however, do not enter the sphere of ordinary consciousness but only appear in their effects, in the impulses and expressions of our will and of our life of feeling. This observation also brings to light a particular aspect of what, in fact, is present in full waking consciousness—the life of thought. And it is precisely this special aspect that becomes more comprehensible to us when we take a closer look at the life that human beings spend *not* on the earth but, rather, between death and a new birth.

When we pass through the portal of death, we undergo certain conditions. I have often described these conditions, which have also been recorded in our literature and which you are familiar with already—at least, from certain perspectives. If we examine carefully and precisely which particular members of the human being are linked to our faculty of thinking, to our faculty of forming mental images, then we find that, in order for us to have thoughts while living on the earth, we need the physical body. It is really the physical body that needs to be set into action if the human being is to have thoughts as an earthly being. However, in order to achieve this objective of having thoughts, the etheric body must also be brought into activity. But these are also precisely the two members of the human configuration that remain behind in bed, unconscious—or so it appears—between falling asleep and waking up. And only when we have attained a certain development of our consciousness, a certain schooling of the soul—which enables a person to view even physical things from their spiritual perspective—only then do we discover that human beings are continually thinking while asleep. If we consider the whole human being, we can say that during earthly life we are never not thinking.

However, when we return into our physical and etheric bodies upon awaking in the morning, our ordinary consciousness is squeezed back rather quickly into the physical and etheric bodies, and the only thing that this ordinary consciousness becomes aware of is that external things then begin to make impressions; that we then have sense perceptions, which we process conceptually; that we then perceive the objects around us with our senses. But if we reach the stage of being able to descend much more consciously into our physical and etheric bodies, then we encounter this thinking when we wake up—the thinking that has been going on continually while we were asleep, albeit without our I and astral body being involved in it. We think—in the sense that our physical body and our etheric body are partaking in a continuous thought activity between falling asleep and waking up. But we are outside of this thought activity with our I and our astral body; we do not consciously participate in it and believe that it does not exist. In this regard, we exist in a state of great self-deception concerning our own human nature.

Now, it is true that we can better recognize a particular aspect when it appears isolated—that is, in an atypical way—from what in ordinary life is beautifully and harmoniously integrated into the whole essential nature of the human being, actually into the whole nature of all beings. Hence, we may be able to recognize—even just based on experiences arising in the external world—not only that we think between falling asleep and waking up, but that we actually think more intelligently while asleep, when we are not consciously present, than when we *are* present. Accordingly, if we survey this entire situation, we may well come to the acknowledgment about our own nature—one could even call it a depressing self-confession—that our etheric body's thinking is poorer when we are present in it with the normal consciousness of our I and our astral body than when we are not in it. We spoil the thoughts that are occurring in our etheric body by being present within it with our normal consciousness.

Therefore, anyone who has insight into these things can certainly confirm stories such as the following. There once were two university students. One was a student of philology who knew nothing about calculating numbers—I have to add this—who understood nothing about calculations at all. The other was a student of mathematics. Now, we know that when it comes to certain elements in the study of mathematics, one needs to sweat a bit over the problems, whereas in philology things tend to come more easily. And this is how it was with these students, who, as often happens with students, shared a room, and slept together in this room. One night, when they had finished the preparations for their exams, the philology student was very pleased with himself; the math student, on the other hand, was not satisfied at all because he could not solve a problem that he needed to solve for a written assignment. He went to bed very dissatisfied, and the following strange event transpired. At a certain hour, the philology student woke up and saw the math student get out of bed, walk to the desk, and continue his ponderings; he also saw him write for quite some time, then go back to bed, and lie down to sleep. The next day, when both got up, the student of mathematics said: "We didn't even have a drink yesterday, and yet I have a terrible hangover today!" The other one said: "It is no wonder, if you get up at three o'clock in the night and do calculations for hours, that you have a strained head the next morning." The first one then responded: "I didn't get up!" He knew absolutely nothing about getting up. Then they investigated and, lo and behold, the student had solved the problem, although he had no awareness at all of doing so.

Such things are by no means just fairytales. I chose an example described in the literature because it can be checked. I could tell you many similar instances. This particular case is not what is important here; what matters is that it actually points to a reality. When consciousness is not present—and it was mentioned specifically that the person in question knew nothing of what happened—the physical and etheric bodies are worked upon through jolts from outside, as it were, and the etheric body then works alone within the physical body on continuing the task.

Now, I know what is surfacing in the minds of many; I know that some of you would gladly see this kind of thing happen rather more often. But as modern human beings we do not have it quite so easy. What we see in a case such as this is that the I and the astral body are only working through jolts from the outside; and that the etheric body, if it can work alone in the physical body, actually proves to be clever, even ingenious, compared to what we achieve—often without much genius at all—when we are present with our I and our astral body. This story was mentioned merely to illustrate the fact that the human being has thoughts all night long—or rather, the physical body and the etheric body of the human being—except that we are not involved in this process with our I and our astral body. For thoughts are formed directly from the outer world through the mediation of the etheric body, and then the physical body becomes the instrument through which the physical earthly human being cultivates these thoughts.

Accordingly, we have to recognize that our life of thought is indeed tied to the physical body and the etheric body. This is not the case with our life of feeling and our life of will. It is merely a superstition when today's official science maintains that our feelings and our will are dependent on the physical and etheric bodies in the same way as our thought life is. I have often spoken of this and I will therefore not dwell on it today; instead, I will only point to the various observations made on previous occasions, which many of you attended.

Now, as human beings living on the earth at the present time, our constitution is not such that we can follow what our I and our astral body experience when—separated from the etheric body and the physical body—they take along with them, from ordinary life, only our will and a portion of our life of feeling. For, what is experienced between going to sleep and waking up actually takes place in a completely different world. It takes place in a spiritual world, a world in which the surroundings are not the kingdoms of nature, the mineral kingdom, the plant kingdom; it is a world in which the surroundings are the higher hierarchies, the spiritual beings, and spiritual events. But insofar as we are human beings living on the earth, we have certainly not yet reached the stage of development that would enable us to follow—on the level of consciousness and self-consciousness—what we experience with our I and our astral body between falling asleep and waking up. This experience remains unconscious but, despite that, is no less alive than what becomes conscious. It is something that is undergone, something that—after it has been experienced—belongs to the inner substance, to the inner constitution of the human being. Consequently, we wake up every morning in a transformed state, a state corresponding to the degree of transformation undergone during the night. We do not simply wake up in the state that was reached in the evening before we fell asleep; instead, we wake up in the state that we have been made into by our life of sleep.

When we then pass through the portal of death, we discard the physical and etheric bodies. Accordingly, the experience we have in the first few days, right after passing through the portal of death—because the withdrawal of the etheric body only takes a few days—is such that we feel as though our thought life was being sucked up by the cosmos. First, we have a brief glance over our previous earthly life. It is then as if we were looking at this earthly life as our world, seeing it in living images. All at once, as though at one stroke, our past earthly life stands before our soul—once the soul is completely free of the physical body and the etheric body, in other words, when the passage through the portal of death has taken place. However, this process continues for several days, the process whereby—after the physical body has been discarded—the etheric body slowly dissolves within the universal cosmic ether. During this time, the impression is such that, at first, there is an animated, distinctly contoured overview of the person's earthly life; that it then grows weaker and weaker, but also becomes more cosmic, as it were; and eventually, after a few days, that it then melts away from the human being.

And through this process, everything that is actually most valuable about earthly life departs from the human being during these few days. All the thoughts we have about the things of the world, about our whole earthly environment, everything that fills our ordinary consciousness—all this melts away from us, melts away within a few days. And to the same extent that this content of earthly life melts away, what emerges instead—to that very same extent—is what the human being experiences unconsciously during the sleep state. Our consciousness now expands its range into this realm; it gradually becomes conscious. If we had no experiences during sleep, then our life—as our conscious life—would come to an end three or four days after death. For, what we considered most valuable during our life on earth melts away; and what emerges from this darkening, dimming consciousness is what we lived through each time we slept but what remained unconscious for us in that state of sleep.

Now, the distinctive characteristic of what we experience during the sleep state is that, from the perspective of this state, the world takes its course in reverse. It makes no difference whether this sleep is long or short, because once we are asleep, this other state of consciousness has a completely different relation to time. Therefore, the characteristic I am describing holds true for all sleep timelines—whether you sleep all night long or only for a few minutes. When we are traversing the time between falling asleep and waking up, we experience in reverse what we had lived through in the physical world between our last time of waking up and falling asleep. We live through it once more in another form; we navigate it in a different way.

With our waking consciousness we have our experiences more with physical nuances—and with feelings about these physical nuances; we live through the sequence of events from the beginning to the end and through each single occurrence or situation as they follow one another, experiencing them in their physical and intellectual nuances. In sleep, however, we experience all of this again in reverse, but now with moral nuances. That is where our moral-religious impulses live; that is where we go through events in such a way that we evaluate each occasion according to how relevant or irrelevant it makes us as a human being. That is where we do not have any illusions—as would be the case if we were to consciously go through it—about the significance of whether we have accomplished something or not, because that is where we evaluate the events of the day in terms of our humanity.

With regard to how it relates to our human constitution on earth, natural science is not actually wrong when it says that there is only causality in the world, only cause and effect, only justification for explaining later events from earlier events—because in our waking life we only see and perceive this stream. However, there is actually another stream contained in the reality of life, although it remains unconscious for our earthly consciousness. Even so, human beings experience this moral world order every night between falling asleep and waking up. That is where we evaluate things morally, particularly as regards our own human value. We do this every night—or, more precisely, every period between falling asleep and waking up—in relation to the preceding time of being awake. And when we have gone through the portal of death, we pass in reverse order through our last night, the next-to-last night, the night before that, and so on, right up to the first night of the time after birth when consciousness awakened for the first time; this takes about a third of our lifetime on earth, since we spent about a third of our life sleeping. The physical, cause-and-effect course of the world subsides for us, and what then rises up before us is what the gods and the spiritual beings think, feel, and will about this course of the world. But initially, we still relate to it through the coloration, the hues, with which earthly life colors everything, because we have to undergo it in the form in which we experienced it during our life on earth. Since we spend a third of our life sleeping, we need about a third of the time of our earthly life for this experience of living through it again in reverse—which then takes its course as I have described it, for example, in my book *Theosophy*, in the description of the soul-land, the soul-world.

Before we enter a world that is purely spiritual, we must first live through everything that we experienced unconsciously during our states of sleep on earth. In this way, we are schooling our consciousness to become able to actually experience things spiritually between death and a new birth. And this experience of living through our earthly life in reverse is, at the same time, a process of loosening our ties to earthly life. Until we have freed ourselves precisely in this way—that is, by going through our life in reverse—we will not be sufficiently free in our consciousness, free in the sense that this consciousness can move among the spirits of the higher worlds in accordance with its full potential. And it is approximately at this point that we will have arrived at the start of our life in the higher worlds. Then, the rest of our life between death and a new birth can take its course in such a way that it is a purely spiritual experience.

Just as we live here among physical beings and physical events, so do we then live in the spiritual world among spiritual beings and spiritual events. There, we live among the spiritual beings who never descend to earth, and among their activities; we also live among the beings who will descend, or have descended, to the earth as human beings—those who have passed through the gate of death before we did, and those who will come after us. It really is true that we meet up again with all the people we knew during our life on earth; and this community of human beings is really a very extensive one. For, since we live through these experiences during our life of sleep, everything that we went through—no matter how briefly—with human beings, during our life on earth, is included in this community. Even though it is true that we are already in the spiritual world during each period of sleep—when we live through earthly events in reverse—it is precisely the fact that we do this as *earthly* human beings that distinguishes this nightly earthly experience from what we then undergo once we have passed through the portal of death.

To begin with, we have to acknowledge to ourselves that what we recognize as the content of our earthly consciousness melts away from us in the course of a few days; and that what we did *not* take note of at all in the course of earthly life—because it was submerged under the surface of consciousness during sleep—then breaks through that surface, inasmuch as we now truly experience it and really live through it. For in those earthly sleep states, we experienced with our I and our astral body only the events of our waking life, as we lived through them pictorially and in reverse order. But when we pass through the portal of death, we immerse ourselves in spiritual substance, just as we immerse ourselves in physical substance when we become earthly human beings. One could certainly say that, just as we receive a physical and an etheric body when we become earthly human beings, so do we receive a higher form of beingness as an outer sheath, as a spiritual sheath, when we have passed through the portal of death. And, through this process, we now experience as a reality what we only experienced pictorially during our sleep states here on earth. It is a real, true experience, just as our experience of living life on earth in a physical body encompasses real earthly life. And it is this real experience—which is a recapitulation, but now as a reality, of the picture-experiences of our sleep states—that forms the basis for the subsequent experiences that we go through in the further course of our life between death and a new birth.

What then follows in this period between death and a new birth—once we have discarded our entire earthly existence, as it were—is the phase during which, as I mentioned earlier, we prepare our next earthly life by developing, in communion with the beings of the spiritual world, the spiritual seed of our next earthly life and, above all, of our next physical body. This is then followed, in turn, by a phase during which the human being becomes more oriented toward earthly life again. After having lived for a long time among spiritual beings and spiritual realities between death and a new birth, the human being then enters a state comparable to that of someone who feels tired and wants to fall asleep. Naturally, this takes place on a completely different level, but I want to explain it by means of a comparison. What I mean is that the human being now feels how the consciousness that exists in the spirit becomes weaker and how it is no longer possible, in that sense, to work together with the beings of the spiritual world; this consciousness is now adjusting again toward an interest in a new life on earth.

Just as we sink into sleep every day, when our consciousness becomes completely unconscious, so do we sink down, as it were, within the purely spiritual consciousness that fills the majority of our time between death and a new birth. In this case, however, we do not sink into unconsciousness but, rather, into being filled with interest in life on earth—but now seen from the other side, from the side of the spiritual world—into an interest in earthly life. This interest in earthly life arises many years, even many centuries, before we descend to life on earth. We already become interested in our future earthly life long before not only our grandparents but even far more distant ancestors, many generations before us, live on earth—from whom we then eventually descend. This interest, which had been focussed on the purely spiritual world for such a long time between death and a new birth, is now transformed into an interest in the course of the generations. At the end of these succeeding generations, we ourselves are then born. Through long periods of time, we actually follow from the spiritual world the ancestral succession, at the end of which our own parents stand. In this way, we grow together with our ancestry from out of the spiritual world.

A day will come when these things will enter general human consciousness, and only then will we see to what extent the often-repeated statements of science—a science which, despite its exactness, is rather inadequate—to what limited extent these statements are valid today with respect to the concept of heredity. Physical heredity can only become comprehensible to us if we know how the forces through which we were already involved in our ancestry from the spiritual world, actually contribute to the physical formation of heredity. If it is pointed out to us, through a science that limits itself to the physical world, that we have certain characteristics of our great-great-grandfather, then we must not forget how, even while this great-great-grandfather was alive, we already took an interest, from the spiritual world, in what this great-great-grandfather was like; and how we grow into what then develops outwardly as characteristics through the succeeding generations. We really grow into it from the spiritual world.

These things will also gain practical significance later on, when anthroposophy becomes a part of the general culture of humanity. We hardly realize how much in the way of despondency and lack of soul-energy arises today in a semi-conscious or unconscious way as a result of our thoughts about heredity—because science, in particular, can only speak about these hereditary relationships in a completely inadequate fashion. But these things have even permeated the arts and have already been assimilated into the common human way of thinking.

Once we become permeated with the awareness that we are not only connected to the physical formation of our ancestors but also to the evolution of our own soul—which follows the entire ancestral development from the spiritual world and helps build this ancestral development—then this awareness will indeed become an inward reality for us. Then, energy and courage will once again come from the spirit into the souls of quite a few of the people who, as a result of today's way of thinking, are experiencing despondency and a lack of energy. For there is not much value to knowing some particular aspects about the spiritual world theoretically. Most of the time, we even clothe what we think about the spiritual world in physical thought forms. It is not a question, however, of forming theoretical thoughts about the spiritual world for ourselves—although we must of course have them first, these thoughts, so that they enter our life of feeling and our will—but the essential thing is that they can then *live* in our mind and in our feelings.

In order to illustrate this, I would like to say the following. As a result of certain time-dependent circumstances, which I have recently characterized in Dornach,[†] the anthroposophical movement worked hand-in-hand with the so-called theosophical movement for a while. It never adopted the teachings of the theosophical movement, but only found an audience within the Theosophical Society. But there are of course certain teachings that are also known to the theosophical movement. Those who only distinguish these things superficially, confuse theosophy with anthroposophy. Despite the fact that many people do this, it should be clear to you that there is a great, profound difference. I would like to characterize this important difference through the following remarks.

Please try to examine carefully what theosophical teachings actually put forward. It is true that these teachings also refer to the members of the human constitution, the members of the essential human being, even using the same names as far as the lower members are concerned—physical body, etheric body, astral body. But if you go deeper into the characterizations, then you will find that the physical body is described as a dense body, the etheric body as a body that is a little less dense and more like a kind of vapor, and the astral body as a body that is even less dense, as an even thinner vapor; after that, you will have to put in quite an effort but you will only come to a vapor that gets ever thinner. Just take a look for yourself and observe how little this [theosophical] literature addresses what the anthroposophical writings expect even of elementary-level readers—namely, to picture the etheric body not as something thinner but, rather, as something that is actually the opposite of the physical body. In the same way as the physical body fills space, the etheric body takes something away from it. Physical matter fills space; etheric substance sucks space away. There is nothing here by way of a definition that would imply an ever-thinner nebula; instead, it is really the beginning of the path to spiritual observation. Some people are actually perturbed by this, because the ever-thinning nebulae offer them a lovely opportunity to create a link to the physical world; the whole thing can then be pictured in physical images, so that whole systems, whole worldviews, can be constructed through this theosophical approach.

Likewise, as I have also outlined earlier, when a human being goes through the portal of death, that person's thoughts melt away within a few days. According to the theosophical view, however, they melt away in a few hours and are one of the first things to be forgotten. The strange thing is that thoughts resulting from a spiritistic approach are not effective at all, not even in the very first moments after death; the human being cannot possibly carry them through the portal of death. The thoughts that people derive from spiritistic experiments are the most materialistic thoughts of all. This is confirmed by the fact that such thoughts are not actually carried beyond death. And while spiritists believe that they receive thoughts from a spiritual world passed on to them by mediums, the truth is that any thoughts derived from spiritism do not even reach beyond death. This is how powerful the illusions are that people indulge in when, one way or another, they want to form ideas about the spiritual world.

The important thing is not that we merely think about the spiritual world. It is true that we must have such thoughts initially, so that the content of the spiritual world can actually enter our soul, but what matters is that these thoughts turn out to be filled with creative life. The usual physical earthly thoughts are abstract thoughts. Most scientific thoughts are very abstract; such thoughts do not actually accomplish anything in the human being—just as little as mirror images can do anything. Such thoughts are merely images. If you and another person are looking into a mirror at the same time and you get slapped in the face, then you will not attribute the slap in the face to any of the reflections in the mirror but, instead, to the real person standing next to you. Thoughts are just like the mirror images—they do not do anything; they do not act as impulses in the reality of life. It is only the moral intuitions in our thoughts that can act as impulses. And this is why, even though we have to start from thoughts, our thoughts about the spiritual world must work as realities—not as thoughts.

It is only when we perceive thoughts as realities, and also experience them as realities, that we actually enter into the real anthroposophical worldview. This is also the very issue that is frequently met with objections. For, if these things are understood superficially, people will say that this whole anthroposophical worldview could even be based on delusions; that human beings are subject to auto-suggestion. They might say, as an example, that some people are so impressionable that the very thought of drinking lemonade fills them with the same sensation one can have when actually drinking lemonade. It is true that there are people who are so sensitive that they need only think about lemonade and they will have the taste of lemonade in their mouth. If this is brought forward as an objection, then it is correct; but just let us hear from people who say that they have actually quenched their thirst by the mere thought of lemonade! This is definitely not what they would say! Mere thoughts do not become realities. Moreover, as long as anthroposophy remains mere thought, it is like an imagined lemonade. But it does not need to remain that way, because anthroposophy is derived from a spiritual reality. It does not simply work as a thought; instead, it works in the same way as the outer reality of physical matter works on the physical body. It permeates and pulses through human will and human feeling. It becomes a reality in the human being. This is the important thing.

Ultimately, nothing special has been achieved if we hold anthroposophy only as a theory. It has to become life. And it is especially in one respect that it can become life, that it fills our souls with energy, perseverance, and courage. It becomes life when—in moments of anxiety about our physical life on earth, of deepest sorrow, of profoundest suffering—we look up to a spiritual world and can then be filled with inner joy, with inner consolation, with inner energy. That is when anthroposophy becomes like a living being; that is when it becomes something that accompanies us, that moves in our midst as a living being. Then it will actually have become what it is meant to be for us; then it will permeate all our activities and inspire us to really enter this world. For we are placed on the earth not only for the sake of physical matter but also for the sake of the spirit. Above all, anthroposophy will then lead to a real knowledge of what we are as human beings.

For, if we simply look at the human being in such a way that, after a person has died, we disregard what has passed through the gate of death and only focus on what is left behind as a physical body and study it in an anatomical sense by dissecting the corpse, by looking at it physiologically—then, in this way, we learn very little about the human being. For, in that case, everything in the human being becomes more or less of equal value—or, put another way, the blood cells become very similar to the nerve cells. It is true, of course, that people still distinguish between them—I do not wish to tell you anything nonsensical—but these distinctions are not made in terms of what is essential. In terms of their essential nature, the blood and nerve cells can only be differentiated if one understands the relationship of this elementary entity, the cell, to the spirit.

Now, with respect to the nerve cells, even the tiniest nerve particles, it can be said that the human nerve organization provides an earthly home, as it were, for what comes from the spirit. When we leave the spiritual world and become citizens of the earth again, we enter our physical body through certain processes, which have already been described. What assists us in our descent into the physical world is everything connected with the human nerve organization. One could say that, as we descend from the spiritual world, we place ourselves into our nerve system. And the characteristic feature of this human nerve organization—of each single nerve cell, of each tiny nerve particle—is that the spiritual element fills the nerve substance in such a way that within the essence of this human nerve organization we have what may be called spirit condensed into matter. It is nearly correct to say that within the earthly human being, a continual exchange is occurring between nerve substance and blood substance. And even if it is not quite like that, this exchange occurs in such a way that the actual blood substance is not accepted within the nerve substance and is continually cast out, meaning that there is something in our nerve substance which, for the duration of our entire earthly life, cannot really be permeated by the spirituality of the earth.

When we are born on the earth, we enter into our nerve organization and, in doing so, we are actually saying: We are the offspring of heaven. Insofar as we are beings living in a nerve organization, we have our roots in heaven; and we gain a foothold spiritually, and thus remain the offspring of heaven, to the extent that we live in our human nerve system. One could say that the spiritual essence that we were before [in heaven] has become more rigid; that it now becomes incorporated into the remainder—the part that is not the nerve human being but, as its extreme opposite, the blood human being. It gets incorporated, but this is a different kind of substance. It is a substance that maintains a continuous intimate reciprocal activity with the spirit, a substance that is continually transfused† with spirit. Whereas the spiritual element becomes rigid in the body's nerve organization, it is constantly being created anew in the body's blood system; this is where the actual earthly metamorphosis lives. These two human entities are joined together, but are entirely distinct from one another, just as positive and negative electricity are distinct from each other. As human beings we carry this polarity within us in relation to the nature of our body's nerve and blood organization. The other organs are metamorphosed organs—metamorphosed out of the blood and the nerves.

It is a completely different thing whether something is occurring in our blood organization, which has then become an earthly process, or whether something is occurring in our nerve organization. However, we are not conscious of this at all because the substance of the spiritual element has become so rigidified that everything is reflected back. It is then actually our thoughts that are reflected back. But we carry this duality, this twoness, within us—that is to say, the fact that we always are a descendant of heaven and a seed of the earth. Offspring of heaven, seed of the earth—they are polar opposites, but they are working together.

Now, please permit me to make use of a comparison. Think of two opposite states. Imagine a scale with the left and right beam of the scale attached at the pivoting point; balance occurs when the weight on one side is as great as the weight on the other side. Whenever you increase the weight in one pan of the scale, you must also increase it on the other side if the scale beam is to remain at the horizontal position. There is one point, however, that is not involved or interested in this at all—namely, the point from which the balance beam is suspended. You can carry the scale around anywhere as long as you hold it at the one point where the balance beam is affixed. You will always be able to see that the left is dependent on the right and vice versa, but also that the suspension point is not bothered by this at all. There, everything is in balance, and whatever happens in the two pans of the scale is completely independent from what is happening right at the suspension point of the scale. You can actually make any kind of movement and, if you have enough dexterity, you could even make a movement at the suspension point—none of this has any relation at all to what is happening on the scale, on the right or on the left side of the balance beam.

This is also how it is with the human being. But in the case of the human being, there is no suspension point; instead, there is a state of equilibrium between what we are as a nerve human being, and the being we become on the earth. There is a connection between these two aspects, a connection that can be investigated. For example, if someone has strongly developed thoughts, then these may be expressed in resoluteness of will. And if someone has strongly developed muscles, then that person will also develop different thoughts about activities of will. And in between, there is a state of equilibrium. This state of equilibrium is not located in the head, as the representative of the nerve human being, nor in the limbs, as the representative of the blood human being. It lies in between and is something like a fulcrum, which is the state of equilibrium between both.

And what is the outcome of this state of equilibrium for the human being? You see, if a scale could move independently, then it would be able to move at its point of equilibrium without being concerned about whether its balance beams hold weights or not. And it is because of this state of equilibrium within us that we live our lives as earthly human beings, despite what natural science has discovered with respect to the causality of the will, the lack of freedom, and the origin of will impulses. Just as it is true that there is legitimacy to the law governing the balance between the right and the left beams of the scale, so is everything true that natural science says about the origin of our will impulses. However, the will itself lies in the fulcrum, in the state of equilibrium. Consequently, one must first develop insight into the true nature of the human being in order to be able to evaluate whether the human being is a free being or not. But this insight only arises if one understands the relationship of the spirit to positive matter on the one hand, and to negative matter on the other, or, one could say, a human being's relationship—both the positive and the negative—to matter. Then we discover that the region between these two realms is where the human being becomes a free being; then we get insight into what it is that enables the human being to rise above causality and also above spiritual determinism.

In former times, there was spiritual determinism. Based on it, philosophy declared that everything in the human being had to be determined by the spirit—and, based on its equivalent in more recent times, by natural causality. Just as the determinists were dabbling around with the nerve human being—and did not realize that different, opposing forces always bring about an equilibrium—so do people today potter around with natural causality. Both approaches lead to an unfree human being. Freedom actually lies in between the two.

What this means, then, is that we can only truly comprehend the physical world if we are able to correctly envisage the precise relationship of this physical world to the spiritual one. It is not enough to simply say that the physical world has its foundation in a spiritual world. That would, at best, lead to the trivial notion: Here stands the physical human being and a spiritual archetype is floating around somewhere. It would not lead to a concept of the physical human being. The only way that the physical human being can be viewed correctly is by realizing that the spiritual world has a completely different relationship to one half of the human being than it has to the other half; and that there is a point of equilibrium in between the two, untouched by either, which creates human freedom.

Essentially, an inner joy should arise in the soul—and I will speak momentarily about what can be effected through thoughts that are drawn as living thoughts from the spiritual realm—an inner joy should arise in the soul if it is able to say to itself: It is as if scales are falling from my eyes when I can recognize that the human being is free, and when I am able to see the reasons for this freedom. As long as people merely understand anthroposophy with brilliant intelligence—and I would not want to deny that anthroposophists have it—as long as people acknowledge it only as a thought, anthroposophy will not yet have come alive. It is only when souls would want to burst with delight at an especially important realization and be joyfully excited at having come to one or another insight, it is only at that moment—provided such people feel themselves to be anthroposophists—that the anthroposophical movement really comes into being. For it can only arise as an anthroposophical movement if it comes to life in the whole human being. Then it also intersects with the aforementioned state of equilibrium.

Now, my dear friends, I would like to let you go at the end of this lecture by leaving you with a mental image that poses the question: To what extent can we, already now, be set inwardly aglow and be joyfully excited through thoughts that are inspired by anthroposophical knowledge? With this point of view in mind, please reflect on the real beginning of the anthroposophical movement!

The Hollowness of Words and the Shallowness of Contemporary Thinking

An Evaluation of Mauthner, Rubner, Schweitzer

STUTTGART, JULY 4, 1923

In our time, there is not much understanding—outside of the realm of the anthroposophical movement—of how one is actually supposed to form a true conception of the soul again. In saying this, I have made a statement which, on the one hand, may sound completely incomprehensible to some, because the assumption is often made that we know what the soul is, that we know what is involved when one speaks of the soul, and so on. And then again, on the other hand, such a statement can also often be taken as something that is self-evident, in the sense that the centuries-old, even millennia-old views of the human soul supposedly have run their course and that we simply must wait with forming conceptions about the human soul until scientific research will have come far enough to be in a position to really explain the nature of the soul.

However, I would now like to counterbalance these two objections with what the recently deceased linguist Fritz Mauthner, whom I have often mentioned, asserted—namely, that people today oftentimes believe that they have a particular viewpoint about one thing or another, when in fact they only have words. It was for this reason that Mauthner wrote his *Critique of Language*.† He wanted to show that contemporary civilized humanity, in particular, has a language that is inherited. We have expressions for just about everything. But if we take a closer look at what lies hidden behind the words, then, in reality, there is nothing. We have a word, and believe that we are describing something with it, but—according to Mauthner—we are not actually describing anything real with that word.

Now, it would of course be nonsensical to apply this critical analysis of language to scientific knowledge, for example. For no one would believe—regardless of whether one knows a lot or little about, say, a horse—that anyone could possibly be misled about the fact that a horse is meant when the expression "horse" is used, in any language. Everyone knows perfectly well how to distinguish the fact that one cannot ride on the *word* horse from the fact that one *can* ride on a real horse. And this already makes it quite clear from the outset that, with reference to the things that exist in nature, such an analysis of language is quite irrelevant, because one will always know the difference between the word and the object in their relation to what can be perceived outwardly. I do not believe that anyone who wants to go for a ride would climb on the word horse instead of on a real horse.

But the situation is really quite different when it comes to everything which, in our present-day civilization, relates on the one hand to the soul—to the life of the soul, to the realities of the life of the soul—and on the other hand to the ethical and moral requirements of humanity. In that respect, one would indeed have to say that there is, at most, just a belief that realities are hidden behind the words. For this reason, it is also quite understandable that Mauthner pondered at length about the question: Should one even still utter the word "soul"?[†] For there is basically nothing real behind what people mean when they use this word, as there is when they use the word horse when speaking of a horse. After all, people no longer have a conception about the life of the soul. Therefore, we should not only leave out the soul from the field of psychology, as nineteenth century soul-research did, but we should completely eradicate the word soul and instead speak of "soul phenomena" in the same way as one would speak of something undefined.

If we intended to mention that there are three persons, Charles, Fred, and Hans, who are sons of the same father and the same mother, and if we wanted to gloss over them with a superficial classification, then we would describe them with the word "siblings." Why then, says Mauthner, should we use the word "soul" when we know nothing tangible about the phenomena of the soul? The word soul describes nothing; one should say "souling" [as in "seeing," "hearing," "feeling"—see Mauthner's explanation in note to page 64]. If, with a bit of luck, this actually were to come about, then one would be rid of the illusion that, when we say "soul," there is something more behind it. For then, in the future, one would no longer say that the human being has an immortal soul. Instead, one would say that, during life on earth, the human being has a "souling" within him or her; one would say, "I am touched to the core of my souling," and so on.

These things are, in fact, extraordinarily serious, far more serious than is usually thought, especially for those people who are striving in full earnestness for an understanding of the spirit. In any case, they show how important it is today that people pay close attention whenever it is mentioned somewhere that one ought to find the right means again in order to uncover the reality of the soul, the truth about the soul.

It is said today that the faculties of the soul principally comprise thinking, feeling, and willing. But people would do well to clarify for themselves what they actually mean by the expressions thinking, feeling, and willing; for they would soon stop believing that they were looking at something real. I would like to speak today about how anthroposophy can explain the fact that, with our ordinary consciousness, we are not at all in a position to view the whole reality in this respect. And what I will indicate today by way of introduction will then be elaborated in the next lecture; for it is my task today, above all, to point first to another side of this question.

If we take an honest look into our inner being, then we have to admit to ourselves that what we carry as thoughts within us is mostly taken from the outside world—and for most people, this is indeed all they carry as thoughts within them. Thoughts are more or less just mirrored images of all the impressions made on the human senses in the outer physical-sensory reality. Just try to make a conscientious experiment in self-observation by asking yourself: How many thoughts do we have in this human consciousness that indicate something—notwithstanding the fact that we have words such as thinking, feeling, willing, God, immortality—that indicate something in the intellectual life of ordinary civilization that is *not* mirrored in the outside world? People really only seek to interpret everything in such a way that it can have a mirror-image in the outside world. And if one tries to explain the spiritual to people today, then many of them will actually expect to see images even of the spiritual, perhaps a film or something similar, because they say: If this is not illustrated for us, if images like those of the sense world are not put before our eyes, then we do not understand anything of the spiritual!

It is in moments such as these, when people expect even the spiritual to be clothed in sensory images, that they are actually more honest than when they, perhaps as soul-experts, speak about the soul. If we survey the various aspects of what I have often discussed, even here in this very building, then we will be able to realize that, looking at our thinking in this way, we are only seeing one side of this thinking. In this sense, one can even speak of a reality—a reality, however, that would be the equivalent of getting to know a person only from behind. Just imagine the grotesque situation that would arise if you only knew a person from the back! Sure, you would know him, but you would not know his essential being. At most, you would occasionally grasp something of this essential being. This might then also give rise to a situation like that of the student who came to Heidelberg as a very young greenhorn and enrolled in a course with the famous Professor Kuno Fischer.[†] Full of joy, the student then rushed over to the barber to get his hair cut before going to the lecture, and, because he was very excited about hearing the famous man, he even mentioned it to the barber. The barber responded to this by saying: "Yes, Kuno Fischer will indeed be writing something on the blackboard today." The student then asked him how he knew that Kuno Fischer was going to write something on the blackboard today. The barber answered: "You see, when the professor intends to write something on the blackboard, he gets his hair parted at the back before the lecture so that he can turn around!"

All the same, if one is presented with clear indications, such as those that reveal something of a person's character from the parting of the hair at the back of the head, then one might actually learn something about that person's inner being, even if one only gets to know him from behind. But firstly, it may not be particularly significant, and secondly, in the case of most people, one would still not learn very much.

As far as our thinking is concerned—that is, the part of the soul that is most important for life on earth—it is indeed the case that we only perceive, if I may put it like this, the back side. The front side escapes ordinary observation. For if we attempt to consider the human being with the help of anthroposophy and ask ourselves: Is it the full extent of our thinking when we form abstract mental images about external sense-perceptible things?—then we begin to realize that there is more to thinking; that thinking, apart from the fact that it comprises a sum of abstract thoughts, also constitutes a sum of forces. Thoughts are not really capable of doing anything and we actually think best when we do nothing, when we sit down quietly, when we cultivate stillness. Thoughts are powerless, just as images in a mirror are powerless. But if you trace the development of the human being from infancy until maturity, and then, in turn, follow the growth processes still present in the human being in later life—for, even though the human being no longer grows taller, growth processes are still always present—if you look at these forces of growth in the human being, then you will find that they are the same forces, but now seen from the other side, that show themselves from the back in abstract thoughts. The human being sends abstract thoughts outward; turned inward, these are the forces that shape the human brain. In the first few years of childhood, the brain is shaped plastically. The forces that work as growth forces in other realms, are the forces of thought. And just as you must, when you see a person from behind, also think about the front (in order to be able to entertain the idea that this is a complete person), so you must, when you think about abstract thinking, *also* think about the forces that form concrete, real thoughts—forces that penetrate the human being, forces that work on the human being.

The essence of a pedagogy that has its foundation in a healthy anthroposophy, is that the educator knows: It is not enough to offer the child abstract notions about one thing or another. For it makes a great difference whether a child acquires a living, pictorial, actively viable concept of something, or a concept that is dead. Dead concepts have an inhibiting effect on the growth processes, while active, vivid concepts have a nurturing effect on the growth processes. And this then brings us to the realization that thinking shows the one side, which is powerless and only mirrors the outside world, but that, if directed inward, we see a vividly active side that permeates the whole human organism with forces. It is in reality the other side of this growth, the spiritual counter-image of this growth. And if we investigate this further, then we find that the human being brings along, from his pre-earthly existence, that which constitutes the other side (which, in relation to the human being, is the back side, but in relation to thinking, is the front side)—that is to say, the human being brings along *not* the dead thinking (which for us only appears on the other side, toward the front) but brings along this living thinking.

In fact, what happens in the transition from pre-earthly existence into earthly existence with regard to this matter, is the following. In pre-earthly existence, the human being develops, unhindered, a system of forces that works from all sides in the spiritual world. Then the human being descends into earthly existence. At that time, this thinking, which is actively present in the spiritual world, transforms itself into the inner organizational forces of the physical body; and toward the outside it sends a reflecting surface, as it were, a surface into which the earth casts its images. This is what actually happens. However, the circumstances at that stage are such that, after the human being has effectively completed the time between death and a new birth, there is actually no further task for this living thinking in the spiritual world. This living thinking has its great task in the time between death and a new birth. When this task has been completed, what then occurs in yonder realm is the phenomenon that I have often described to you, that is to say, the soul turns toward life on earth. At that time, this thinking also has a new task—the task of forming the human body. And the significant thing about the human being's thinking on earth, about the human thinking that comes down from the spiritual realm, is that it is now directed—as a creative, formative force—toward the human body. Accordingly, in our true, genuine thinking we have a legacy from the spiritual world, but one that becomes something only on the earth, because in the spiritual world it no longer has a task. We owe it to this fact that our earthly thinking can become so clear. If this thinking still had a task as it does in the spiritual world, then it could not become so clear on earth.

Now let us move on to the other faculty of the human soul, to feeling. In regard to it, you will all have noticed—even independently from what I have said about it, also here in this room—that feeling is not as clear as thinking. Feeling is something that occurs in a way that is similar to dreaming, although it appears in a different form. The state of soul while in the process of feeling is basically very much the same as during dreaming, except that feeling occurs in an entirely different form. Why is this so? The reason is that in the case of our feeling, too—just as is the case with our thinking—we only have the back side during our life here on earth. But with feeling, the front side is not directed only toward the human body; rather, as we descend from pre-earthly existence—from the existence between death and a new birth—to earth, we also retain as a legacy that which lies behind feeling. That aspect still remains focussed on the spiritual; it does not merely have an earthly task. This is why, when we fall asleep each night, we do not take our thinking with us into sleep; but we do take our feeling with us. And if you look at dreams in the right way, then you will find that they are pictures, since logical thinking is no longer present; feelings, however, continue to be present. Every time we sleep, we immerse ourselves in the entire spiritual world. We do not take our thinking with us, but we do take our feeling with us, and even more so our will.

It is, of course, quite understandable that the realm of the will is beyond our reach during the day. I have often said that the human being can resolve to do something, can have a thought. But how the thought then glides further down into the body, how a will impulse to move a hand actually brings that about—this remains as obscure as our condition during sleep remains obscure. At the same time, however, it is in the will that the human being retains the most from the realm of the eternal. And, again, it is in the will, which expresses itself in human activity—for, if the human being is not active, no will is involved, only a wish—it is precisely in actions of will that we can see the earthly human being working in an outward direction. Seen from the other side, the will represents something entirely eternal. Thinking also represents an eternal element, but one that has been turned toward an earthly activity. The will, however, continues to exist in the realm of the eternal and works upon the destiny, the karma, of the human being as it unfolds through repeated lives on earth.

I wanted to describe for you, with these initial words, how we can find our way to a real knowledge of the soul, so that we will have realities again behind the words thinking, feeling, and willing, so that we point to something real again. Just as we use the word horse to refer to a physical horse in the outer sense, so we can, if we penetrate the life of the soul with anthroposophy in this way, find our way back again to reality, to the realities. This is the path, and—because the noblest forces are activated when someone has the will to comprehend it—this path will simultaneously lead to what I emphasized at the end of the last lecture, namely, that anthroposophy will never be understood if it remains a theory; that it will only have been understood when, in acquiring anthroposophical knowledge, the human being becomes a different person; that it will only have been understood when a true transformation comes to pass, when the human being, with respect to morality and universal humanity, becomes a different person.

What we are striving for in this way is opposed by something different today. And I feel that I have an obligation to speak to you about this, because anthroposophy now has a presence in the world and we must be alert to what is happening. We should not always keep our windows covered, but must also look outside. In that sense, it is a spiritual duty to speak about these things. In all those instances today where people believe that clear concepts can only be obtained from natural science, anthroposophy tends to be dismissed with claims that it is fantasy, speculation, pure fiction. And these are the people who say that they alone have clear thoughts!

Irrespective of the fact that, as one becomes familiar with anthroposophy, one naturally develops an inner certainty with respect to the truth through the study of anthroposophy, it is nevertheless important from time to time to evaluate for oneself how "clear" today's thinking actually is! This is what I would first like to illustrate for you with an example, because as anthroposophists we should be fully aware of what constitutes contemporary culture and civilization today. I will use an example that speaks for itself. If we were to examine the logic of, say, a person who writes in the newspaper, then this would not prove very much. Instead, I will take an important contemporary scientist and say explicitly that I do not want to say anything malicious or disparaging, because I fully recognize that we are dealing here with an important scientist and with a serious matter that he is addressing. And in doing so, I would like to draw your attention to the "clarity" that prevails in this respect today.

In October 1910, the well-known scientist Max Rubner[†] gave his inaugural address at the university of Berlin entitled "Our Goals for the Future." He spoke about the intellectual goals of the future. This was not just anyone speaking but, rather, someone who is fully involved in his research and who, from the point of view of today's civilization, must be regarded as a serious and capable researcher. At the end of his speech, he also summoned the students and attempted—in a way that was beautiful in and of itself—to make it clear that they should really devote themselves to their studies. But he did so by using the clear concepts—and I mean "clear" in quotation marks—that such a researcher is able to use today based on the current way of thinking. I would like to draw attention to a few details. He began his appeal to the students by saying: "We all have to learn; we bring nothing to the world other than our instrument for intellectual work, a blank slate, our brain, each with a different disposition and different potential for development; we receive everything from the outside world."

This is a view that is often encountered today. It basically says: If you want to speak of the life of the soul, look at your brain; it is a blank slate; it must receive everything through the impressions of the outside world. What this really says is that, when we come into the world, we have our brain as a blank slate; we have to expose ourselves to the impressions coming from the world; then these impressions enter into us and the page becomes inscribed. "Therefore," Rubner said to his students, "just expose yourselves to the impressions of the world, freshly, bravely, and cheerfully, and the blank slate that you have brought with you will be filled."

He then went on to tell them how they should do this. He said: “No brain can grasp everything that our combined ancestors have experienced and learned, what billions of brains have contemplated and concluded in the course of human history, what our intellectual heroes have helped to create. . . .” In other words, the students should only take note of what the intellectual heroes have helped to create. But now, all of a sudden, the intellectual heroes supposedly are creating something and the uninscribed brains [of the students] must meet up with the inscribed brains of the intellectual heroes! This would mean that, as soon as a person pieces together two sentences, one of which is on page 23 and the other on page 24, these sentences would no longer be in agreement! For if the intellectual heroes *also* had uninscribed brains, then it would no longer be possible to speak of their brains making impressions on uninscribed brains, as these impressions supposedly come from brains that have created something—and this is precisely what is being denied, since everything is said to have been received only from the external world. Now, however, the outside world apparently also includes everything that human brains create. It is important to examine such statements carefully!

And then it continues: “What we learn provides the basic material for productive thinking.” Now, put these two sentences together: “We receive everything from the outside world,” and the second, “What we learn provides the basic material for productive thinking.” This is not just a regular newspaper writer speaking; this is how a person of merit, a rightfully acknowledged researcher, speaks from the perspective of contemporary civilization! At this point, it is only of marginal importance to point out how he explains the functions of the brain—when, for example, he says, “There is always something refreshing about working in a new, previously unexplored area of the brain.” This is why Rubner told the students that they should also occasionally look around for other subjects, which they had not yet explored, because: “. . . Some areas of the brain only become productive when they are tilled repeatedly, but ultimately bear the same good fruit as others that are more easily opened up. . . .” So now the soil that is tilled does not produce the plough, after all! If you really immerse yourself into these thoughts, you are no longer able to think at all. But Rubner finds that this way of thinking is quite natural.

Now, in order to show you the implication of what he is saying, I would first like to mention something else. When someone is actively engaged in sports, we observe this person making various movements. If you are particularly interested, you can even take a snapshot of these movements. But if you look at this situation objectively, the following can be affirmed. If one traces the internal organic processes taking place while someone is doing sports—that is to say, what is taking place on the inside between the nerves and the muscles as a kind of destructive and restorative process—then one finds that this is not only much more important with regard to the human being, but that it is also infinitely more interesting than what can be captured in a photograph. I am not saying anything against sports as outer physical exercise. But what the athlete is on the inside is truly much more interesting than what he is on the outside. What this activity causes inside the organism—this is where things start to get interesting.

Now, the truth is that with respect to the movements of the human limbs, the situation is the reverse of what it is in relation to thinking. With thinking, the situation is such that what is carried out, meaning, what is taking place, what is the actual fact—this is the essential aspect, and what lies in the organism is the inessential. With sports, what takes place outwardly as a fact is the less interesting aspect; what the organism does internally is the more interesting one. With thinking, that is to say, what presents itself as thinking, what thinking really is—this is the interesting aspect, and what the organism does during this process is something that is relatively elementary. Therefore, if one has insight into these things, one can no longer speak of thinking in the same way as one does of muscular movements.

But when all this is viewed superficially, externally, what do people say? Then things are explained like this: "Thinking strengthens the brain; the brain improves in performance through practice, just like any other organ, in the same way as our muscular strength improves through work and sports. Studying is sports for the brain." You see, by exposing this one aspect, it can be shown that our civilization defines itself through its most important element, through the way it thinks about things. Nothing else will wake us up to what is actually happening in the present time.

Now I would like to cite a person who—in a manner that can actually be called brilliant, notwithstanding certain limitations—has developed strikingly negative thoughts about our contemporary civilization and who is able to characterize this particularly well by saying that it is ultimately the flawed way of thinking, the way thoughts are formed and shaped, that has brought our civilization to decay and to the abyss. And I have to say that the person capable of writing the book *The Decay and the Restoration of Civilization*—Albert Schweitzer[†]—is indeed in a position to judge such things. Anyone who is familiar, for example, with Albert Schweitzer's book *The History of Research into the Life of Jesus*, published in 1906, and the way in which Schweitzer is able to approach even the Apocalypse—so that he is already well ahead of other theologians—will have to admit that Schweitzer is quite capable of having a sound judgment about the actual value of contemporary intellectual life.

And now he has written this book, the first part of which has just been published. The first chapter is entitled "The Guilt of Philosophy for the Decline of Civilization." And the sentences that are meant to characterize our current intellectual life, the life of our civilization, are truly razor-sharp! The very first sentence reads: "We stand in the midst of the decline of culture. The war [WW I] did not create this situation. It was itself only a manifestation of it. What was provided intellectually has been converted into facts—facts which now, in turn, are having a deteriorating effect on the intellectual life in every respect." Here is a human being who has insights into the worthlessness of contemporary culture! And he continues: "We strayed from culture because none of us gave any thought to culture. . . . This is how we passed over the threshold of the new century with unwavering notions about ourselves." And then he asks himself: Why are we seeing this degeneration of our culture? Why are we living in this demise of culture? He then comes to the realization that we do not have to go very far back in time—to the time when intellectualism experienced its first period of bloom—to find that people still had a "whole worldview," that they still spoke of ethical and moral aims in such a way that these aims had the same sources as the laws of nature. People looked at the laws of nature and then approached the sources of morality with the same conceptions, meaning that they had a "whole worldview" that encompassed the moral and the natural realms equally.

You will remember how often I have pointed out that the decline of our culture is an outcome of the fact that we have a one-sided view of nature that places the Kant-Laplace theory[†]—the idea that everything developed out of a primordial nebula—or something similar, at the beginning of our Earth evolution. According to this theory, the human being, too, was formed out of this primordial nebula; then, what we call moral ideals—illusions—arose; and, one day, when "heat death" occurs—which *must* occur in keeping with purely physical laws—there will be a large field of corpses, and what will be buried with them is what emerged as cultural ideals or as moral ideals. Accordingly, our morality is no longer an inherent part of this worldview. It is no longer included in it; it is something that can only be captured in abstract thoughts.

Schweitzer also knew that these views had essentially developed around the middle of the nineteenth century. He expresses this quite clearly: "It is now obvious to everyone that the self-annihilation of culture is underway. . . . The Age of Enlightenment"—by this he means the time when intellectualism experienced its first blossoming—"and rationalism had established ethical and rational ideals about the development of the individual toward true humanity, about the individual's place in society, about society's material and spiritual tasks, about the conduct of peoples toward one another and their merging into a humanity united by the highest, spiritual goals. . . But around the middle of the nineteenth century this interaction between the ethical ideals of rationalism and reality began to diminish. Over the course of the following decades, it gradually came to a standstill. The abdication of culture took place without a fight and without a sound. Its ideas lagged behind the time, as if they were too exhausted to keep pace with it."

And now, Albert Schweitzer wants to make it clear that if people no longer have effective thoughts, then culture must perish; and since philosophy seems to contain influential thoughts, he attributes the reason for the decline of culture to philosophy. He knows—and describes it in this book—that, even if Hegel and Kant are only read by a few, their thoughts nevertheless govern the thoughts of thousands, for they are transmitted to the broadest masses of humanity through all sorts of unobserved pathways. It is actually not an exaggeration to say that if the simplest mountain farmers have only just started to read the most popular books today, then Kant is already inside them. People always believe that philosophy only affects those who read the philosophers; but that is just an outer illusion.

This is why Schweitzer says: "The decisive factor was the failure of philosophy." But then he treats this philosophy with some compassion after all and says: "Philosophy should have been thinking, but because thinking itself has strayed and because people have forgotten how to think, one need not be surprised that philosophy could no longer think either." In this way, he treats philosophy a little more leniently. "Philosophy did not realize that the power of the cultural ideas entrusted to it was now in dispute. At the end of one of the most outstanding books about the history of philosophy, published at the end of the nineteenth century"—the same one, incidentally, that I have discussed here, too—"philosophy is defined as the process in which, 'step by step, and with an ever more brilliant and confident consciousness, cultural values, whose universal validity is the object of philosophy itself, are contemplated.' In doing so, however, the author forgot the most important thing—namely, that in earlier times, philosophy not only *thought* about cultural values, but also allowed these values to flow into public opinion as active ideas, while from the second half of the nineteenth century onward, these thoughts increasingly became its guarded, unproductive asset."

But then he becomes more lenient. After all, why should philosophers be blamed for not thinking if no one else is thinking either: "The fact that thinking was unable to establish a worldview with an optimistic, ethical character and to base the ideals that make up culture on such a view was not the fault of philosophy but, rather, a fact that arose in the course of the development of thinking. But philosophy became accountable to our world for not acknowledging this fact and for holding on to the illusion that it really supported cultural progress." Thus, Schweitzer no longer blames the philosophers for not being able to think, since people generally are no longer in the habit of thinking either. But he does blame the philosophers for not noticing this at all. They should at least have noticed it.

"According to its ultimate purpose, philosophy is the leader and guardian of universal reason. It should have been its duty to acknowledge to our world that ethical, rational ideals no longer gain a foothold in a comprehensive worldview, as they once did, but are left to their own devices for the time being and have to assert themselves in the world solely through their inner strength. . . . Philosophers philosophized so little about culture that they did not even notice how philosophy itself, together with its era, was becoming more and more cultureless. In the hour of danger, the watchman, who should have stayed awake sustaining us, was asleep. This is how it came to pass that we did not stand up for our culture."

As a matter of fact, I think that I have also told you quite a few things about this state of being asleep; I have already spoken about it here from a wide range of perspectives.

In the next chapter, Schweitzer discusses the culture-inhibiting elements within us. Here he develops some very interesting ideas. He finds, to begin with, that human beings have become unfree as a result of what they have absorbed as culture in recent times. Now, one can certainly empathize with these feelings because people have increasingly started to follow certain trendsetters and to have complete faith in the authority of science and so on. But then Schweitzer claims that human beings are not focussed in their thinking. I think that this does not need to be discussed much more either; Schweitzer is probably right in saying that the power to focus has really diminished in our civilization. But then he calls the human being incomplete. Now, people might well respond to this by saying that if Schweitzer really thinks that we are unfree and so unfocused, and that we are not even complete human beings, then we cannot concede that to him! But what he really means is this: What people learn today is a speciality, whether one is a scholar or just some other person, so that only certain aspects of one's abilities are developed, not the complete human being. This is why we go around as incomplete—that is, not at all as whole—human beings. And then he finds, as a fourth point, that humanity has declined to the highest degree; and, as proof, he provides some nice examples. But he is generally of the opinion that unfree, unfocussed, incomplete human beings also do not develop the humanity in their ethical life. He then finds yet another culture-inhibiting element in the form of over-organization and the annihilation of human individuality. For, so he asks, how much does still depend on the individual today? Everything only depends on what is mapped out by some organization or other. Schweitzer rightly reproaches our time for being particularly prone to over-organization.

However, then he wants to move on from this by answering the question of how we are supposed to return to culture again. What needs to be done to find our way to culture again? At that point he poses the question: What must this culture, to which we should find our way, be like? He answers this by saying that it must be ethical and optimistic. Now, imagine that you want to build a house. You go to an architect who says: You have to describe to me what the house should be like so that I can draw the plans for you. Then you tell him: The house has to be solid, weatherproof, beautiful, and comfortable to live in. Now, one cannot draw plans based on these comments, but you believe that you have actually said something when you say: The house must be solid, weatherproof, beautiful, and comfortable to live in. Unfortunately, one cannot do anything with these statements. And one can do just as little with the statement: A worldview must be ethical and optimistic. It is the same thing, exactly the same.

Once, as a small boy, I was in a village and there was a trial. Chickens had been stolen from one of the village dignitaries. The judge then tried to determine what the penalty should be by asking for a description of the chickens. And so, he asked the person concerned what kind of chickens they were. The answer was that they were truly beautiful chickens. Yes, but that is not enough; you have to tell us in such a way that one can get an idea of what the chickens might have been worth. "Well, they were very nice chickens." Yes, but would it not be good to know, for example, whether the chickens were thin or fat. "Well, they really were very nice chickens." And this is how it continued; nothing more could be had from this man other than that they were very nice chickens.

Now, we are here discussing a truly outstanding mind who fittingly characterizes the decline of culture in an extraordinarily subtle and apt way, and who actually recognizes a great deal that people today do not want to acknowledge. For example, he knows—and it is a good thing that someone other than an anthroposophist says this—that "generating a comprehensive summary of knowledge and validating its findings for a worldview is not really his concern. In the past, every scientist was also a thinker who meant something in the common intellectual life of his generation. Our time has reached the point where we are able to differentiate between science and thinking. This is why we still have scientific freedom, but almost no science that still thinks." Again, it really is good that someone else says it for once. But you see, despite all this insight, he does not get any further than the beautiful chickens. Remarkably characteristic! What actually emerges again as a truly fruitful worldview, appears here as something that must be "ethical and optimistic"—just like: "solid, weatherproof, beautiful, and comfortable to live in!"

Schweitzer does certainly embrace a wide range with this negative characterization. He notices, for instance, that there are people who have already experienced that this kind of thinking, this brain-sport, does not lead to the sources of existence; and that this is why they say that they prefer to dismiss all this thinking and rather arrive at the truth via a path of feeling or faith, via a mystical path. He recognizes this, and since he himself is a sharp thinker, at least up to a certain point, he poses an interesting question. He says: "Philosophical, historical, and scientific questions, which an earlier rationalism could not yet cope with, descended upon this rationalism like an avalanche and buried it along the way. A new worldview, a worldview based on thinking, must work its way out of this chaos. It must do this by allowing everything that factually exists to work upon it while executing all possible manner of reflection and thought in aiming to find the ultimate meaning of existence and life, and seeing whether some of it can be deciphered." If only he were to execute a little "reflection and thought" himself, instead of "the house should be beautiful and weatherproof"!

"The ultimate knowledge through which human beings understand their own existence within universal existence is, so people say, of a mystical nature. In saying this, people believe that knowledge no longer comes about through ordinary reflection, but rather is, in some way, experienced. But why assume," he then asks, "that the path of thinking ends at mysticism? It is true that earlier forms of rational thinking have always stopped when they came close to the realm of mysticism. . ."

At this point we might ask ourselves: What is the aim of anthroposophy? It aims to start from clear—mathematically clear—thinking, and not to stop at mysticism but, rather, to penetrate by means of thinking into the domains that are to be opened up for the eternal. But even then, people are still saying that the house should be strong, weatherproof, and comfortable to live in—when it is actually right there in front of them, but they cannot find their way in. It really should be possible to say this in full objectivity and without being immodest. But these are not actually the worst thinkers; these are the best, the sharpest thinkers! We must not close our eyes to such things. We should not always speak aimlessly of making anthroposophy comprehensible to this or that person, when people are talking in this way.

But then Schweitzer continues: "Thoughts that are thought through to their conclusion will lead, somehow and somewhere, to a living mysticism that must necessarily be thought by all people." (Like: "Proper construction will result in a good house, just the way I want it!") Then he goes on to say that he finds people unfocussed and that he wants to clarify what people should do in order to get beyond this terrible state into which culture has fallen: "Reflecting on the meaning of life is already important in itself. If such reflections were to develop again among us, then the ideals stemming from vanity and passion, which now proliferate like evil weeds in the convictions of the masses, will wither away without hope of retrieval. How much would be gained for today's situation if all of us were to spend only three minutes every evening looking up meditatively at the infinite worlds of the starry skies. . ."—incidentally, there is no note here stating that one can find a more accurate description in *Knowledge of Higher Worlds*; no, it just says that we must somehow get to the point where people take three minutes to collect their thoughts—". . . looking up meditatively at the infinite worlds of the starry skies and, when attending a funeral, devote ourselves to the mystery of life and death instead of walking behind the coffin in thoughtless conversation."

Then, after having drawn the reader's attention first, it ends with: "One cannot really offer people anything that is, in fact, a worldview—although we do indeed need such a worldview." I would just like to know why we need a worldview if one is not supposed to tell people about it! "The great revision of the convictions and ideals with which, and for the sake of which, we live, cannot be accomplished by talking the people of our time into other, better ideas than the ones they have. . . ." Imagine that it is not permitted to talk people into better thoughts than they already have; rather, that one must leave them to themselves! Just let them ponder; just let them think different thoughts when they walk behind a coffin; just let them reflect! In that case, people will indeed simply continue to do what they have been doing up until now, meaning that they will not know what they are supposed to think about in these three minutes, and so on.

"Thinking, thus far, has sought to understand the meaning of life based on the meaning of the world. It may well be that we must accept that the meaning of the world is to remain undecided and that we must give meaning to our lives out of the will to live, as it exists in us. . . ." It may well be indeed! "Even if the paths that must be taken in order to reach our goal are still obscure, the direction in which we must go is clear. Together, we should think about the meaning of life; together, we should struggle to come to a world- and life-affirming worldview, in which our impulse to act—an impulse we experience as necessary and valuable—finds justification, orientation, clarification, deepening, moral values, and strengthening, and then, as a result, becomes capable of establishing and realizing definite cultural ideals that are inspired by the spirit of true humanity." They will be beautiful chickens indeed!

No one will be able to say that I intend to dole out caustic, intentionally negative criticisms. I took the first example, Professor Rubner, precisely because I wanted to choose an individual who must be acknowledged as regards his scientific achievements, where it would be foolish not to do so. The second example I took was chosen so that I was able to say that I consider the person who wrote this book to be one of the sharpest thinkers, a person who has the most right to speak in such a way. I do not want to dole out criticism in a derogatory way; something like that would be alien to me. One must make an effort to point to things that characterize the facts as they are. However, when Albert Schweitzer says: "Philosophy should have been keeping watch, but it was precisely philosophy that was asleep," then we have no choice but to say that he himself continued this sleep.

Let us wait and see what the second volume of this work will be like; but, having seen the first one, the second volume will likely not be much different. He perpetuates the sleep and lets his dreams develop out of this sleep. These dreams are wishes, *not* realities. It must be our aim to go beyond mere illusions, beyond mere phrases, and on to the realities. You can see how depleted the words of our language have become. This is why we have to begin to speak about the soul as we did this evening; then the words will be filled with content again. Otherwise, it will indeed be as Schweitzer said: "Philosophy is not to blame for the decline of culture, but it is to blame for not even noticing it." Now, Albert Schweitzer is of course not to blame for the fact that our words have become so depleted that they no longer hold concepts within them, that there are no realities left in them anymore. But he can be held responsible for the fact that he did not even notice it. He did not notice at all that he was using words that have been completely depleted.

I felt obligated, in light of this newly published cultural deed of Albert Schweitzer—and I do not mean this maliciously but very much in earnest—to draw attention to the decline of culture in such a poignant way. I felt obligated to indicate what the junction point must actually be like—the point from which one can form a true judgement about what, on the one side, is not actually real, and what, on the other side, has to be done. Now that we have gone through this episode, next time we will speak about concrete themes of anthroposophy.

The Four Members of the Human Being

Intellectual Thinking versus the Moral-Religious Experience

STUTTGART, JULY 11, 1923

We will take our starting point from the fact that the human being is a multi-membered being, a being composed of several members, that is to say, from something that is very well known to us. We will take our starting point from the premise that within the anthroposophical movement we are always striving to understand in what sense the human being is made up of various members, and to what extent each member needs to be understood on its own, so that a true understanding of the whole human being will only be possible if we are able to combine the insights we have developed about each single member into a united whole.

Leaving everything else aside for the moment, we know that the human being is organized into the physical body, the etheric body (also called the body of formative forces), the astral body, and what we refer to as the I. Now, this is not—or at least should not be—a mere categorization of the human being and of human essential nature; rather, what we itemize as the four members of the human essential being actually stems from very different worlds and can only be understood in terms of the inner conditions of these worlds. And only when we have understood how the physical body, the etheric or formative-forces body, the astral body, and the I are formed out of their respective worlds, only then are we in a position to gain an understanding of the entire human being—by letting the attained insights into each of these individual human members resound harmoniously together. The physical body of the human being must be understood purely from the perspective of the physical world, and the etheric or formative-forces body, in turn, must be understood from the perspective of the etheric world, and so on. If we are not extremely precise with regard to this, if we do not acknowledge that things are exactly as I have indicated just now, then we cannot come to an understanding of the complete essential nature of the human being.

Let us leave the human physical body out of consideration for the moment. We can do this because all outer education and science today is aimed at understanding the physical body of the human being. But no attempts are made today to understand, in the same sense, the etheric or formative-forces body of the human being. At most, people develop the idea that this etheric or formative-forces body perhaps consists of a finer substance than the denser physical body and that this finer etheric substance is simply intermixed with the physical body. But that is not how these things really are; they are completely different as regards their essential nature. This means that someone who—in order to be able to form concepts about the functioning of the physical body—would have understood everything that can be understood based on physical science, would still know nothing about the etheric or formative-forces body. For, if we simply observe the human being, it is not really possible to find the laws of the etheric body in the proximity of the earth. We cannot look for the laws of the etheric body in the vicinity of the earth itself.

When we see a stone falling vertically, we say that gravity is at work, that the stone is moving in the direction of the centre of the earth. And just as our approach to this situation is correct if we look for the causes of the falling stone near the earth or in the earth, so would our approach be *incorrect* if, in searching for the causes of what takes place in the etheric or formative-forces body, we were to stay in the vicinity of the earth. In point of fact, we must look for what is at work in our etheric or formative-forces body *not* on the earth but, rather, in the vastness of the universe—as it were, on the surface of a sphere that is infinitely far away from us. There, forces are working in from all sides. Just as physical forces work outward from the center of the earth, so do these forces work inward from all sides and determine our etheric body.

You will remember what I have described with regards to how human beings transition from their pre-earthly existence to earthly existence. The human being descends and has already sent the laws governing his physical body down to the earth. Then, so I said, the human being gathers his etheric body from the vastness of the cosmic ether. At this time—that is, before acquiring the physical body, which had been sent ahead—the human being consists of I, astral body, and etheric body. But in terms of the laws governing the etheric body, the human being has not formed this body from the earth but, rather, from the four regions of the world. One can say this representatively, but it really means that it is drawn together from all sides. And so, when the human etheric body is formed, its laws become effective from all sides of the world periphery, from the circumference.

Now we come to something which, right from the outset—when it is explained—contains an element that is extraordinarily shocking for people today, something that is very astounding. You will agree with me when I say the following. If we light a flame here, however strong it may be, the intensity of the light will mean less and less to us as we move further away from the light source; finally, there will be a point at a certain distance where this light source is hardly relevant anymore, where it has become so weak that, at any rate, we are no longer able to read—a point where, even if there is a light somewhere at a great distance, we can say for all practical purposes that there is no light. Everyone will acknowledge that this is so. Similarly, modern science also acknowledges that gravity decreases with the square of the distance,† that it becomes weaker the further one goes out into the periphery. But what people today do not consider at all is that, here on earth, we put into words the laws that apply on the earth; but that these laws, which we express as earthly human beings, are also diminishing, are becoming weaker and weaker and, finally, at a certain distance no longer exist at all for all practical purposes. No matter how cleverly you formulate natural laws for earthly conditions, no matter how cleverly you establish historical principles for what happens on earth, these laws—the laws of nature and of history—are no longer applicable at a certain distance from the earth, just as the gravitational force or the intensity of a light source becomes irrelevant at a certain distance. Therefore, it would be naive for someone to claim that the same natural laws that are valid on earth also apply to a star that is said to be so many light years away, because the validity of our natural laws only applies to earthly conditions and ceases when we penetrate into cosmic space. But the laws of the etheric originate in the far reaches of cosmic space. If we expect the laws there to be the same as the natural laws of the earth, then we will never understand etheric existence. As soon as we speak of the human etheric body, we must already speak of something that follows laws which are completely different from what constitutes the natural laws of the earth.

Herein lies the very aspect that is so striking and shocking for modern human beings; nonetheless, it must be comprehended, little by little. Otherwise, today's humanity will simply become wrapped up in earthly conditions and will not be able, with its soul nature, to transcend these earthly conditions. I would now like to describe this aspect for you in a form in which one can say it—or at least ought to be able to say it—having spoken about anthroposophical truths for some time now within a specific circle. For, if one were to say what must now be said in front of any other group, people would assume that one had taken leave of one's senses. However, this is not actually an accusation. Because, as long as people stay "with their senses," they also stay with the science of the sense-perceptible. Strictly speaking, then, one should be able to take such things seriously, since the genius of language works quite correctly. Someone who presents spiritual science could, at most, be accused of "having taken leave of the spirit." To say that someone has taken leave of his senses is not an accusation at all. The only thing that matters is that one should be "with the spirit" in full consciousness. But if it is said that someone only has a legitimate consciousness if he stays "with the senses," then one must forego spiritual science.

Nowadays, people all around are proclaiming: There are certain remarkably simple laws that one comes to in the end. People call them axioms or something similar—the names are not important at this point. I will refer to some of these axioms. One axiom states that the whole is always greater than any of its parts. This is self-evident, people say, and anyone who sins against such an axiom has taken leave of his senses, since the whole is greater than any of its parts. Another axiom states that a straight line constitutes the shortest distance between two points. With respect to earthly conditions and to the sensory world this applies to the fullest extent. If we go to the most extreme abstractions, then one comes to statements such as these: The whole is always larger than any of its parts, and: The straight line constitutes the shortest distance between two points.

But when you soar into the etheric, you must truly pierce through from the sensory world into another world where even the most trivial laws of the sensory world no longer apply. As soon as you enter the etheric world, the law stating that the whole is greater than any of its parts no longer applies. For in the etheric world, the situation with respect to the human being, for example, is as follows. If we observe the etheric aspect behind any single part of the whole human being, if we observe the liver or the lungs and look for the corresponding etheric parts, then each individual part of the human being is significantly larger than the whole human being is on the earth. And if you ever were to believe that [in this world] the human being would be bigger than his liver, then you would never be able to penetrate through to the spiritual. For in the spiritual realm, a whole is created as the result of the larger parts working together to form something smaller, so that it is precisely through the interaction of the larger parts that the whole is formed.

This will perhaps become even clearer to you with regard to the other example: that a straight line constitutes the shortest distance between two points. Yes, this is true in the physical world. There, if you have one point here and a second point over there, then the straight path is the shortest. However, when you come into the etheric world, any path that is made along curves, any meandering path, is the easy one; but any path that is taken in a straight line becomes impaled. It continually gets pierced; this path, the straight path from one point to a second point is actually the longest of all paths. This is why, in relation to the etheric world, a statement like the one that says, "a straight line is the shortest path between two points," is a principle that ensnares you in the physical, that makes it impossible for you to escape from the crusted layer in which you are encased.

As long as you do not truly acknowledge the fact that in the etheric world everything is different and even the opposite of what it is in the physical world, you will not be able to approach the spiritual world with true understanding.

People are quite pleased to know the members of the human being's essential nature: physical body, etheric body, astral body, and I. But then they would like to be able to use the exact same kind of thinking with respect to the etheric body as they used for the physical body. But that simply will not work because, as one moves further and further away from the physical world—which, by the way, is identical with the earthly world—the validity of the natural laws decreases proportionally, and completely different laws take their place instead. I just want to draw your attention to the fact that even already in approaching this second member of the human being's essential nature, it becomes absolutely necessary to adopt an entirely different way of thinking.

But as soon as we find our way into this other mode of thinking, we must—in the most all-encompassing sense—take this other way of thinking in earnest. No matter where you go in the physical world, you will find all sorts of things—maybe not atoms, but you will find things like cells and similar things. But it would certainly not occur to anyone that you would be able to find thoughts under a microscope, for example, or in a telescope. These must be found in other ways. You can examine the brain under a microscope until the end of time, but you will not find any thoughts in it; they cannot be discovered with a microscope. And it is this very fact that provides the evidence that with the microscope, and actually with all such observations, one can only discover the physical world; for the etheric world consists entirely of thoughts. The etheric world is the activity of thoughts working as forces. And as soon as one advances from the human physical body to the etheric body, one will find that this etheric body consists quintessentially of thoughts; but that the thoughts work as forces. We are completely suffused with thoughts, permeated by thoughts everywhere; but the thoughts work as forces.

This, however, has a very important consequence for the perception of the human being. For imagine that you lie down to sleep. So now, in the bed, there lie the physical body and the etheric body. The etheric body is filled with thoughts; it is a kind of distillation, a kind of extract from the ether of the world—and the ether of the world is an active world of thoughts. This is why it is justified to say that the human etheric body is actually something extraordinarily clever, if I may use the expression, something that is filled with luminous and non-contradictory thoughts. And when, as a human being, we leave our physical body and etheric body with our I and astral body, we actually leave behind a very clever being. The only thing, which is critical, is that when we are asleep, we do not realize at all how clever the entity is that remains lying in bed. By day, we are not so clever; this is due to the fact that during the day we submerge ourselves with our I and astral body into the very clever etheric body and continually dumb it down. For, insofar as we are imperfect as human beings, this imperfection stems from our I and our astral body. Our astral body and our I are not able to soar upward to the inner soundness, clarity, and cosmic aptness of the etheric body. If one could make the etheric body speak and if one were then to write down in shorthand just as faithfully—or possibly less faithfully—what this etheric body reveals all night long about the secrets of the universe, then this would be something incredibly clever, even still cleverer than what could be written down.

Thus, cosmic thoughts work as forces in the human etheric body; and we are only ever able to make use of a small portion—and it is always very little—of what is unfolding in our etheric body. The degree depends on, and is proportionate to, what we have in our astral body.

And yet, what are we with regard to our physical and etheric bodies which remain lying in bed when we are asleep and have withdrawn with our I and our astral body? There in the bed, we are a being composed of a physical body and an etheric body, meaning that we carry within us only the laws of the plant world. And in what can be discerned about ourselves when we look back down, as it were, and see how the wisdom of the whole world shines out from our sleeping etheric body in radiant spirit-clarity, in what can be observed about the human being when we look back in this way, we basically have before us, on a small scale, everything that we also have before us when we look at the earth—inasmuch as it exists as a physical sphere but lets the plant world spring and sprout forth from itself and inasmuch as this plant world is etherically stimulated from all sides by the world thoughts that are active in the weaving of the world ether.

This is the infinitely sublime picture of the cosmos, the cosmos that actually spreads out before us once we are able to look at everything that sprouts from every single plant on our earth—sprouts as though, I would like to say, from spiritual flames of fire, while drawing lines and undulating waves up to the farthest regions of space. This means that we actually have before us the earth's globe with forces sprouting into it from the most distant regions of space—forces that coax the vegetation out of the earth—and that these forming forces of the earth are being replicated in every single sleeping human being.

However, when we place this picture before us, we must think away everything contained in our I and in our astral body, and we must think away from the cosmic picture the image of the animals with their astral bodies. What is in our astral body simply does not belong to what is, on the one hand, earthly and, on the other, etheric; it belongs to a completely different world again, a world that we do not seek in the same way as we seek the etheric. If we were to describe it pictorially—and these things can only be described pictorially, because otherwise we get caught up in earthly conceptions—then we would have to ask how we can come to a conception of the world ether. We can form an idea of the world ether by simply following what exists here on the earth in an outward direction, by travelling further and further outward. (One must of course do this in a spiritual sense.) Here on earth, the activity of the ether is in reality barely perceptible, because on earth this activity is weakest. Just as, for example, the effects of earthly light become the weakest at a great distance, so the effects of the cosmic ether are weakest near the earth. As soon as we go out into the distant realms of the universe, the true nature of etheric activity becomes more and more a reality.

If we go out into the vastness of the cosmos, then it begins to dawn on us that the physical aspect of the earth is woven into the etheric according to laws that are quite different from those found on earth. But if one were to go all the way out to the limits, where the ether radiates its forces inward from the outside, then one would experience something curious. People whose thinking is not very thorough, and rooted in the physical, will say: "If you move from the earth in a radial direction out into the cosmos, then you can continue into infinity." Or, those who are familiar with the more recent developments in geometry might say at most: "If you move outward into infinity, then you will come back on the other side; it only will take quite a while." But this is just something thought out, because in reality it is not like that. In reality, one actually comes to an end, even if the path can, speaking superficially, be called infinite in accordance with earthly standards. In the universe there is a transition from earthly law to cosmic law—which radiates inward. The universe is a closed whole, and when you reach the end—all you have to do is think about it pictorially—then, in all directions, you will encounter the inside of the surface of a sphere. This is where the astral shines in. The astral begins to work from the outside in, by taking hold of the etheric.

However, even there you will not come to anything that is the I. If you pursue the path from the world, then you will first come to nature, to physical nature, to earthly nature; from there to the etheric; and at the end of the etheric, you will come to the astral. But you will not yet come into the world to which the human I belongs. This world does not exist in this region of the cosmos, which as such can be found by the astral senses; rather, the I belongs to yet another world, which in turn has its very own laws. Accordingly, when we speak of the essential nature of the human being, we must be quite clear that the different members that make up the human essential being belong to entirely different worlds. It is not a matter of simply differentiating these members but, rather, of depicting the fact that within the human being's essential nature, the beings of radically different worlds converge together. This means that, the moment you want to think about the differentiation between waking and sleeping, you should also begin to think about the differentiation of these distinct worlds. For, what we actually have in our I and in our astral body does not belong to the same world to which the other two members of the human being belong—the members that lie in bed. What we have left behind lying in bed—this we have passed on to the mineral and the plant world for the duration of sleep. What we carry with us as I and astral body—this we have taken out of the plant and the mineral world and lifted into another world, which is neither the world of the plants nor that of the minerals.

And what occurs then while we are asleep? While we sleep, exactly the same thing is taking place within the members that lie in bed as what is happening outside in the world in the mineral kingdom and in the plant kingdom—as long as the plants are not eaten by animals. For, in that case, the astral element comes into effect, working in from the animal world. But if we disregard human beings and animals and take into account only the earth and its plants, then we have here the world to which we surrender our physical and etheric bodies during sleep; and in that sense, everything that takes place in the mineral and plant kingdom also takes place in our physical and etheric bodies.

Suppose we were unable to sleep. I have mentioned before that people sometimes claim that they cannot sleep, but that they do in fact sleep, even if their sleep is interrupted and they wake up often—because the amount of time indicated by some people as the time during which they apparently have not slept is of such a size that, if it were true, they should have been dead long ago. In point of fact, sleep is necessary for the whole human being. In any case, if we did not sleep—let us just assume this—then we would continually be busy, with our astral body and our I, in our physical and etheric bodies. However, the physical body and the etheric body simply cannot tolerate this. The physical body follows the laws of the earth. The astral body does not belong to the earth at all; it continually works on the physical body in a way that is at variance with the laws of the earth. If a human being were unable to sleep, then the physical body would become completely unfit because it would then be worked on incessantly by extra-earthly laws. This would be just as if someone in the physical world were to perpetually cultivate a field with pickaxes and spades and, in doing so, completely pulverize it; for this is how our astral body would begin to work on the physical body. The physical body must re-enforce the earthly laws within itself so that it becomes solidified in a certain way. And the etheric body is dumbed down by the astral body. I do not mean this in such a bad way.[†] There are also clever people and one does not always have to blame people for being clever; but, seen from a cosmic perspective, this is actually how it works. Then, the etheric body must be exposed to the cosmos once again, so that it can rid itself of this dulling influence for a while. In this way, human beings must become a mineral and plant cosmos, as it were, so that what exists within us can flourish, so that a particular state will have been prepared when we awaken. (I am here speaking about normal life. Of course, even when abnormal phenomena occur, human beings still sleep and are awake.)

Now, what kind of state will have been brought about when we wake up? The condition that is brought about arises as a result of the fact that our soul—that is, the astral body and the I—initially cannot fully enter into the physical body and the etheric body; for they can never go all the way into them. Oh, what clever individuals we would be if we could go all the way into our etheric body! But it would also deplete us; we could not bear it. It really is true that this astral body is basically terribly selfish. The etheric body—which, by its very nature, is actually identical with the cosmos—is not egoistic. It is not jealous either, nor does it need to be. But the astral body is subconsciously terribly envious of the etheric body—which is so wise and holds the thoughts of the whole world within itself. The astral body is terribly envious.

But provisions have actually been made so that the senses remain independent, so that the I and astral body remain independent during the day. Thus, the I and the astral body gradually gain the possibility of submerging themselves more deeply into the physical body and the etheric body. However, this actually fills them with a longing to leave again; then the I and astral body wish to sleep and therefore become tired. It is actually only due to the fact that we are not absorbed by our physical and etheric bodies while awake, that we are able to maintain ourselves as independent beings. For, if the human being would be absorbed with respect to the I and astral body, then we would know nothing of ourselves and of the world; rather, we would then be in the interior of our physical organism, which extends to the skin, and follow the processes in our physical organism; but we would only know something about our inner existence.

We would know, however, that sublime, wisdom-filled thoughts are gushing into our interior—but even then, we would not be able to get beyond these thoughts. If we were fully absorbed in our physical and etheric bodies, then we would be entirely unaware of any other human beings, of animals on the earth, of other beings on the earth. If we did not maintain our independence as a result of not completely entering into our physical and etheric bodies, then we would never be able to establish relationships with the world; then we would only be able to know something about our physical body and our own etheric body.

People reflect on things and wonder: How is it that we can say that the table is outside us? We would never be able to state that the table is outside us if we submerged ourselves completely in our physical and etheric bodies. We would never become aware that the table is outside us; we would only experience what is inside us, that is to say, within the skin of our body. A whole universe would shine into us, a universe that is self-contained, etheric, and full of wisdom. And the ability to assess that something exists outside us arises from the fact that we ourselves are outside us when we sleep. Then, when it is outside the physical body, the I becomes accustomed to an existence outside the physical body. When the I slips back in, it has a perception of the outside world. That we are able to perceive things outside us at all—this we owe to the fact that we can sleep. We become accustomed to an existence outside ourselves because we place ourselves there in sleep.

Philosophers reflect on what affirms existence, on why we even say that something exists, or why we say, "I am." If I were completely absorbed by my physical and etheric bodies, then I would not even be able to say, "I am." But because I can make myself independent of the physical and etheric bodies between falling asleep and waking up, I am also getting used to living with the world outside. Just as we are conscious of having a memory, just as I consciously remember today that I saw someone yesterday and ascribe a reality to this memory, so do I ascribe a reality, an outer reality, to what is customarily outside me—because I am also at times outside me, during sleep.

This means that we have to think about things from a completely different perspective than we do today. Then we will be able to really know how much depends on the circumstance that human beings are not absorbed by their physical and etheric bodies. Only then can we truly understand that even our feeling of freedom is essentially determined by the fact that we also have the ability to be outside of our physical and etheric bodies. People who think as natural scientists, who do not consider the autonomous state of an I and an astral body during sleep, will never be able to come to an understanding of freedom, for [they would not realize that] the human being would not be free if we were at all times united with our physical body and our etheric body. How should people know anything about freedom if they know nothing about the times during which the human being makes the astral body and the I independent from the physical and etheric bodies? If we could not sleep, we could not be free. Only what we bring with us from sleep into our waking state makes us free.

People today have absolutely no conception of this world in which the I and the astral body are during sleep. But if we know that all the things of which people are able to form mental images lie in the realm of minerals and plants, then we know that modern science can really only come to conclusions about the sleeping, *not* the waking human being—and about the sleeping human being only insofar as science has developed concepts about the etheric like the ones I have presented today. Once people know this, they will realize that they should then also be able to develop concepts about the I and the astral body. Today, as I already indicated recently, we only have words for these things.

How do we come to concepts about the I and the astral body? Let me use a trivial comparison. In this way you can, firstly, give your thoughts a little rest while this trivial comparison is presented and, secondly, we will definitely come to a better understanding if I interpolate this comparison. Just imagine that any being, a human being or any other being that depends on food, did not feed itself but refused food altogether. It would become thinner and thinner, until finally it would be just skin and bones. This is beautifully symbolized for us through the following story. There once was a farmer who had decided to wean his ox off the habit of eating. And he had already come quite far with this habit-breaking regimen. He gave the ox less and less every day, and had every hope of getting to the point where he could give it only one straw a day. He would have succeeded too, but the ox died before he could complete the experiment. You see, a being that no longer receives nourishment eventually ceases to be.

But this is how things have developed in the course of historical development with respect to the human soul, or—as we refer to the realm of the soul—the I and astral body. People have gradually lost any concepts that can be applied to the soul.† And so, the soul has become a mere word. I already mentioned to you last time that Mauthner, who wrote the *Critique of Language*, did not even want to use "soul" as a word anymore. The word he wanted to use was "souling."†

Now, let us remember the times during which there was still a living awareness about the fact that the concept "soul" needs nourishment, if it is to exist; that one needs something for the soul that must be given to it, just as one needs nourishment for a living being. The concept of the soul has died completely because, ultimately, people's concepts no longer contained any nourishment. Let us look back to such times. I would like to remind you of a well-known saying of Paul's: "And if Christ be not risen, then is our preaching vain, and your faith is also vain,"† meaning that human beings would have to die in soul—for this is the basis of this saying—if it were not for the power that lies in the resurrection of Christ, if this power had not come into the world. But this power that is granted to souls is a spiritual power. And if we take our start from such thought-images, then we will have to ask ourselves: What is it that should then be added—as nourishment, so to speak—to our concept of the soul, so that it becomes a living concept? We must integrate into this concept that which, on the earth, is not earthly—namely, ethical-religious contents, moral contents. These are what keeps the soul alive, just as the body receives nourishment.

How far removed is today's humanity from saying to itself: If the soul does not receive spiritual nourishment, then it will die with the body! In Paul's time there was still a living awareness of the fact that the soul would be in mortal danger if it were not to receive spiritual nourishment. This idea must enter the world again through anthroposophy. For you can be sure that, if someone is looking for proof of the immortality of the soul today, he or she would be looking for it in a similar way as natural science does. It would not even occur to such a person to say: Over the course of life on earth, the soul becomes more and more similar to the physical body and the etheric body; and, in order to be able to maintain itself, it must receive spiritual nourishment—that is to say, moral-religious content—because in that way it conquers the transitory nature of the physical and etheric bodies. The fact that the spiritual, the moral-religious element in the spiritual, has something to do with the life of the soul—this is something that will have to be understood by humanity again. Then, people will also be able to attribute substance and reality to the moral-religious element.

From this you can see what has actually been triggered by the age of intellectualism. What is it, then, that the age of intellectualism has brought about? You see, when the age of intellectualism had not yet arrived, human beings were still somewhat submerged in their physical and etheric bodies. The fact that human beings are no longer submerged at all is foremost the achievement of the intellectualistic age. Since that time, people have really only had mirror images in their thoughts. The essence of abstract, intellectualistic thinking is that it contains nothing within itself because it is a mirror image. The thoughts of earlier human beings still had power. Out of this power, people created myths. Myths still penetrated down into reality. With abstract, intellectualistic thinking one can think everything precisely, but this thinking does not gain any content; instead, what we have with intellectualistic thinking is merely a drawing of the world. Accordingly, the situation is such that the intellectualistic age has led human beings completely toward the outside, allowing them to experience only mirror images of reality. The moral-religious realm cannot be experienced at all if one wants to experience it intellectually, because moral-religious things must be *done* by human beings. If moral-religious things are not actively pursued, then one cannot experience these mirror images. What this means, then, is that the human being, precisely in order to experience the substance of the moral-religious element as a reality, must grow beyond intellectualism and into a real inner experience. This can only be done if we resolve to stand in full clarity with the aims of spiritual science.

I would like to repeat here what I already had occasion to say elsewhere. In certain parts of the world, people are now finally recognizing that there is a difference between our present age and a hundred years ago. People speak of Goethe† as he lived, let us say in 1823, without emphasizing something that is only now beginning to emerge as a beginning awareness in America, where it is even more evident than in Europe. You only have to think of Weimar as it was when Goethe walked around in it—and all the other places where Goethe went—and realize that there were no telegraph wires all around, no telephone lines and so on. At that time, the air was not interspersed with telegraph lines or electrical wires. Now, just imagine how refined the instruments are that receive the electrical forces coming from everywhere and think about the fact that people have many such devices in front of them and all around them. Over in America, people are beginning to have an inkling that the physical human being is affected by the fact that we are surrounded by electrical cables and the like. Goethe walked through the world without his body having any induction currents in it. Nowadays, you could go somewhere far away, but it would be impossible to go far enough without electrical cables following you. This continually induces currents within us. Goethe did not live in such currents. All these effects take the physical body from humanity, make the physical body such that the soul cannot enter it at all. We really have to be clear that in an age when there were no electrical currents, when the air was not buzzing with electrical cables, it was easier to be a human being. For, at that time, these ahrimanic forces were not constantly present—forces that take your body from you even when you are awake. At that time, there was also no need for people to make such an effort to find their way to the spirit. For it is only when we come into ourselves, that we actually come to the spirit. Therefore, in order to be a human being at all, it is necessary to expend a much greater spiritual competence today than was the case a hundred years ago.

However, it would never occur to me to be reactionary and say: Let us do away with all that stuff, with all the modern cultural achievements! That is not what is meant. But modern human beings need this direct turning-toward-the-spirit—as outlined by spiritual science—so that through this intense experience of the spirit, we become the stronger ones against the forces that are emerging with modern culture, forces that aim to solidify our physical body and take it from us. Otherwise, what will happen is that human beings will miss out, one could say, on establishing a connection with the evolution of humanity.

This intellectualistic age burst forth, for the good of humanity, at a time when human beings were still able to be somewhat immersed in their physical bodies. If we had maintained the soul constitution that human beings had in the thirteenth and fourteenth centuries, then, with that type of soul constitution, it would never have become possible for us to grasp intellectual thoughts at all. Then, we would no longer have the older conditions, but neither would we be able to develop abstract intellectual thoughts; they would go up in smoke, evaporate. We would become alienated from the old conditions and would not be able to think; consequently, we would move around in the world as dreaming beings, staggering around in the face of the most important world concerns. We would wander around like tumbling dreamers. But this is actually what might lie ahead for humanity if it does not sharpen and strengthen its inner spiritual capacities.

The way in which humanity would suffer from this kind of progress would be such that people would immediately feel pain whenever they were trying to think. In the sixteenth century, people were still so inwardly robust that they were able to have crisp intellectual thoughts. They still took great pleasure in thinking intellectual thoughts. Today, we are very close to the point where people say: "Oh, thinking about things is so difficult; please put the whole story on film for me so that I do not have to think, so that I can watch it in its various stages!" This is when strange things could happen. I really do not mean this in a funny way. This is something, as you will see in a moment, that is very much within the realm of possibility. Just think, if you were to film the entire multiplication table, then people could always carry a device in front of them and as soon as they attempted to calculate something, the right number would start up with the help of a specific sound, and they would have the whole thing in front of them as a film. Little by little, people no longer will want to think, because it will begin to be unpleasant; thinking becomes unpleasant. People much prefer to dream rather than think. And if outer things such as these, the outer development of culture, were to continue without a strong inner spiritual element arising within this development, then it would indeed be the case that all people would become like stumbling dreamers. This is meant very seriously; such a thing is in the offing for humanity. And it is this very thing that can only be counteracted if we are truly committed to approaching the spiritual world courageously and boldly, in the way that spiritual science intends and can put into effect. It is still entirely possible today that we, as humanity, can galvanize ourselves inwardly to such an extent that we can come to inner activity. But all those who understand this must work in full earnestness and with all means at their disposal.

Please do not interpret the things that I am saying in a negative sense, in a negative way. I certainly do not want to take anything away from modern culture. The more these things are developed, the more enthusiastic I am about them. I do not want to eliminate the telegraph or films; that does not even occur to me. But it is absolutely necessary to take into account that everywhere in the world there are always two things confronting each other. The world is completely dominated by externalization. This requires a counterbalance. Just as we must dry ourselves after having bathed, so we must immerse ourselves in the spirit when we are confronted with a culture in which outer depiction is becoming ever more prevalent. It is precisely when we are entrapped externally in something that no longer works *through* us but, instead, works *upon* us in such a way that we literally switch ourselves off in soul and spirit—this is precisely when we are summoned to become all the more active inwardly.

The best way to find these thoughts, which we need, is to make it quite clear to ourselves that the human being is such a complicated entity because spiritual beings from the most diverse worlds are flowing together in this human being in order to form a complete being. When I had written my *Outline of Esoteric Science*, a very important contemporary philosopher[†] sent me—I have already mentioned this earlier—a long article about "this *Esoteric Science*." And when I began to read it, right from the start it contained clever things like: "This division of the human being into physical body, etheric body, astral body, and so on, is just an abstraction." But that is just as clever as someone saying: It is an abstraction to say that water consists of hydrogen and oxygen. It is no wonder, then, that we have to say that one cannot discuss these things with people who think like that. We must always be able to gauge the impossibility of discussing factual matters with our contemporaries. Such discussions are fruitless discussions. Admittedly, they also are the more uncommon ones. The more common cases are those where opponents come forward with personal slander and lies. In those cases, it then becomes a matter of expounding the lie as a lie to the world, the slander as slander. But discussions are of very little use. For it is precisely because of the essential nature, both of anthroposophy and of what such opponents have to say when they want to discuss things, that no bridge can be built between them, that anthroposophy must assert itself through its own strengths in all areas. We must be just as vigilant in rebuffing slander and lies as we must clarify for ourselves that anthroposophy can only make its way through the world by working with all intensity out of its own inner strength—in other words, when dealing with opponents, we must be vigilant whenever untrue methods are used in such attacks. On the other hand, certain opportunities may well arise that make it necessary to point out whether something is justified or not; you can do this, for example, when you are merely dealing with a fictitious opponent. Some people have actually used this approach by copying the refutations contained in my writings, except that they left out what was positive in them. It is certainly true that one can find factual refutations in my writings. For it is necessary to have a clear insight into these things and not to start dreaming when it comes to this realm.

Now, please forgive me for the fact that almost every lecture, even if it attempts to lead into somewhat more remote areas, must nevertheless end with this kind of an appeal. It will be most harmful for the Anthroposophical Society if it develops too much of an inclination to sleep; it must be vigilant. Human beings become plant-like when they sleep. But the Anthroposophical Society also takes on a plant-like existence when it is asleep with regard to its real concerns. And just as little as human beings can endure being plants all the time and sleeping through their whole lives, so little can the Anthroposophical Society endure it when people are always asleep. Wakefulness needs to be developed too. And I would like to recommend this without distinction to both the Anthroposophical Society and the Free Anthroposophical Society.† Otherwise, it may well turn out that both societies only developed side by side because, if they had stayed together, the members of either society would have disturbed each other's sleep too much; and if you are independent, then others disturb your sleep less and you can sleep all the better.

It will be a matter of both societies coming to the realization that they must now wake up through their own inner forces and not be glad that the other one will no longer disturb their sleep. Of course, I do not mean to be offensive, but sometimes one has to say such things and actually say them, even to the Free Anthroposophical Society as well. If either one of them is not to become the favored child, then both should be treated kindly. And so, what I would like is that this be given sufficient consideration. I think that some people already know what I actually mean. People often say that they do not know what I mean, but I still believe that if the will is there, you can know what I mean; and even when I urge you to be awake, you can know what I mean, no matter how unpleasant it may sound.

So, my dear friends, send your delegates to the Delegates' Meeting of the Anthroposophical Society in Dornach, to be held from July 20 to 22 [1923]. Send them very awake. For we will need wakefulness in the future, complete wakefulness in the Anthroposophical Society as a whole.

Three Stages in the Awakening of the Human Soul

PRAGUE, APRIL 28, 1923

Today, I would like to add something from a more esoteric perspective to what I was able to say in yesterday's public lecture.† What I would like to speak to you about today is actually meant as a kind of esoteric addendum.

When a human being leaves the existence which I referred to yesterday as pre-earthly existence, and grows, beginning with embryonic life, into physical-earthly existence, we see how in this physical existence the soul-spiritual element—which initially is hidden—begins to assert itself from out of the physical body, and how the child, as it were, sleeps its way into the physical-earthly world. We see that the life of the child, in its relation to the surrounding world, is still a kind of dreaming; that it only gradually awakens. We find, however, a threefold structure in the stages of this awakening that manifests at particularly prominent points in time. And we will be able to see something of this threefold structure if we observe it with the kind of inner joy, the devoted love with which anyone who is in the full sense a human being always observes a child. But the full significance of this threefold structure, this triad, only really becomes clear if one is able, through spiritual science, to observe the soul-spiritual life in the physical-bodily existence. This triad consists in learning to walk, learning to speak, and learning to think. You know at which age the child goes through each of these three developments, because this is the logical sequence of events. We will soon see why this logical sequence must occur as it does. It can be different, but this sequence of events is certainly the natural one.

"Learning to walk" is a term that only refers in a very one-sided way to a series of abilities that the child acquires simultaneously. The child enters the world in such a way that it lives in a state of balance that is utterly different from the one in which it later moves around in the world. This latter state also includes the correct use of the arms, as well as the right adjustment of the whole organism to the posture suitable for human beings in relation to the world, and to the ability to move around in a way that is appropriate for human beings in earthly existence. This is what the child must learn first. The forces required to achieve this mobility of the organism then give rise to the capacity of the human being to find a position of equilibrium with respect to the solid, the fluid, the gaseous substances. And all of this contains the foundation, the ground, for something else. As the human being takes on these activities—learning to walk, acquiring balance, learning to use the arms and fingers—the movements thus occurring in the entire organism have an effect on the system that forms the basis of human speech. It tenses the muscles, moves the blood, exerts an influence upon the human etheric body, is transmitted to the physical, etheric, and astral organs of breathing, then proceeds further and exerts a certain formative activity upon the brain. One might say that it transfers itself to those organs which produce speech from the inside of the child, as it imitates its environment.

Speech is the human being's transposed movement and transposed balance. Someone who can attain cognitive insight into reality, through observation of the soul-spiritual, will be able to see how the dexterity—that is to say, *not* the resulting skill but rather the effort that the child must make in order to acquire the dexterity of its hands in grasping—how this dexterity continues to work in the melodious element of speech. The rhythm of speech comes to expression in the way the feet are set down in the movements of walking. It is very meaningful to observe whether a child that is learning to walk, first steps on the heel of the foot, on the ball of the foot, or on the toes. What shoots forth (*herausschiesst*) as the child's thinking grows out of speech. Walking, speaking, thinking—these abilities develop out of the child's dim, dreamlike state of consciousness. When the human being is born and is not yet able to do these things, this force is nonetheless working in the child as a final aftereffect of the way in which it was present in pre-earthly existence. Spiritual science can show us how this force is present in pre-earthly existence. The earliest speech sounds are not sounds that reflect thinking; they are sounds that arise from bodily comfort or discomfort.

How, then, did walking, speaking, and thinking exist in pre-earthly existence? If we observe the manifestation of this thinking, as it flows out of the child, and trace it further back, then we will find that it disappears into an indefinable darkness. It only appears again in the last period before earthly birth. This is where the observer sees the soul-spiritual essence of the human being in a spiritual interaction with a multitude of beings—those that have been described in my *Esoteric Science* as Angeloi, the Angels.† It is an interaction that can be described by saying: In this realm, thoughts are not just thought and expressed in an abstract way; rather, a living stream of thoughts is flowing back and forth from being to being. In this way, there is a living communication with the Angeloi. From what has flowed into the human soul as a force, something develops which is slept through, as it were, by the human being during the earliest stages of life, but which manifests later when it emerges as the force of thinking, the force of forming concepts. And we have this so that we can establish the proper way of communicating and interacting with human beings. Just think of what we would be if we were not thinking beings, what we would be as human beings among each other! Everything that we are as human beings among each other, stems from the fact that we are thinking beings. Here on this earth, we communicate with each other as human beings through the thoughts that we put into our speech. The way in which we communicate here through thinking—this is what we have acquired from our pre-earthly interaction with the Angeloi. There, we can also have such association with the other human beings who are in pre-earthly existence, just as we associate with the Angels. This takes the form of a direct thought-speech. However, our communication with the hierarchy of the Angels is on a higher level, since this offers not only fulfilment for the soul but also a force which then reappears in the thinking that the child acquires in the third stage of its earthly life.

Now let us look at the second stage, at the ability to speak. It is not as closely tied to the nerve-sense system as is thinking. Speaking is linked to the chest system, the rhythmic system of the human being, to what manifests in breathing, in the circulation of the blood. If we look at the forces that struggle out of the child when it imitates the outer world in learning to speak, and trace them back to pre-earthly existence, then we find that as human beings we acquired these forces through the interaction that we were able to have, during pre-earthly existence, with the hierarchy of the Archangeloi, the beings who govern the various peoples—beings who have this task precisely because they have the kind of relationship with human beings that has just been described. These forces, which we acquire as the result of our interaction with the Archangels, sink down into obscurity and only emerge again in the forces of our earthly life of speech, through which we communicate with other human beings. What would we be among each other as human beings if we were without language, if we were not able to pour the etheric element of our thought-waves into the coarser air-waves that facilitate speech? The forces that cause our rhythmic system to become the bearer of a more condensed manifestation come to us from the hierarchy of the Archangeloi. This is how we can trace these things by going back to pre-earthly existence. Accordingly, we can express not only in abstract terms that the human being lives among spiritual beings, but we can actually describe the very specific form in which one or another rank of beings has given us a specific gift for earthly life. We are thanking these spiritual beings—that is to say, we put ourselves in the right relationship to these beings—when we say: *For my thinking, I thank the Angeloi*; *for my speech, I thank the Archangeloi.*

Let us now go back to the first thing that the child learns—to walking, to learning to maintain a balanced posture. There is more connected with this than is commonly thought. Connected with it is the fact that a very specific physical process is activated by the I, a process that turns the child from a crawling into a walking being. It is the I that raises the human being to the upright position; it is the astral body that is at work within the sense of speech in the upright being; it is the etheric body that permeates all of this with the force of thinking. But they all work into the physical body. If we look at an animal, whose spine is parallel to the surface of the earth, then we see that its conduct, its movements, its behavior—everything that develops from the astral—is something entirely different from what it is in the human being who, as a being of will, acts out of his upright, vertical nature. The conditions which, in the case of the human being, are occurring in the I, in the astral body, and in the etheric body in this way, are really a kind of combustion process in the physical body. And here is actually a case in point where our physical science, if it had the desire to perfect itself, would be able to find some alliance with anthroposophy.

It must be said that the combustion processes in human beings are altogether different from those in animals. When the spark of an organic being works horizontally, it erases what comes from conscience; it cannot work into what comes from the moral realm, from conscience. The reason that, in the case of human beings, conscience is streaming through these processes, is that in human beings this spark, this flame of will, is standing upright on the earth. The child puts itself just as much into this incoming jolt of the moral element, the conscience-based element, as it adopts the external, physical position of balance. As the child learns to walk, the human moral nature shoots into it—and indeed, even the religious element that permeates this essential nature. These are truly noble forces that work into the child when it transitions from crawling to walking! If we trace these forces back through the dimness of the child's consciousness, then they lead us to an even higher level of human interaction with those beings whom we call the Primal Powers, the Archai. Everything that we went through in our pre-earthly existence continues to have an effect. If we want to add a third part to the prayer-like formulation: For my thinking, I thank the Angeloi; for my speaking, I thank the Archangeloi—then we must say: *For my being placed within earthly existence in accordance with physical and moral forces, I thank the Archai*, who have been endowed with this power by still loftier beings.

And now we are able to have an answer for our question: How does it transpire that the human being, who possessed a light-filled consciousness before birth, enters earthly life with a dimmed consciousness? This dampening of consciousness occurs because the forces of walking, speaking, and thinking—and these can be condensed into one concept—are placed into us by the higher hierarchies in order to be transformed. We can see from this, therefore, how the very aspect that makes us human beings, the aspect through which we become human beings among one another, reveals that we have a connection with the higher divine-spiritual worlds. In a certain way, we enter these divine-spiritual worlds again and again during our earthly life. It is really the case that we have to say to ourselves: The state of sleep—from which dreams arise in a playful way—is at least as significant for the actual essential nature of the human being as the waking state. When the human being transitions from the waking state into the sleep state, it is especially these three abilities, which we have made our own in the manner described, that begin to grow silent. Our forming of mental images, our speaking, and our being active all grow silent. However, it can then also be observed that, to the same extent that our thoughts disappear from our consciousness as we fall asleep and our thinking becomes silent, we come near to the Angeloi; and that, as our speaking ceases, we come near to the archangelic beings. And to the extent that we are completely at rest, through the cessation of our activities, we come near to the beings of the rank of the Archai, the Primal Powers.

What is important, however, is that during this state of sleep we approach these three hierarchies in a worthy manner, that we come near to the Angeloi, Archangeloi, and Archai in a worthy manner. And it is indeed this subject in particular about which one would have to speak to human beings of the present time. For, *how* we come close to the Angeloi depends largely on how we shape our thinking while awake; *whether* we are able to come close to the Archangeloi in a worthy manner depends on the way in which we use our speech-forces; and *whether* we are able to come close to the Archai in a worthy manner depends on the way in which we use our capacity to move, as well as our sense of morality.

We are living in a time where people no longer want to have anything in their thinking that goes beyond the physical world, where they want to be stimulated by the outer world. Independent, pure thinking, such as I described it already thirty years ago in my *Philosophy of Freedom* as the foundation needed for moral understanding, is rarely found and regrettably very little cultivated in today's children. But through the kind of thinking that Goethe and Schiller† would still have called idealistic, we can get away from the mere waking world of earthly existence and still retain something for the sleeping state. We have as much strength to approach the Angels during sleep as there is idealism in our thinking. And we are as powerless to take the steps that should be taken toward the Angels as there is materialism in our thinking.

In the same sense, it should be noted how those who do not find the strength—through idealism developed in the waking state—to come close to the Angel-beings, then fall prey to ahrimanic elemental beings during sleep; for their thinking is then compelled to turn to these beings. It is so beautiful how children learn to think so directly, in a way that most people can no longer even picture conceptually! The thinking of a child, right after it has learned to think, is full of spirituality. It is wonderful to see how, up to the time when they are being gobbled up by materialism, sleeping children ascend, as if on wings (*wie im Fluge*), directly toward their Angel-being; to see how they connect with their Angel-being during sleep. Accordingly, we can say that during sleep, we seek—albeit only through idealism, through spiritualization of the world of thought—those worlds from which we have developed, so that we may learn to think as human beings among human beings here on the earth.

And when we consider speech, we find that, just as idealism in our thinking is important for our interaction with the Angeloi, so is idealism in our soul disposition equally important for our interaction with the Archangeloi-beings during sleep. If we are able, when addressing another person, to pour goodwill into our words, as well as a benevolent disposition that empathizes with the soul of the other—a disposition that does not pass by the other person but, rather, responds to him or her with the interest that one can have in human beings—then this disposition, which can be described as an idealistic-benevolent one, is what also gives speech its harmonious, benevolent sound. When the astral body and the I have transitioned into sleep, it gives this astral body and the I, which also are involved in our speaking, the power to come close to the Archangeloi-beings, whereas an unsocial, egotistical soul disposition disperses these forces into the world of the ahrimanic elemental beings—with the result that, when we fall asleep and have not used language in the right, idealistic manner, we are actually making ourselves less human.

The same applies when we use our actions, our deeds, in a way that is humanly kind and, at the same time, based on the full awareness that the human being is not only a being who lives in the flesh but also a being who, according to his inner nature, is a spiritual being. For, out of this awareness arises the recognition that other human beings are also spiritual beings. By acting on the basis of this conception, we gain for our sleeping state the forces that bring us close to the Archai in the right way, whereas, if we are incapable of performing humanly kind actions, if we are only conscious of ourselves as physical beings, then the relevant forces will be scattered in the world of the ahrimanic elemental beings—with the result that we alienate ourselves from our actual human essential nature.

This is how, as human beings, we bring a triad of gifts with us from our pre-earthly existence; and it is also in a threefold way that we reconnect these gifts to their archetypal forms between falling asleep and waking up, when we remain unconscious but return again and again to the proximity of these beings. This is actually quite similar to how, here on earth, we have to give shape to our interactions with other human beings out of three sources—the source of thought, the source of speech, and the source of actions. And during our sleeping life, we relate in a threefold way to the spiritual world—to the Angels, to the Archangels, and to the Primal Powers.

What we there establish in union with these beings is of crucial importance for our passing through the portal of death. For it is possible to discern, through spiritual vision, that human beings are able to come ever closer to the beings of the ranks of the Angeloi, the Archangeloi, the Archai. And things would definitely become very bad for a future humanity if it were to succumb entirely to the ahrimanic elemental beings, if a materialism of thinking, speaking, and acting were to become more and more entrenched. But thanks to the spiritual world, human souls of the present time—at least, this is the case for most people today—still possess enough of an inherited good soul disposition in their thinking, speaking, and acting that all of this cannot yet be ruined by today's materialism. Very materialistic people do not have much in their present earthly life that would let them get close to the hierarchies, but what wells up from their past lives is what leads them there.

Humanity could quite easily meet with another kind of outcome, however, if it does not develop a spiritual view of life. Bringing idealism into one's thinking, speaking, and acting provides the human being with the possibility of establishing new relations, as it were, with the three ranks of divine-spiritual beings, the Angeloi, the Archangeloi, and the Archai—which the human being needs for the period between death and a new birth. Otherwise—if this does not come to pass—a human being who did not have a connection with the Angeloi in the present time would have to be born at a future time as a being whose thinking is paralyzed; a human being who did not enter into an interrelation with the Archangeloi would have to be born as a being without the ability to speak; a human being who did not have a connection with the Archai would, in this future time, have to be born paralyzed in limbs and paralyzed in moral impulses. It is within the power of earthly humanity either to drag down the whole of earthly humanity through materialism in civilization and culture, or to raise it to a loftier height through spiritualization—a higher stage which I have called in my *Outline of Esoteric Science* the Jupiter existence† of earthly beings.

Anthroposophy is not a theory. Every word, every thought passes into the whole of our thinking life, into the whole of our human soul-being. We cannot do otherwise than to have the thought: You are actually a crippled being if you do not have the right relation to the higher beings. This also gives us a feeling of responsibility for our moral life in relation to the spiritual world; and it is from this world that the human being derives the right sense of responsibility in relation to the physical world. It only comes from this world. If you consider what occurs for the human being in this way, how we come close to the Angeloi through the idealism in our thoughts, how we come close to the Archangeloi through our words, through the idealistic disposition contained in our speech, how we come close to the Archai through the idealism embodied in our actions—in short, how we struggle our way up toward the three hierarchies during sleep—then you will also be able to comprehend what anthroposophical research shows us: that human destiny is woven in this way. We carry all this through the portal of death, and later it becomes conscious. After death, we must form our thoughts in association with the Angeloi; with our acquired soul disposition we must secure our concepts, our mental images after death. The way and manner in which we take our place, through speech, in the midst of humanity gives us the ability, the power, to come together with the Archangeloi. And through the way in which we use our limbs we must, by interacting with the Archai, acquire the possibility of having self-consciousness after death. This is how we live our way into this world, and this is how we weave what then develops into the clear power of consciousness between death and a new birth.

Now, if we observe a child during the earliest years of life, then we see the continuing effects of a previous earthly life. We do not just look into its pre-earthly life but also into its previous life on earth, and it is only then that we acquire a view of the entire earthly life. That is when we really see the child—how it learns to walk, how it learns to use its arms, whether it steps on the ball of its feet or on the heels. Then we are not only seeing the child as it appears to the physical eye, but we also see how certain actions were previously carried out with tenderness, with gentleness, with a compassionate heart, and how this gives the child a firm step in its present life; or, alternatively, how an insecure, wavering gait is the outcome of insensitive, pitiless conduct in a previous life. Every step the child takes, its struggle to develop a particular way of walking, reveals to us that this shaping of its gait is the outcome of a previous life on earth. We learn to recognize the physical as an image of what is living in the child as a moral impulse from a previous life on earth. It is the most amazing thing one can observe—this learning to walk! The main measure of destiny comes to expression in learning to walk. However, as I mentioned yesterday [in the public lecture], the freedom of a human being is no more affected by the fact that we are born with our destiny than by whether one has blonde or brown hair.

In learning to speak something else is expressed. It indicates a connection with pre-earthly existence as well, but it is difficult to characterize. Because it is difficult to express, I shall clothe it in more conventional words for you. When, as human beings, we pass through the portal of death, we have given a particular moral shape to our essential being. Every time we were asleep, we were always weaving our own essential being, and now we begin to see for ourselves what we were weaving during those times. Once we have passed through the portal of death, we are able to come close to the Angeloi, Archangeloi, and Archai in the right way. But there is something else that is then being added, a further element that human beings receive from the second rank of the hierarchies. These beings pour into the human being—as an additional, more impersonal destiny—that which places the individual within a specific language in his or her next life, that which integrates him or her into a particular national context. Individual destiny is connected with what the human being *is* through associating with the Archai. The capacity for speech we receive from the Archangels. But which language we speak—this we receive from still higher beings, from the Exusiai, Dynamis, and Kyriotetes.

If we look at thinking, at our capacity of forming mental images, then we find that it is connected, as I have shown, with the Angels. These beings can confer the gift of thinking upon human beings. But they only acquired this capacity during the Earth phase; they did not have it during the Moon phase. In the course of this process, a certain development is occurring for the Angels themselves; through it, they themselves come into a close relation with the Seraphim, Cherubim, and Thrones. Through this relation, they are acquiring the capacity for a direct association with the Thrones, Cherubim, and Seraphim—and these beings do not bestow a faculty that is imparted only to a specific human community; rather, it is a faculty that is given to all of humanity. The faculty of thinking is, of course, something that is common to all of humanity. This is why there is logic—the same logic throughout the entire world.

Walking, in which personal destiny is expressed, we receive from the Archai, out of their own forces. The forces of speech we receive from the Archangels, but in this giving they are guided by the second rank of the hierarchies. The ability to think we receive from the Angels, but they bestow this onto us through the influence of the highest hierarchies.

This is how all these things are interwoven in the world order, and we can only understand the human being if we are able to see a being that is interwoven with the world order. In this way, we comprehend not only the individual human being but also the essential nature of a language family, be it a living or a dying one, as well as the nature of thinking, be it an imperfect or a more perfect way of thinking. On the earth, the human being exists within a certain dualism. Entities and beings are seen and understood as being dependent on certain natural laws. And based on this, the human being develops an awareness of a relationship with a divine entity. Here on this earth, there is no connection between a physical and a moral world order. But if we look back into the life before birth and toward the life after death, then we enter a world where these two realms have merged into one. And one cannot rightly judge what we ourselves are as human beings if one is not able to properly understand oneself as a spiritual being. We cannot arrive at a unified worldview if we cannot see beyond birth and death, if we do not see into the higher worlds. In order to understand our whole, complete being, we need a consciousness that is permeated by the knowledge of our connection with the spiritual world.

These are the things that I wanted to speak to you about today in a more esoteric way.

Anthroposophy as a Path toward a Deeper Understanding of the Mystery of Easter

PRAGUE, APRIL 29, 1923

As human beings, we perceive the condition of the soul, the whole life of the human soul, far too much only as it is experienced by human beings of our age, that is, of the nineteenth and twentieth centuries. And what we know from history is, for the most part, the external events and less the history of the human soul itself. The changes that are occurring in the soul life of humanity are given little consideration.

Now, it must be said that earlier ages did not have cause, in the same way as we do at the present time, to occupy themselves with the history of the life of the human soul. Our own age—which, if we consider it as a great historical moment in time, begins in the middle or actually already in the first third of the fifteenth century—presents human beings with very special responsibilities that can only be undertaken with today's consciousness, whereas human beings of earlier times were able to take on their tasks by means of a certain instinct, albeit a humanly formed instinct. You have heard on various occasions, and perhaps read in lecture cycles, that in ancient times, humanity possessed a kind of instinctive clairvoyance; that the evolution of humanity has consisted in the fact that this instinctive clairvoyance was lost; and that the present-day state of soul—which is an intellectual one and has primarily developed the human forces of reason—has taken the place of this instinctive clairvoyance. I do not mean to say that, because of this, the forces of feeling and of the will are not active in today's humanity. But what actually constitutes the greatness of our contemporary civilization, what we are experiencing especially in our present time, appeals to the forces of reason, the forces of the intellect. However, human beings living today have every reason to consider the question: "What does it mean for the human soul when civilization is entrenched in the intellect?" This question can only be answered comprehensively if one takes into account, at least to some extent, the indications about pre-earthly human existence mentioned yesterday in a different context.

As human beings of the present age, we experience our thought-concepts as something very abstract, as something that we do not experience inwardly to the same degree as the thought-concepts that were living within human beings in the age of the ancient, instinctive clairvoyance. And if we look at the pre-earthly existence of human beings with our abstract, intellectualistic concepts, then we find that what currently is abstract thinking was something entirely different during this pre-earthly existence. When, in our pre-earthly existence, we had as yet no physical body, no bodily organism, when we still had a soul-spiritual essence, our thoughts were something completely different. At that time, thoughts still had a soul life, and we experienced a thought in such a way that we knew: These thoughts are spread throughout the whole world and we scoop them up from this world and draw them into our own soul existence.

Today, people believe that thoughts are something that they create with their brains. This is just about as clever as if someone who is drinking a glass of water were to believe that the water came from his tongue, that he was not taking it in from the outside. In truth, thoughts are something active, something living, the active forces in all things, and we only scoop them up, draw them in from the world. Our organism, our organic system, is only the vessel into which we draw the thoughts by means of our I. And it is only during our earthly life between birth and death that we can succumb to the error, to the erroneous notion, that we ourselves create thoughts, that we do not draw them in from the world. As long as we live in pre-earthly existence, we know that the world of thought fills everything in our surroundings, just as the air does during our life between birth and death; we know that we breathe in thought-forces, as it were, and breathe them out again, that they are something active and productive.

It is of the utmost importance that we become conscious of the fact that the forces of thinking in pre-earthly life are something completely different from those in earthly existence. When we come upon a corpse in the world, we do not say to ourselves that this corpse could have been given the form that it has as a corpse through the kind of forces that we call the forces of nature. We know that it is the remains of a living human being; that it was necessary for a living human being to have been in existence. We know that a natural force can never give a corpse the form that it has; that a corpse can only be the remains of a human being who was alive. What we are able to observe in regard to the life of thinking in human beings, as we possess it in earthly existence, also provides a basis for understanding that the forces of thought developed during earthly life cannot arise of themselves in our physical organism; that they are instead the remnants of the living forces that we possessed in pre-earthly existence. With the same certainty with which one can say that the corpse is the dead remains of a human being who lived, one can also say: The abstract thinking that we have today is the dead remnant of what we possessed during pre-earthly existence in the form of living thinking. Living thinking dies when we are born—or, more specifically, when we are conceived—and what becomes active in us as forces of thinking is the corpse of the living thinking that we possessed in our pre-earthly existence. We can only fully and correctly understand earthly thinking if we regard it as the residue of pre-earthly thinking, just as we regard a corpse as the remains of a human being who was alive.

This awareness that human thinking is the remnant of a living thinking must gradually permeate humanity more and more. For it is only then that we see ourselves in the right way as human beings; only then do we look back in the right way at our pre-earthly existence, just as one looks back from the corpse, in which only the forces of nature are still present, to the living human being in whom higher forces are living. But one can only see this whole situation in the right light when one realizes that this kind of thinking, as we have it today—a thinking that tends toward abstraction—has only been developed since the fifteenth century. Of course, it developed in different ways for individual peoples and ethnic groups, but generally speaking, the situation was such for civilized humanity that it evolved toward this dead mode of thinking during the first third of the fifteenth century; that this way of thinking became more and more dead and then reached a certain culmination of this deadness in the last third of the nineteenth century.

In point of fact, if we look further back in evolution, then we find that human souls in these ancient times, as they passed through conception and birth, still carried something from their pre-earthly existence over into their earthly existence. The living nature of ancient myths, of old folk legends, of the old formative forces of the soul—which are not the same at all as our present-day forces of fantasy—could not have developed if something of the living pre-earthly thinking had not radiated into it, if earthly thinking had already become entirely abstract. Indeed, it can be said in a certain sense that even today, a last remnant of pre-earthly thinking still exists in the time of early childhood, which then is lost in the course of life.

But these human beings of more ancient times were also completely different in their whole constitution of soul, compared to present-day human beings. Just try for the moment to truly envisage that, even today, you existed within this living thinking; that you would be able to experience a clairvoyance such as human souls had in earlier times; that you would be able to experience imaginations, but that these imaginations would work so powerfully upon you that you would experience yourself merely as a vessel for divine-spiritual forces: You would never attain an awareness of freedom. The true sense of freedom was only developed, for the first time, in civilized humanity. The fact that human beings could become free we owe to the circumstance that it is not a living thinking that is at work in us—at least not in the waking state—but, rather, a dead thinking into which we can inject whatever we ourselves want to inject, out of our own free will. It is no longer the case, as in earlier times, that spiritual beings are thinking within us; we are beginning to think for ourselves. However, beginning to think for oneself means to inject human will into this thinking, and if one encounters dead thinking, then one can pour free will into this thinking. And so, the human being had to advance toward a dead thinking in order to be able to become a free being in the course of earth's evolution. You see, when we consider the development of the human soul life in this way, we realize that there is meaning in the structuring of the whole human evolution on earth.

Now let us go back to slightly older times. What took place with respect to our thinking in the first third of the fifteenth century—inasmuch as it became ever more dead, more abstract, and intellectual—is something that had been prepared gradually and over long time periods. Such things do not occur all at once. They go through a time of preparation, through a kind of beginning, and then reach a climax. Now, it can be seen quite clearly that a first beginning of this abstract thinking occurred in the fourth century AD. What I mean is that in the fourth century after Christ, the first traces of a particular belief began to assert themselves in human consciousness—the belief that the human being produces thoughts. The ancient Greeks would never have believed that. The Greeks were still quite conscious of a certain living quality in their thinking and were aware that thoughts are everywhere within things; that they themselves were merely drawing these thoughts out of the objects. The notion that the human being produces thoughts arose as a result of the fact that thoughts became ever more lifeless. And these lifeless thoughts—with which one can, in a manner of speaking, do whatever one wants—occurred for the first time in the fourth century AD. This process then continued gradually in this way until the fifteenth century, when the consciousness that we still have today had become clearly established.

What does this mean, however, with regard to the evolution of humanity? In the fourth century AD, the first beginnings of an intellectual, abstract thinking emerged. But this actually means nothing other than that the Mystery of Golgotha, the appearance of Christ upon the earth, occurred at a time when the human soul still was filled with living thoughts. In this respect, humanity has certainly lost a great deal in terms of its consciousness. And although it is true that humanity has attained freedom through this, it has nevertheless lost very much indeed. When Christ appeared on earth, he was received on this earth by a certain number of human beings who still possessed an inwardly living, inwardly active thinking, who still possessed remnants of their pre-earthly existence in their thinking. Accordingly, their bearing toward the Mystery of Golgotha was entirely different from that of human beings of later times.

Just give some careful consideration to the fact that, up until this time, people said to themselves—they did not express this in distinct words because everything was more enveloped in pictures at that time, but they had a certain awareness—they said to themselves, "I am now on the earth. As an earthly human being, I have thoughts here on this earth. But this thinking indicates another world to me; it points me back through birth and conception to a pre-earthly existence, to the world from which I have descended." People experienced themselves as a continuation of what they had been in pre-earthly existence. They knew quite clearly that with their earthly life they were continuing an earlier, pre-earthly existence—notwithstanding the fact that, at that time, human beings were already looking into this world of pre-earthly existence as though through darkened glass. This awareness that the human being is a being who comes down from the heavens to the earth was essentially lost in the fourth century after Christ.

And it was also from this viewpoint that people looked at the event of Golgotha as well. When the initiates—who still existed at that time but were not as wise as the initiates of the ancient Mysteries, even though they still possessed some remnants of the old Mystery wisdom—when the initiates spoke of Christ to the people, this led them to the following realization: Jesus Christ had previously had his home in the world in which we existed before we descended to the earth. This was his world, and in earlier times he had never left that world. It is indeed something inherent to earthly human beings that, already since very ancient times, they had to descend to the earth; and that, in doing so, they had departed from Christ in order to come down to the earth. When Christ was mentioned in the ancient Mystery centers—these Mysteries had always spoken of the Christ-being, even if the name "Christ" would not have been used—then people's thoughts needed to be directed upward to pre-earthly existence and they had to be told: If you wish to know something concerning Christ, then you must not hold onto your earthly consciousness; then you must look upward to pre-earthly existence.

It will be necessary to recount a few things about this pre-earthly existence in order to comprehend what I intend to say today. We stand here on the earth as earthly human beings; we look up at the sun and form conceptions about this sun; we even develop certain hypotheses about it—such as, that this sun is a ball of gas, or something similar. From an earthly point of view, it is actually quite obvious that people develop such ideas for themselves; but then they believe that this is also valid from all points of view. Before we descended to the earth, we also saw the sun, but from the vastness of the cosmos, from the other side, as it were. Seen from there, it was not a physical object, but rather the quintessential embodiment of spiritual beings; and the most significant of these beings, for people living before the Mystery of Golgotha, was Christ. Accordingly, one can actually say the following. When, in pre-Christian times, the students of the Mysteries were initiated into what later was transformed into the Mystery of Golgotha, it became clear to them that human beings, while in their pre-earthly existence, saw the sun and perceived Christ; that, when they had descended to the earth, they saw the sun from the other side, but that Christ was concealed from them; and that they could only be guided upward to Christ through the Mystery wisdom.

In the first period of Christian evolution, people felt that the essential nature of Christianity consisted in the fact that the great spirit of the sun had not remained the spirit of the sun; that, through the Mystery of Golgotha, he had actually left these regions—which can only be experienced by human beings while they are outside the physical body—and had entered earthly existence; and that he was the only one from among the divine-spiritual beings who had entered earthly existence himself. Moreover, using the methods of spiritual research, we can distinguish human beings who, even in the first period of Christian development, experienced very deeply in their souls that Christ had descended from the realm of spiritual beings—beings who do not need to go through birth and death, for whom birth and death are only a transformation—and that he had gone through birth and death.

This descending of Christ to the earth was the most essential perception initially experienced during the first period of Christian evolution. This descent was of much more significance for the human beings of that time than what followed this descent. The fact that Christ wanted to be in community with human beings, that he wanted to share in the two most significant experiences—birth and death—was felt in the circles of the initiates to be the true religious impulse. They could only feel this because human beings still had some degree of an inner, living way of thinking; because up until the fourth century AD, thinking had not yet been completely paralyzed, had not yet become entirely abstract; and because this living thinking still permeated the whole human being in the same way as, in a physical sense, breathing does today. This is why people were able to perceive that Christ had actually fulfilled the human destiny of coming down to the earth, which the other divine-spiritual beings had not done—because undergoing birth and death is not something intrinsic to the gods, but only to human beings. The sublime element in the belief of the initiates of the first Christian centuries was that they perceived that Christ had really become a human being, meaning that he had actually taken on human destiny, that he was the only one of the divine-spiritual beings who shared this destiny with human beings.

But it is also necessary that the human soul be presented with discernible evidence that this soul, insofar as it belongs to the world of pre-earthly existence, cannot actually die. This is why the very occurrence that we associate with the resurrection of Christ has come to pass—namely, the victory of Christ over death, which stands as the archetype of the victory of every human soul over death. And inasmuch as the old idea of "unbornness" [an existence before birth] had blended, as it were, with the new idea of the resurrection—which, incidentally, had already been present as well, but no longer existed with the same intensity since the event of Golgotha—it became in a sense the expression for what is of the greatest importance in the earthly evolution of humanity.

When thinking was still a living thinking, human beings were not the least bit afraid of death. To them, death was not an extraordinary occurrence. It is something of monumental importance in the history of human evolution that death was viewed quite differently, that is, as something completely self-evident; whereas, when human beings gradually lost the awareness of a pre-earthly existence, the abstract way of thinking, which has the physical body as its instrument, increasingly brought a fear of death and, with it, the belief that death is something final. Ancient humanity did not really need the idea of resurrection, but rather that of a descent to the earth in common with the Christ. But as human beings advanced more and more toward abstract thinking, they increasingly needed a perspective beyond earthly existence, a perspective in the direction of immortality. And this perspective arises for humanity when the reality of Christ's resurrection is viewed in the right way. I have presented this reality, this fact, in books, lectures, and lecture cycles in many different ways. Both facts—the descent of Christ into birth and death and the fact of the resurrection, that of the victory over death—could still be sensed and perceived quite clearly by humanity up until the fourth century after Christ, because living thinking was still present. From this fourth century onward, however, as abstract thinking became ever more prevalent, humanity became increasingly incapable of uniting its thinking with the content of the Mystery of Golgotha.

It is actually the destiny of the evolution of humanity that, in the era in which humanity gained its freedom through abstract thinking, the understanding of Christ Jesus, which was present in the first centuries after Christ, had to be lost as a consequence of this thinking—a thinking that is dead in relation to the spiritual world. It was lost, mainly because the writings referred to as Gnostic† writings—a term that has now become almost a derogatory one—have been eradicated root and branch, save for a few remnants which are not of much use as literary sources. What had been thought in the first centuries by those who still had some knowledge of living thinking, was destroyed; we know of it only from the writings of their opponents.

Just imagine what it would be like if, through some fluke, all anthroposophical books and writings disappeared and the essence of anthroposophy had to be judged only from the writings of its opponents! That is how much people who rely only on external documents know about Gnosticism today. The tremendous understanding of Christ comprised in Gnosticism was completely lost to humanity. Above all, the awareness that Christ had a connection to the sun and that Christ descended and experienced a common destiny with humanity on Golgotha was completely lost. All of these interrelationships, especially the feelings connected with these things, were lost to humanity. And what increasingly emerged instead were the abstract interpretations and abstract thoughts.

One of those who struggled toward an understanding of Christianity, based on the character of that era, is Augustine.† In Augustine we have a human mind who could no longer understand the ancient ways of viewing nature. You know that Augustine is said to have been a Manichaean.† Augustine himself speaks of this. But what lies behind all these things can no longer be properly understood with our outer way of obtaining knowledge. What Augustine calls Manichaeism, what is called Manichaean teaching today, is only a fading residue of an ancient teaching that thought of the spirit only as a creating power, and recognized no difference between matter and spirit. There was no spirit that did not create, and what it created was perceived as matter. Nor was there any concept of mere matter in these ancient times; on the contrary, there was spirit in everything.

What Gnosticism understood in this way was something that Augustine could not understand, what later times no longer understood, and what our present time no longer understands either. It is true: there is no matter by itself. This is how the Gnostics understood it, and they viewed everything pertaining to the descent of Christ in the light of this understanding. Augustine could no longer do anything with this view. The era had passed. The possibility of doing anything with it no longer existed because the documents had been destroyed, and the ancient clairvoyance had also died out. And so, after a long, almost superhuman struggle, Augustine came to the decision that he could not arrive at the truth on his own, but had to submit to what the catholic church prescribed as truth, in other words, submit to the authority of the catholic church. And this mood—think of it, to begin with, as a mood—remained, and was sustained particularly by a thinking that became more and more abstract. Very slowly and gradually thinking became weakened.

And the Scholastics† in their greatness—and they truly were great—still lived with a last trace of the insight that earthly thinking descends from an extra-earthly thinking; that the human being lives within a heavenly thinking. But, as a consequence of this development, the possibility of grasping the life-giving quality of the event of Golgotha was gradually lost. And it really is a fact that the progressive theology of the nineteenth century, because it aspired to become scientific in the modern sense, lost Christ, and that this theology was quite content to eventually just have "the simple man from Nazareth."† Henceforth, Christ was now only "the highest human being on earth." People were no longer able to form a concept of Christ's indwelling within Jesus.

This means that the development since the fourth century AD has actually consisted in a gradual loss of the connection of the human being to Christ, the kind of connection that had existed in such a living way for many people in the first centuries of Christianity. It also meant that, in the end, people understood less and less of the content of the gospels. Human beings living in the first centuries of Christianity would have found it quite strange to speak of contradictions in the gospels. To them, this would have been as if a person who is familiar with someone's picture taken from the front, were presented with a photograph taken in profile, and would then say: "That cannot be a picture of the same individual." This is how it would have appeared to human beings living in the first centuries after Christ if one had spoken to them of contradictions in the gospels. They knew very well that the four gospels simply present a picture taken from four different sides. People today would say that these are exclusive presentations, that they are different from each side. In the spiritual world everything is, of course, far richer.

Increasingly an age approached when people no longer have any understanding, in the old sense, of the event of Golgotha. Now, it is of course a fact that the nature of the event of Golgotha is such that it can only be understood from a spiritual point of view. And it is indeed interesting that historians generally avoid mentioning the event of Golgotha. Today, we have the historian Ranke,† considered a very distinguished historian, who declares: "We do not talk about it; we leave it out." If one omits from history the most important event of all, then no history can come to pass. Even if one has no relationship with the spiritual world, and therefore cannot understand the Mystery of Golgotha, one would still have to acknowledge its tremendous influence. Nowadays, however, history is written without chronicling the tremendous impact of the Mystery of Golgotha. The ability to look at the Mystery of Golgotha in the right way is increasingly disappearing.

We can, however, also consider this matter from a completely different perspective; we can say to ourselves that, in the course of its development, humanity entered a stage where it became a necessity to have Christ in their midst. More and more, people lost the awareness of their connection with pre-earthly existence. It was no longer in their view. Eventually, human beings knew only that they existed after their birth on earth. That is when Christ came—in order to reveal to them, through his descent, that there is a pre-earthly existence, in order to give them a perception of what could no longer be a living reality in their own consciousness. Since human beings no longer had this association in their own consciousness, they needed to attain a new relationship to it through their connection with Christ, who had gone through the event of Golgotha. Christ had, in a sense, given himself to humanity at a time when a new era was gradually approaching—the era during which humanity was to ascend to freedom. As thinking became more and more abstract, it was no longer possible to view the Mystery of Golgotha through the faculty of thinking. But the content of the New Testament stories was so captivating, so appealing to the human heart, that what could no longer be grasped with thoughts could still exist for a certain period of time through purely external traditions.

If we survey the first period during which Christianity was expanding, then we see that traditions existed that were actually derived from the gospels, and that a childlike soul disposition increasingly took hold of the images of the events in Palestine. But we also see that, as experiences became cognitive in nature, the experience of the Mystery of Golgotha also dwindled. To the same degree that dead thinking emerged, the childlike memory of the occurrences in Palestine also became obscured, and human beings began to lose their connection with Christ Jesus. They were content, however, if they could still maintain a relationship with the human being Jesus. And now we stand within our own present time, where—although people do not really notice it yet—the awareness of the connection with Christ Jesus has actually been lost. Bound by tradition, people still adhere to their confessions, but do not have a living inner connection with Christ Jesus. You only have to observe how external the yearly festivals have become! For most people today, Easter has become an outwardly observed festival, whereas in earlier times, the Easter festival was of such a nature for human beings that they experienced something in deepest inwardness that can actually be called a memory of the Mystery of Golgotha.

Christ gave himself to humanity at a time when it had to develop a consciousness of freedom. In a certain sense, humanity has achieved this. But this freedom would become merely external if a connection with Christ could not be found again. This, however, can only be found if we begin to pursue a spiritual way of knowing. Spiritual knowledge, as it is pursued by anthroposophy, will find the connection with Christ Jesus again. This connection can only be found spiritually. What happened on Golgotha is not only an event that deeply affected the physical, earthly history of humanity; it also is a spiritual event. No person can understand the event of Golgotha unless he or she is prepared to understand it in a spiritual sense. It is for this reason that anthroposophical spiritual science is at the same time a preparation for a new understanding of Christ and the Mystery of Golgotha. If we consider these facts in this light, then we will be reminded of the deeply significant words from the gospel: "Lo, I am with you always, even unto the end of the world" (Matthew 28:20). From these words radiates the assurance that Christ was there not only when the event of Golgotha took place but that he will also be there, and remain with human beings, as a spiritual being who can be found in the spirit. Accordingly, we should not only regard what shines forth from the gospels as Christian; rather, we know that Christ is with us, and if today, armed with spiritual insight, we listen to what the spiritual world reveals to us about him, then this is a revelation of Christ. This is just as much a Christ-revelation as what we gain from looking at the gospels.

"I have yet many things to say unto you, but all of you cannot bear them now" (John 16:12). This is a reference to that future time when Christ is to be seen anew. And now this time is approaching; it is already here! Humanity would lose Christ if it could not, through spiritual science, gain Christ in a new way. Through spiritual knowledge, we must again begin to understand much of what people in ancient times had connected with the Mystery of Golgotha, but which had been lost because the spiritual understanding of it had been lost. Just observe how human beings, affected by today's intellectualism, struggle with the words that Christ is supposed to have spoken, namely, that the Kingdom of God has come down to earth,[†] that a completely new life is about to begin. Nowadays, it is considered so immensely clever to say that, after all, everything on earth has remained exactly as it was! This is clever of course, but one really ought to ask a different question, gleaned from the spirit of the words of Christ: "Is one really speaking in the true sense of a Christian spiritual understanding if one believes that some sort of external spiritual kingdom is to be established?" An outer spiritual kingdom would actually be physical! People do not notice this contradiction. It is highly noteworthy that in this day and age people have actually become quite clever, but are not able to really assess the cleverness within their own field.

Even though it leads us away from our actual theme, I would like to call your attention to something quite interesting. The Viennese geologist Eduard Suess,[†] a distinguished research scientist, speaks in his book *The Face of the Earth* of the fact that the face of the earth must have been completely different; that the stones must have been much more alive than today; that we actually are already walking on a dead earth at the present time; that the chunks of soil on which we walk belong to a dying world. This geologist assumes that, at one time, the earth was more alive and gradually transitioned into a dead state. Here, in regard to an entirely different field, Suess says something quite similar to what Christ said concerning the spiritual life of the earth. If this were the only thing in store for the earth—that it would disintegrate in a distant future, that it would be reduced to dust in the cosmos—then we would all be included in this turning-into-dust.

On the other hand, if the earth were to have the same future as the human being—"the body disintegrates into dust, but the spirit lives on"—then, with an earth like that, we would actually be looking at what leads over into the Jupiter existence. We would really be looking at a new earth.

With regard to the physical, this view of the earth's turning-into-dust is correct, but with regard to the soul-spiritual, other laws apply. To the ancient initiates at the time of the Mystery of Golgotha, it was clear that the ancient civilization, the ancient Mysteries, were at an end; that the way in which ancient human beings had lived with their gods was over; that the way in which they had lived with the manifestations of nature was at an end. But the gods bestow upon human beings the possibility of moving toward a future in the spirit. Whatever knowledge had been derived from the earth in ancient times is now a thing of the past. A new time must come, when human beings must initiate a kingdom by means of their own will, when human beings must be able to give life again to dead thinking through their own efforts. This was a prophecy at the time of the Mystery of Golgotha. Outwardly, this kingdom came about. It can only be understood and taken up, however, by human beings of the present time. Today, we must feel that the Kingdom of God, of which Christ speaks, must be perceived by us on earth because Christ is working on the earth. This must come to fulfillment on the earth, and the fulfillment of this Kingdom of God must be grasped with earnestness, precisely in this age—our present time. We experience in all fields how humanity is increasingly confronted with the peril of being cut off from the spiritual worlds, and from its true being *if* it does not find access to the spiritual world. Through natural science, we cannot access the essence of the human being.

Take the great divide that exists today between older people and youth. There has always been a contrast, but it was never as pronounced as it is today. There is one thing in particular that must be understood about this situation. Many people say that older people cannot advocate for the young because they have not retained their childlike nature. That sounds exceedingly lovely, but it is not so. Young people do not demand of us that we should act as though we were as young as the young people themselves; for, in that case young people would instinctively say: "Whatever these old people can do, we can do too. In that case we do not need them at all; then we might as well stay among ourselves as we are." What we must learn is how to grow old in the right way, how to use the aging human body in full freshness. Young people do not love aged children; what they love is human beings who have grown old in the right way. Young people want to look up to older people precisely because there they can see something different, something they do not have themselves. But as humanity we have lost the ability to be really spiritually alive. When the real fire of childhood is at an end, we dry up. The body is just getting older, but we act within the old body in the same way as we did when we were children. We must attain the ability, even without our body coming to our aid, to spiritualize our thoughts out of our spiritual understanding, to create anew the living thoughts through our own will, to bring about the resurrection of thinking within us. What exists in us as dead thinking must, through these efforts, become living thinking. Then this living thinking will be able to penetrate the Mystery of Golgotha; and only then can we, through a real sacrifice of our thinking and feeling, reproduce within ourselves the living words: "Not I, but Christ in me." †

These words indicate something very powerful, also for our age. We have achieved I-consciousness though non-living thinking. This could not have been achieved through the living thinking of older times. We now have this I-consciousness, but it must be set aglow inwardly and be spiritualized through and through by learning to speak the words, "Not I, but Christ in me," in the right way. We must be able to receive Christ into our innermost being—this inner being that we must develop through spiritual cognition. This is something that we as human beings can only accomplish today if we can permeate ourselves with the real intentions of anthroposophical life. In point of fact, anthroposophy does not aspire to be a new religion. The Christian religion already exists. When human beings are led to Christ, they are not founding a new religion; but they are in need of a new path to Christianity. And a new path to Christianity opens up through anthroposophy. It is anthroposophy that can open this new path—a path that is so necessary today—to an understanding of the Mystery of Golgotha.

This is what I wanted to add to what has been said here. For it is absolutely appropriate if, from time to time, we try to let this central event of the entire evolution of humanity—the Mystery of Golgotha—arise before our souls in the right way, illumined by anthroposophy. For truly, the course of humanity's development has unfolded thus: The earth has evolved up to the Mystery of Golgotha; then, from out of the spiritual cosmos, a tremendous fructification of the earth takes place, bringing about entirely new conditions for the continuing life of the earth. Only by bringing this religious nuance into the anthroposophical understanding can we raise it to the level that it must reach if it is to meet the deepest longings of human beings today.

Having been granted the opportunity, during our gathering here, to deepen our understanding of the most important event of humanity in this way, I would like to express my deep satisfaction and gratitude that I have once again been able to be in your midst. And I would also like to express my feeling that what we have contemplated here while spatially together, will also live on when we are spatially apart. Anthroposophy aims to be a symbol for the entire spiritual life of human beings as well. We should be able to feel through anthroposophy that our being together in the same space must also be seen as the starting point for a non-spatial togetherness in which all those souls in the world who are interested in anthroposophy can come together. Such a soul-spiritual community does indeed exist for those who seek it today. And within this community, Christ will be able to work most intensively, now that he has united himself with the evolution of the earth in the Mystery of Golgotha and has waited for an age that can understand him not merely out of tradition, but also in thoughts, feelings, and will-intent. And all of this is then permeated with the special will that I would like to call Christ-imbued will: "You shall not take the name of the LORD your God in vain" (Exodus, 20:7). Acting and thinking out of this impulse, in community with all like-minded human beings, in spiritual thoughts, will then also lead to a real community with respect to outer matters.

THE REVELATION OF ASCENSION AND THE MYSTERY OF PENTECOST

DORNACH, MAY 7, 1923

IN THE COURSE of human evolution on earth, mighty images have been placed before humanity. These images, arising from the various world religions, actually require a certain esoteric knowledge if they are to be fully understood. Over the years, we have seen all four gospels interpreted in that way, based on anthroposophy, in the sense that we applied anthroposophic-esoteric knowledge in order to bring to light the deeper content and meaning of the gospels.[†] Generally speaking, what really matters in this respect has been presented in the form of pictures—for the very reason that pictures refuse to let themselves be communicated in the same narrow, rationalistic way as is the case with concepts and ideas.

When it comes to concepts and ideas, people think that once they have grasped a concept, an idea, they have understood everything that is relevant. In the case of an image, an imagination, it is not possible to have such an opinion. A picture or an imagination conveys life. One might say that it works in a living way like a living being itself—say, a living being like a human being. We may have come to know an image from one side or another, but we will always, again and again, get to know new sides as well. And we will not be satisfied with all kinds of definitions purporting to be comprehensive; rather, we will endeavor to look for characteristics that aim to focus on the image from various sides and bring the image ever closer to human comprehension.

Today, I would like to bring two pictures, which are already quite familiar to you, place them before your souls, and characterize a few things related to these pictures. The first picture is the one that depicts the disciples of Christ Jesus on the day of the Ascension, looking up and seeing Christ vanishing in the clouds (Acts 1:4–14). This image is usually understood to mean that Christ went up into heaven, has left the earth, and that the disciples were then, as it were, left to their own resources—just as all of earthly humanity, for whom Christ went through the Mystery of Golgotha, finds itself on its own after his Ascension.

One could easily come to the conclusion that this contradicts the reality of the Mystery of Golgotha in a certain way. We know that through the Mystery of Golgotha, Christ resolved to unite his own being with the earth, that is to say, from the time of the Mystery of Golgotha onwards to remain forever connected with the evolution of the earth. Therefore, the powerful image of the Ascension could be seen as being at variance with what the esoteric view of the Mystery of Golgotha reveals regarding the connection of Christ with the being of the earth and with humanity. Today, we will try to overcome this [seeming] contradiction with the help of actual spiritual facts.

The second picture that I would like to bring before your souls today is that of the scene taking place ten days after the Ascension, when the disciples had congregated together and tongues of fire descended upon each of their heads, so that they felt inspired, as it is commonly expressed, to "speak with other tongues" (Acts 2:1–13). What this means in reality, however, is that the disciples now were able to impart the secrets of what happened on Golgotha to every human heart, regardless of its creed or affiliations. Today, we will keep these two pictures before our souls and try to give a few indications—it can, of course, only be a few—about their characteristic qualities.

We know that the evolution of humanity did not begin on the earth. We know that the Earth phase of evolution was preceded by the Moon phase of evolution; that it was preceded by the Sun phase; and that this, in turn, was preceded by the Saturn phase of evolution—as you will find it described in my book *An Outline of Esoteric Science.*[†] We know that, although the evolution of the human being did indeed descend as far down as the physical body during the Saturn phase, this physical body was essentially only a body of warmth at that time, meaning that a whole range of warmth differences and warmth effects was concentrated around the soul-spiritual entity—as it was during that time, in the sense of the descriptions in my *Esoteric Science*. We know furthermore that during the subsequent Sun phase of evolution, the human being acquired an air-formed body and during the Moon phase a kind of fluid, watery body; and that it was only during the Earth phase of evolution that a solid earth-formed body, in the actual sense, was acquired.

Now let us consider the Earth phase of evolution. We know that the Earth phase of evolution is taking place in seven successive stages. The first stage was, in a sense, a recapitulation of the Saturn phase, the second a recapitulation of the Sun phase, the third a recapitulation of the Moon phase; we have previously also called this stage the Lemurian era. The actual Earth phase of evolution began with the fourth stage. We are now living in the fifth evolutionary stage. It will be followed by two others, a sixth and a seventh (see Plate 1 in the appendix).

Stage 1	Recapitulation of the Saturn phase of evolution
Stage 2	Recapitulation of the Sun phase of evolution
Stage 3	Recapitulation of the Moon phase of evolution Lemurian era
Stage 4	Beginning of the actual Earth phase of evolution Atlantean era
Stage 5	Post-Atlantean era
Stage 6	Sixth era
Stage 7	Seventh era

Now, the middle of the Earth phase of evolution falls in the middle of the Atlantean era, meaning that in our present age, the earth has already passed the culmination, the actual mid-point, of its evolution. You will realize from this that the earth is actually already in a descending phase of its development. In our time, we must therefore always take into account the fact that the earth is in a declining stage of its evolution. I have often pointed out that this indeed conforms entirely with the findings of modern, matter-based geology. In his book, *The Face of the Earth*, Eduard Suess† draws attention to the fact that the chunks of soil on which we walk today actually belong to an earth that is already dying.

During the Atlantean era, the earth was, so to speak, in the middle period of its existence. At that time, the earth was teeming with inner life, and one would not have been able to find the structures that one finds today as rocks and stones, which crumble away. Instead, one would have found the mineral element working in the earthly realm in the same way as the mineral element works today, say, in an animal organism, where it will *only* form various kinds of deposits if the animal organism is diseased. If the animal organism is healthy, the only deposits that are formed are, for example, in the bones. But even in the bones there is still an inner life. They do not have the kind of deadness that turns to dust; they do not, like our mountains, like the rocks of our mountains, crumble into dust. This crumbling of the rocks of our mountains is simply evidence of the fact that the earth is already in a death-process, in a process of dying.

As I said, this is now known even by traditional, materialistically inclined geology. Anthroposophy must now add to this knowledge the fact that, in reality, the earth has been going through this process of decline since the middle of the Atlantean age. And we must regard as "earth" everything that belongs to the earth—the plants, the animals, and, above all, the physical human being. The physical human being belongs to the earth. And inasmuch as the earth's evolution is in a process of descent, the development of the human physical body is also in a process of descent. Expressing this differently, in more esoteric terms, this means that by the middle of the Atlantean age, everything that had originally been laid down in the warmth-body of Saturn had reached a state of completion. The human physical body was completed by the middle of the Atlantean period. Since then, its development has been one of descent.

Now, it is of course a fact that evolution does not proceed uniformly; that certain ethnic groups or peoples experience a particular phase of evolution somewhat earlier or later than others. Speaking generally, however, it was essentially the case all over the earth that, when the time of the Mystery of Golgotha approached, the development of the human being's physical constitution was such that humanity as a whole was faced with the prospect of no longer being able to incarnate on the earth, that is, of no longer being able to participate in the declining evolution of the earth.

It was known in the schools of the initiates—and can, of course, be known today as well—that around the time of the Mystery of Golgotha, the human physical body had declined to such an extent that human beings who were incarnated at that time, or were incarnated shortly thereafter (until about the fourth century AD), were faced with the danger of leaving the earth desolate and empty, of finding no possibility in future times to descend from the world of spirit and soul and to build a physical body out of matter provided by the physical earth. This danger was present, and as a consequence, humanity would have failed to achieve its true earthly destiny. The combined efforts of the ahrimanic and luciferic powers had, in fact, accomplished so much that, at the time of the Mystery of Golgotha, earthly humanity would have had to die out. But, as a result of what occurred through the Mystery of Golgotha, humanity was, one might say, healed of [the danger of] dying out. The human physical body has been imbued again with the appropriate new freshness, enabling human beings to continue their further evolution on earth in such a way that they can once again come down from soul-spiritual worlds and have the possibility of living in a physical body. This was the very real and actual effect of the Mystery of Golgotha.

On various occasions, I have already indicated that this effect is to be understood in this sense, including once in a series of lectures held in Karlsruhe, entitled *From Jesus to Christ.*† It was this lecture cycle in particular that gave rise to the greatest hostility, because—out of a sense of esoteric duty—certain truths were revealed in it, truths which many people wish to keep concealed. Indeed, one could say that the hostility toward anthroposophy, coming from certain quarters, started on account of these very lectures. These lectures described, from a particular side, the real effect [of the Mystery of Golgotha]. This same fact can, of course, be expressed in many different ways. In the above-mentioned lecture cycle, I expressed it differently, but what

I am describing today is actually the same thing, just viewed from a slightly different perspective.

The real fact is that, through the Mystery of Golgotha, forces fostering the growth and wellness of the physical human being were quickened anew. This brought about the possibility for human beings to receive, during the sleep state, an impulse that they would not otherwise have received. As you know, the overall development of human beings on earth occurs in both the waking states and the sleep states. During the sleep state, the physical body and the etheric body remain behind. From the time of falling asleep until that of waking up, the I and the astral body make themselves independent. And it is precisely in this process of becoming independent during sleep, that the influence of the Christ-force takes effect in those human beings who, through the cultivation of the required soul-qualities, have prepared themselves for the state of sleep in an appropriate way. This means that the effects of the Christ-force are working primarily during the sleep state.

Now let us consider the point in time that is pictorially indicated in the Bible in the image of the Ascension. At that moment, the disciples had become clairvoyant to such a degree that they were able to behold what is, in truth, a secret of the evolution of the earth. The secrets of the earth's evolution actually pass by the ordinary consciousness of human beings. Ordinary consciousness is quite incapable of knowing whether, at a particular moment in the development of humanity, something of the utmost importance for the evolution of the earth is taking place. Many things are in fact occurring, but ordinary human consciousness is unaware of them. And what the depiction of the Ascension scene actually signifies is that, at that very moment, the disciples of Christ had become capable of witnessing something of untold significance, something that was happening, as it were, behind the scenes of the earth's evolution.

What they saw at that time, revealed to them—in the form of an image—a panorama of what would have happened to human beings if the event of Golgotha had not taken place. They beheld as a spiritual bodily reality what would have happened if the event of Golgotha had not taken place, namely, that human bodies would have fallen into earthly decay to such a degree that the future of humanity would have been endangered. This is what would have become of the human physical bodies. And it would have impacted the etheric in human beings as well, because these human etheric bodies would have obeyed the pull of their own innate forces. For the etheric body is actually something that is not being pulled toward the earth; instead, it is continually being drawn upward toward the sun. As human beings, our constitution is such that our physical body has the earth's heaviness, while our etheric body has the sun's lightness. The etheric body continually aspires to strive toward the sun. If the physical human body had become what it would have had to become *without* the Mystery of Golgotha taking place, then the human etheric bodies would have simply obeyed their urge to strive toward the sun, and humanity would inevitably have ceased to exist on the earth as earthly humanity.

Before the time of the Mystery of Golgotha, the sun was—in the sense of what has been described here on previous occasions—the dwelling place of Christ. This means that, inasmuch as the etheric body of the human being strives toward the sun, it is actually striving toward Christ. Now picture to yourselves the scene on the day of the Ascension. With the eyes of the soul, the disciples saw Christ ascending heavenward. In other words, a wondrous soul-vision arose in the disciples. They saw how the etheric forces of the human being, which strive in an upward direction, become united with the power, with the impulse, of Christ; how at the time of the Mystery of Golgotha, human beings were confronted with the peril of seeing their etheric bodies move toward the clouds, toward the sun; but also, how Christ supports and holds together what is moving toward the sun.

This image must be understood in the right sense. This image is actually a cautionary intimation that, although Christ remains united with the earth, he nevertheless belongs to those forces in the human being that actually strive toward the sun, forces that forever wish to get away from the earth. But the Christ-impulse holds human beings firmly on the earth.

What appeared before the disciples' soul-vision in this image of the Ascension, therefore, is what would have occurred without the

Mystery of Golgotha. Imagine that the Mystery of Golgotha had not taken place and that large groups of human beings had become as clairvoyant as the disciples were at that moment. Then they would have seen how the etheric bodies of some human beings were moving away from the earth toward the sun, and they would have realized that this is the path that the etheric bodies are taking; that what is earthly-etheric in human beings is being drawn away toward the sun.

But the Mystery of Golgotha has actually taken place. Christ has rescued, for the sake of the earth, what was striving toward the sun. And what becomes manifest in this sunward-striving movement, now taken hold of by Christ, is precisely the fact that Christ remains connected with earthly humanity. But there is one more thing to consider here. Through the Mystery of Golgotha, Christ has actually placed a cosmic event into the evolution of the earth. Christ came down from spiritual heights, linked himself with humanity in the human being Jesus of Nazareth, went through the Mystery of Golgotha, and united his evolution with the evolution of the earth. It was a deed that took place for all of humanity.

It is important, therefore, to recognize correctly that the Mystery of Golgotha took place for the sake of humanity. Clairvoyant vision will never fail to perceive how the etheric forces of the human being, which always want to rush away from the earth, unite with Christ for the sake of humanity, so that Christ may hold them within the earth's evolution. This is how this event applies to humanity.

But now consider the following. Let us assume for the moment that only a small number of human beings had been able to acquire knowledge of the facts related to the Mystery of Golgotha, and that therefore a large part of humanity—as is actually in fact the case—had not recognized the significance of the event of Golgotha. Then we would see the earth populated by a small number of people who truly believe in Christ and a large number who do not acknowledge or recognize the essential content and meaning of the Mystery of Golgotha. What, then, is the situation for the latter? How do those who do not recognize the Mystery of Golgotha relate to this Mystery of Golgotha, or rather, how does the Mystery of Golgotha, the deed of Christ, relate to these human beings?

In actual fact, the deed of Christ on Golgotha is an objective occurrence, and its cosmic significance does not depend on what human beings believe in relation to it. An objective fact, as such, is real in its essence. If an oven is hot, it does not become cold because a number of people believe it to be cold. The Mystery of Golgotha represents the rescue of humanity from the disintegration of the physical body, irrespective of what people believe or do not believe about it. Thus, the Mystery of Golgotha took place for all human beings, including those who do not believe in it. This is the first thing to be kept in mind.

You will have understood these things correctly if you realize that the Mystery of Golgotha took place in order to provide the physical body of human beings with fresh forces, in order to renew and refresh earthly humanity to the extent that it needed to be rejuvenated. This is what has come to pass and what made it possible for human beings on the earth to find bodies in which they can incarnate—at least for a certain time period, albeit one that will extend far into the future. This event made it possible for human beings to live as beings of spirit and soul in these newly rejuvenated earthly bodies, and to appear on earth again and again.

Now, the Christ-impulse—which is meant to have significance for the spiritual nature of the human being too, not just for the physical—can extend to the waking state. But it would not be able to reach the sleep state if the soul had not been receptive to taking up the knowledge of this Christ-impulse. One could say, then, that the Mystery of Golgotha would have taken place for the waking state of human beings, even if people had not absorbed the knowledge of this Mystery of Golgotha. But in that case, this event would not have taken place for the sleep state of human beings. And the inevitable result of this would have been the following. Human beings would indeed have reincarnated on the earth again and again. But if they had not acquired any knowledge of the Mystery of Golgotha, the condition of their sleep would have been such that their soul-spiritual nature would have had to lose its connection with Christ.

This actually brings us to the contrasting situation of those people who, for all intents and purposes, have no desire to know anything about the Mystery of Golgotha. Christ accomplished his earthly deed on Golgotha for the sake of their bodies, in order to make it possible for them to live on the earth. He did it even for the pagans of that time, for those who did not believe at all. However, in order to have an effect on the soul-spiritual nature of the human being, it is necessary that the Christ-impulse be able to penetrate the human soul even during the state of sleep. In order for this to occur, a human being needs to develop a cognitive receptiveness of the meaning of the Mystery of Golgotha. The true spiritual effect of the Mystery of Golgotha can therefore only come about as the result of a true recognition of its meaning and content. This means that the following needs to happen for earthly humanity. It needs to recognize that, on the one hand, Christ takes hold of the etheric body, which is continually fleeing and soaring toward the sun; but that, on the other hand, the soul-spiritual nature of the human being, the I and the astral body, can only receive the Christ-impulse between the time of falling asleep and that of waking if they prepare themselves for it by acknowledging this Christ-impulse while awake.

Summarizing the above, we can now say: We let the image of the Ascension arise before our soul. The disciples, having become clairvoyant, perceive the inclination of the etheric bodies of human beings to ascend toward the sun. Christ unites himself with this impulse to soar, and holds it. Thus, the mighty picture arising in the Ascension image is that of *the rescue of the physical-etheric nature of the human being through Christ*. But, at the same time, this image also shows the disciples withdrawing, becoming absorbed in thought, becoming pensive and deep in contemplation. For in their souls lives the knowledge that everything that happened through the Mystery of Golgotha occurred in first instance for the physical-etheric nature of human beings. But what is happening, they wonder, with the soul-spiritual? How, and from where, will human beings receive the power to absorb the Christ-impulse into their soul-spiritual nature, into the I and the astral body?

Through the Mystery of Golgotha, the Christ-impulse has taken effect on the earth in such a way that it can only be penetrated and grasped through the forces of spiritual cognition. No matter-oriented cognitive power, no matter-based science can comprehend the Mystery of Golgotha. The soul must, in fact, acquire the power of spiritual cognition, the power of spiritual perception, the power of spiritual sensing, in order to be able to really understand how the Christ-impulse united, on Golgotha, with the impulses of the earth.

And, in order to make it possible for this to occur, Christ Jesus fulfilled his deed on Golgotha. He fulfilled it in such a way that, ten days after the event of the Ascension, he sent human beings the possibility of now also permeating their inner soul-spiritual nature, the I and the astral body, with the Christ-impulse. Thus, the image of the festival of Pentecost, of Whitsun, is the image of *the permeation of the soul-spiritual nature of the human being with the power to understand the Mystery of Golgotha*, that is, *the sending of the Holy Spirit.* Christ accomplished his deed for all of humanity. But it was to individual human beings, who are meant to understand this deed, to each human being individually, that Christ sent the Spirit—so that the soul-spiritual may find access to the deed that was fulfilled for all human beings in common. Through the Spirit, the human being must—inwardly, as a being of spirit and soul—acquire the Christ-Mystery.

These are the images of the two events that took place in sequence, one after the other, in the history of the evolution of humanity, and they stand there in such a way that the Ascension image tells us: The deed on Golgotha was fulfilled for the human physical and etheric bodies in a universally human sense. [The Pentecost image tells us:] The individual human being must make it fruitful for him- or herself by receiving the Holy Spirit. In this way, the Christ-impulse becomes individualized for each single human being.

And now something else can still be added to the characteristics of the picture of the Ascension. Spiritual perceptions, such as the disciples had on the day of the Ascension, actually always relate to something that human beings have already experienced in one or another state of consciousness. After death, as you know, the human being experiences the departure of the etheric body. With death, the human being lays aside the physical body, but retains the etheric body for a few days; then the etheric body dissolves and actually unites with the sun. This process of dissolution after death constitutes a union with the sun-element, which permeates and streams through the space in which the earth also has its place. And, since the time of the Mystery of Golgotha, the human being sees Christ in, and together with, this departing etheric body, because Christ has become its rescuer for future earthly existence. This means that, since the time of the Mystery of Golgotha, the Ascension picture stands before the soul of every human being passing through death—the Ascension picture, which the disciples were able to see as a result of their special state of soul on that day.

For those, however, who also take up the mystery of Pentecost, who allow the Holy Spirit to draw near to them, this image becomes the greatest consolation they can experience after death; for they now understand the true reality of the Mystery of Golgotha, and the image becomes a comfort for them. In a certain sense, this image of the Ascension tells the human being: You can entrust all your subsequent incarnations to the evolution of the earth; for, through the Mystery of Golgotha, Christ has become the savior of the evolution of the earth.

But for those who have not grasped the essence of the Mystery of Golgotha, who have not penetrated it with the I and the astral body—that is, through cognition and feeling—this image becomes a reproach, and it will remain a reproach until they will have recognized that they, too, must learn to understand the Mystery of Golgotha. It is, in a sense, an admonition after death: For your next earthly life, try to acquire the kind of forces that will enable you to understand the Mystery of Golgotha. It is, of course, only natural that this image of the Ascension initially appears as an admonition, because human beings can then endeavor, in subsequent earthly lives, to apply the very forces about which they have been admonished and to acquire an understanding of the Mystery of Golgotha.

You can now perceive the difference between those people who—with their inner forces of faith, cognition, and feeling—recognize and affirm the Mystery of Golgotha and those who do not. For, the Mystery of Golgotha has indeed been fulfilled for all human beings, but only in respect of the physical body and the etheric body. The sending of the Holy Spirit, the mystery of Pentecost, signifies that the soul-spiritual nature of the human being can only partake of the fruits of the Mystery of Golgotha if he or she rises to a real understanding of the essence and meaning of the Mystery of Golgotha.

However, because this is the case—the fact that the essence of the Mystery of Golgotha can only be understood through spiritual cognition, *not* through knowledge of the material world—it also means that the real festival of Pentecost can only be grasped if people recognize that the sending of the Holy Spirit is actually a call to humanity to gradually struggle its way through to spirit-knowledge. For it is only through knowledge of the spiritual that the Mystery of Golgotha can be understood.

The fact that it must be understood—*this* is the challenge of the mystery of Pentecost. The fact that it came to pass for all human beings—*this* is the revelation of the mystery of Ascension. Accordingly, these two things stand, in their chronological order of occurrence, within the evolution of humanity, when interpreted in its true Christian sense, as *the revelation of Ascension*, which reveals that Christ accomplished his deed for all of humanity, and as *the mystery of Pentecost*, which summons each human being individually to take up the impulse of the Mystery of Golgotha.

Thus, it can truly be said that, with regard to these things, anthroposophy provides everything required to gain the right understanding of the mystery of Pentecost in its connection with the Ascension-revelation. And if we perceive that anthroposophy stands as a kind of herald illuminating these spring festivals in particular, then we have added yet another much-needed facet to the many nuanced aspects that anthroposophy holds for us.

This should convey to you something of what, in an anthroposophical sense, can create a mood in which the right feeling for the festivals of Ascension and Pentecost can arise. The images that such festivals place before the human soul are like living beings—inasmuch as we can come closer and closer to their real essence and can get to know them better and better. If we learn to fill the year again with such spiritual understanding of the festival seasons, then the whole year will be imbued with a content that is concrete but also cosmic-spiritual. And human beings will then be able to experience cosmic existence already in their earthly existence.

One could say that the festival of Pentecost is, above all, also a festival of flowers. And if we experience it in the right way, then we will go out wherever flowers are springing up—opening themselves to the influence of the sun, opening themselves to etheric and astral influences—and we will perceive, in the earth adorned with flowers, the earthly image of what streams together in the image of the Ascension of Christ and in the subsequent [Pentecost] image of the fiery tongues above the heads of the disciples. The human heart, as it opens itself, can be symbolized by the flower opening itself to the sun; and what streams down from the sun to give the flower the required forces of fertilization, can symbolize the fiery tongues streaming down over the heads of the disciples.

And it is especially through this power—the power that can once again arise from an understanding of the festivals, from a true contemplation of each festival time—that anthroposophy can work on human hearts and be instrumental in bringing about the kind of soul disposition that may perhaps be the right one in these days of the spring festivals.

The Mood of Saint John's

The Heightened Awareness at Saint John's Tide

DORNACH, JUNE 24, 1923

In the short lecture that preceded the eurythmy performance this afternoon,[†] I already pointed out how we can see, even from the relationship that modern humanity has to the festivals of the year, that we have entered the age of materialism. However, we must then take the meaning of materialism in a much deeper sense than is usually the case. The fact that people are infected with materialism is not actually the most dangerous characteristic of our present time; the much more dangerous characteristic is the superficiality of our age.

This superficiality does not only arise with respect to spiritual worldviews; it is also present in relation to materialism itself and can be seen in its superficial manifestations. For example, this afternoon I pointed out how something like the soul-mood which people in earlier times experienced at different times of the year, also manifested in the festive ceremonies of those earlier times. Different moods of soul were brought into the various festivals—into the winter solstice festival, the spring festival, the St. John's festival, the Michaelmas festival. These moods of soul, which should permeate human beings when they consciously experience the course of the year, were embedded in the special ceremonies that were like rituals, or had, to a certain degree, been infused with something similar to a ritual.

In this way, the human soul was given what we are now only given in terms of our body. We all participate in going through the course of the day. When the sun sends its morning-gold, as morning's dawn, ahead of its own appearance, then we eat our breakfast. When the sun is at its highest, when, in its own exceedingly loving way, it pours out its warmth and light over the people of the earth, then we devote ourselves to our midday meal, and so on through five o'clock tea and supper. In these festive events of the day, we participate in the daily course of the sun, inasmuch as we experience within ourselves the fiery ride of the sun around the world.[†] We experience with the sun what it accomplishes on its fiery ride around the world, inasmuch as we undergo the sensation of hunger and of satisfying it. And in this way, a very decisive way, a mood arises for the human physical organism at certain times of the day. We could call breakfast, lunch, tea, and dinner the festival times of the day. The human physical organism participates in, and co-experiences, what takes place in the relationship of the earth to the cosmos.

In a similar way, people co-experienced and took part in the course of the year in earlier times, when the life of the soul was still experienced more intensely because of the old instinctive states of clairvoyance. Certain things from one sphere even played into the other one. You only need remind yourselves of what still remains of these things: Easter eggs, St. Martin's goose, and so on. This is where the lower region, the region of the physical body, plays into the soul region—which is actually meant to experience the course of the year in a way that pertains to the soul. Now, a materialistic age would likely still be open to having a St. Martin's goose, or other seasonal favorites like it, available throughout the year—although one cannot, of course, say the same with regard to Easter eggs.

But this is not how these things, in their relation to the actual moods of the festivals, were intended in these earlier times; rather, they were tailored to moods of the soul, to soul-hunger and soul-gratification. The human soul needed something different at Christmastime, something different at Eastertime, at St. Johns tide, and at Michaelmas. And one can certainly associate the structural content of the various festival-rituals with, on the one hand, a recognition of the hunger experienced by the soul precisely during the corresponding periods of the year and, on the other, with the gratification experienced by the soul during these very periods of the year.

And so, we are now able to say: If we consider the *daily* path of the sun, then we can see it in connection with what benefits our body. If we consider the *yearly* path of the sun, then we can see it in connection with what benefits our soul.

If the festivals are to be given new life again, then this revival must, of course, come to pass from a much more conscious state of soul—from an awakening of the soul, such as is sought through an anthroposophical understanding of the world. We cannot simply renew the ancient festivals in a historical sense; we must rediscover them out of our own soul-being through a new knowledge and view of the world. Now, in addition to the body and the soul, we also distinguish the spirit in the human being.

However, when we speak of the soul today, it becomes difficult for modern human beings to form any definite concepts at all. The topic then becomes blurred and moves into something undefined. We have, of course, not only been confronted with the fact that, in the nineteenth century, people actually began to speak of a psychology—a science of the soul—without a soul. Fritz Mauthner,† the great literary critic, has even concluded that the soul is something so indefinite that, in reality, we do not know a soul; that we only know of certain thoughts, sensations, feelings, which are experienced within us, but that we do not know of a unified soul within all this. Mauthner concluded that we should therefore no longer use the word "soul" in the future; that we should, when speaking of this undefined inner tousle, no longer say "soul," but rather, "souling" [as in "seeing" or "feeling".] This implies that Fritz Mauthner actually recommended that a future Klopstock,† writing a poem like *The Messiah*, should no longer say, "Sing, immortal soul, the redemption of sinful humanity. . ." but, instead, "Sing, immortal souling, the redemption of sinful humanity. . ." if that would even still have any meaning at all within this "science of the souling"! All this would mean that, in the future, we would not have a science of the soul but, instead, a science of the souling!

Now, it can really be said that modern human beings no longer know anything about this connection of the soul to the yearly course of the sun. Even in this respect human beings have become materialists. We do adhere to the body's festive events, which follow the daily course of the sun. It is true that the festival seasons are celebrated out of traditional customs, but they are not experienced in a living way. Besides, apart from having a body and a soul—or in Fritz Mauthner's sense a "souling"—we actually also have a spirit.

Now, in the course of world history there are historical epochs, as you know. These historical epochs, which extend beyond the course of the year and span centuries, become alive for the human spirit, if it is able to really experience them. In ancient times, people absolutely experienced their influences. Anyone who, carried by the spirit, is able to understand in the right way how human beings in earlier times approached the course of time in thought, will be aware of something that was said everywhere. It was said that, at any particular turning point in time, a certain individuality had appeared and had once again revealed the spiritual out of the heights of the world; that this spiritual element then had entered people's lives, just as the light of the sun gives life to the physical world; and that, once such an era approached its time of twilight, something new would once again have emerged.

These historical epochs are connected with humanity's development of the spirit in the same way as the sun's yearly path is connected with the development of the soul. Of course, if such a development of the spirit is to be understood again in a living way, then this must be done by learning to understand—through a consciously developed knowledge of the spiritual—how changes and metamorphoses arise in humanity's course of development. Nowadays, people tend to completely overlook how such metamorphoses arise. In one way or another, people are outwardly impacted by their effects, but inwardly they are not really interested in these changes—which originate in the spirit and come to expression in the external events of the world.

All one has to do is observe how in our time a certain way of thinking, a certain way of feeling and perceiving, is emerging among children and young people, a way that was still foreign to a previous generation. All one has to do is observe how mighty changes are taking place in relation to the course of humanity's development, which—if one looks at the corresponding elements—can definitely be compared to the course of the year. This is why we should listen to what a particular epoch announces as its requirements; why we should listen perceptively when a new age arises and requires something different from what earlier ages have required. But this is precisely the kind of organ that human beings do not possess today, or only to a very limited extent.

The great interconnectedness of life can be revealed and stand before our souls, if we learn to approach the moods of the festivals again in the right way—meaning, out of our present-day consciousness—if, for example, we allow something like the St. John's mood to really penetrate our souls, and if, out of this St. John's mood, we try to acquire the very soul-quality through which we are able to have encouragement and support from the cosmos, as it is helping us in these endeavors.

It is, of course, a reality that modern humanity has become more or less indifferent to the things that are associated with the great events in world evolution. Today, people no longer have a sensitivity for insights into the great interconnectedness of the world. This shows the intrusion of the spirit of pettiness—one could even say the intrusion of the spirit of microscopy and atomization—into phenomena which, when they are spoken of as I must speak of them here, naturally generate an impression of a paradox.

I would like to point out a particular phenomenon in connection with the mood of St. John's. This connection may appear somewhat remote, but I would like to mention it nonetheless. What could be more obvious, even if one does not have a well-developed organ for perceiving the course of the year, than to have certain impressions in response to the rapid growth of plants and trees when spring arrives, when everything green is budding and sprouting, and all this growth, all this sprouting and budding then unfolds ever further, forming leaves and blossoms. All this lively growth—which creates the impression as though the cosmos, through the sun's influences, were summoning the earth to open itself to the universe—all this is occurring at St. John's tide. Then the sprouting and budding begin to recede again and we approach the time when the earth draws its growth forces into itself, when the earth withdraws from the cosmos. And it is quite natural for us to form the picture, from the impressions we receive of the course of the year, that a blanket of snow belongs to winter; that it is an innate part of winter that the plants, as it were, hide their real nature in the earth's soil; and that it is an innate part of summer that the plants come up from the soil and grow toward the cosmos. What would be more natural than to develop the thought—and in a deeper sense this is actually the case, albeit in its opposite meaning—that plants sleep in winter, and that they awaken in summer?

At the moment, I do not want to speak of this sleeping and waking in terms of correct or incorrect concepts. I just want to speak of the impressions we receive, giving rise to the idea that summer is all about the unfolding of the vegetation, and that winter is all about the vegetation withdrawing and hiding in the earth. Still, as a result of this idea, people develop a kind of feeling for the world. [In summer,] we are drawn into an experience of feeling connected with the warming and illuminating power of the sun when we perceive the sun's warming and illuminating power again in the greening and flowering plant cover of the earth; in winter, we are drawn into an experience of feeling as though we were earth-hermits with respect to the cosmos, when the plant cover is not there and a snow blanket closes the earth off from the cosmos, summoning us to inner activity. In short, inasmuch as we feel and sense in this way, we tear ourselves, with our earthly consciousness, away from earthly existence, as it were. And through this, we place ourselves into the larger interconnectedness of the universe.

But then modern-day research comes along—and I have no intention of criticizing it and what I am about to say is not to be taken as a reprimand, but rather as praise for this research as such—but, as I said, then modern-day research comes along and shrugs its shoulders when great cosmic interrelationships are mentioned. "After all," so people say, "why should we feel elevated by the divinely light-giving, warming power of the sun when the trees are sprouting and turning green, when the earth covers itself with its vegetation? Why should we have to feel a connection with the universe because these plants are sprouting up from the earth?" People feel perturbed by this. People feel perturbed about sentiments appertaining to the cosmos. Experiencing such feelings can no longer be reconciled with a consciousness that is matter-oriented. "After all, a plant is just a plant. And it is simply a stubbornly inherent characteristic of the plant that it only flowers in spring and is prepared to bear fruit in summer. How does that actually happen? And now this is supposed to involve not just the plant, but the whole world? If we are meant to feel, sense, or know something regarding these things, are we then supposed to be concerned with the whole world, not just with the plant? That is not appropriate! As a matter of fact," so people say, "science is already making an effort *not* to focus on the substances that are present in powder form or in crystal form, but rather on the atomic structures, on the atoms, on the electromagnetic atmosphere and so on! This means that science is putting an effort into concentrating on something that is complete, closed off, *not* on something that reaches into the beyond. And now we are supposed to concede to the plant that we need feelings that extend out into the cosmos; that it is a terrible thing when we cannot restrict our field of vision to just one single object! After all, it has become customary, when using a microscope, to have everything else around closed off and to focus only on one small field of vision, to have everything taking place in this small, restricted point of focus. It ought to be possible, after all, to look at the plant on its own, not in connection with the cosmos!"

And now, lo and behold, around the turn of the nineteenth into the twentieth century, researchers achieved something extraordinary in just this field. People certainly knew, already at that time, that particular plants could be made to overcome summer and winter conditions when grown in hothouses, greenhouses, and so forth. On the whole, however, people had not fully grasped, at this turn of the nineteenth into the twentieth century, that plants actually need a certain period of winter dormancy. Discussions were held at that time about how all this related to tropical plants. Those researchers who denied any connections to the cosmos, claimed that tropical plants grow all year round. Others, who still held on to the old conservative views, maintained that when people are exposed to the lush green world of the tropics, they are inclined to believe that tropical plants grow all year round because these plants undergo dormancy at different times, and some for no more than eight days; that, therefore, one hardly notices when a particular species is dormant. This gave rise to extensive discussions about tropical plants and how they grow. In short, one could notice a tremendous unease with respect to this connection of the plant world to the cosmos.

Now, it was especially at this turn of the nineteenth into the twentieth century that the most interesting and ingenious attempts were made in this direction. It actually became possible to remove the stubbornly inherent characteristics, the cosmic "stubbornness," of a great number of plants—not only of those that are recognized as annuals, but even of trees, which are much more resilient in that respect. It actually became possible, by generating certain conditions, to change plants that were known as annuals into perennials, in other words, to overcome their dependency on cosmic conditions. In the case of most of the forest trees in our temperate climates, it has actually become possible to create conditions that triggered trees—specifically those trees of which it was assumed that they needed this wintertime, that they needed to stand there in winter, leafless and bare—into becoming perpetually green. This had, in fact, been the assumption of certain materialistically inclined explanations. In this respect, people have really achieved something extraordinarily ingenious.

It was discovered that the cosmic element could be forced out from trees by bringing them into enclosed spaces and feeding the soil with adequate nutrients, so that plants, which otherwise find nothing in winter when the soil is so poor in nutrients, would then be able to find and absorb their nutrients under these conditions. It was discovered that, if enough moisture, enough warmth, enough light is provided, the trees would grow.

Only one tree from the region of central Europe defied this research-push at the beginning of the twentieth century. This was the beech tree, the copper beech. It was harassed from all sides to let itself be locked up in enclosed spaces! It was provided with the required nutrients, with the necessary moisture and warmth, but it remained stubborn and demanded its winter rest in spite of these attempts. But it was all alone in this resistance.

And in this twentieth century, in the year 1914—and I shall not speak presently about the outcome of the World War but rather about another great historical event—in 1914, we have to record the great, tremendous fact that Klebs,† an exceptionally gifted researcher in this field, has succeeded in forcing the "cosmic stubbornness" even out of the beech tree. He actually succeeded in growing a beech tree in an enclosed space, by providing it with the necessary conditions in this enclosed space, such as the appropriate, measurable amount of sunlight. And lo and behold, the beech tree did not resist and even complied with what the researchers had aimed for.

I am not citing a phenomenon here that would give me reason to speak disparagingly; for, who would not have admiration for such tremendous diligence of research? Besides, it would of course be madness to try to refute these things. They exist; this is how they are; this is unquestionably how they are. Therefore, it is not at all a question of agreement or refutation; it is instead a question of something else altogether. After all, why should it not also be possible to generate hair growth somewhere else than on human beings and animals, provided the necessary conditions for hair growth could be found somewhere on neutral ground? Why not? All that is required is for the appropriate conditions to be established somehow. Incidentally, I am quite sure that many men today would prefer to have hair growing on their heads rather than have it produced externally through some kind of growth procedure! But one can, of course, imagine that this could also become possible. Then it would ostensibly no longer be necessary to connect what happens on the earth to the cosmos in some way.

One can, of course, have all due respect for this research, but it is also important to develop a deeper understanding of these things. Aside from what I presented here some time ago about the nature of the elements, there is something else I would like to speak about today. We must be clear that, for example, the following is the case. We know that, at one time, the earth and the sun formed one body. That was, of course, a long, long time ago—namely, in the time of the Saturn evolution, the time of the Sun evolution. Then there was a brief recapitulation of this condition during the Earth phase of evolution. However, something has remained in the earth that stems from this time. It is something that we are taking out of the earth again today. And we are not only taking it out (from this stage of recapitulation, which occurred during the Earth phase) when we use coal to heat our rooms, but we are also taking it out when we use electricity. For it was during the time when Sun and Earth were one—that is to say, during the Sun phase, which came after the Saturn phase—that the foundation was laid for the fact that we have electricity on the earth. In electricity, we have a force that has been connected with the earth since primeval times; it is a force that is of the sun, a sun-force that is concealed in the earth.

If this is the case, why should not even the stubborn beech tree, provided it is subjected to enough force, be willing to condescend and utilize the sun's radiating light-force that is gained from the earth in the form of electricity, instead of using the forces of the sun that are streaming in from the cosmos?

And it is precisely when we consider these things that we will really notice how much we need to deepen the full range of our knowledge. As long as people were able to believe that the forces of the sun come only from the cosmos, they could also—through direct observation of the actual plant growth each year—develop an awareness of the plants' connection to the cosmos. In our present age—in which, as a consequence of materialistic viewpoints, people want to sever any ties between the cosmos and those influences that can easily be recognized as cosmic influences—in our present age it is necessary, when encountering the seeming independence of plants, to have a science able to remember that there was a cosmic connection between earth and sun in earlier times, but that it existed in a different form. Inasmuch as we become, as it were, microscopically confined on the one hand, we need an all-the-more intensive broadness of understanding on the other; and it is precisely from a consideration of the details that it becomes clear how much we need this broader vision.

What this entails is not that we, based on our anthroposophical knowledge, oppose the progress of research in a kind of amateurish way. However, this progress of research must, by its very nature, lead us more and more to that "earthworm existence" of which I have often spoken here, which prevents us from having an unobstructed view into the distance. We must, therefore, gain a broader view, a great cosmic-historical view, so that we can become aware of the connection between the earth and the sun, *not* only in the present Earth phase of evolution but also in that long bygone era, which we call the Sun phase of the cosmic evolution of the earth. For all these things, we need a counter pole. We do not need a tirade against research, but rather a spiritual, a spirit-based, counter pole. This is the right standpoint for us to take. And I might even say that it actually constitutes a St. John's mood as well, if we inscribe this into our hearts and minds, if it becomes clear to us that, today, we must live in what is really a world-historical St. John's mood, and that we must turn our gaze outward into the widths of the cosmos. We need this. We need this especially in relation to knowledge about the spiritual. Nothing can be achieved today by simply talking about the spiritual, but only by really penetrating into the actual phenomena of the spiritual world. What can be gleaned from the cosmic evolution of the earth by calling attention to the evolutionary phases of Saturn, Sun, Moon, Earth, and so on, has tremendous significance in terms of knowledge, even in historical terms.

If, on the one hand, matter-oriented science, through such brilliant research findings as those of Klebs, draws our attention to the fact that even the stubborn beech tree can be made to forego sunlight and grow in winter under electric light—as it otherwise only does under the light of the sun—then, if we have no spiritual knowledge, we reach the point where we crumble everything in the world into little pieces and narrow our field of vision. Then we have the beech tree standing before us, with the electric light facilitating its growth, but we know nothing except what is revealed to us within this narrowest of fields.

If, on the other hand, we have assimilated spiritual knowledge, then we will come to a different conclusion. We will then say to ourselves: "If Klebs withholds the real sunlight from the beech tree, then he has to give it the ancient sunlight in the form of electricity." Then, our view is not narrowed; on the contrary, our view will be immensely expanded. Those people, however, who no longer want to know anything about the soul's course through the year, may simply say that one day is like any other, with breakfast, lunch, tea time, supper time; they might say that it is nice if there is something better at Christmas time, but that, basically, things proceed in the same way, day after day, all year round. People only look at the course of the day, that is, at the external physical aspects related to the human being, and say: "Who cares about connections with the cosmos? Let us emancipate ourselves from such a worldview! Let us be clear that even the stubborn beech tree no longer needs the cosmos; that, if we lock it inside an enclosed prison, it will grow without the sun—provided we give it enough electric light!"

No, it will not! It simply will not grow without the sun. When we are doing something like this, we must know how to look at the sun in the right way. But then we must also be clear that this involves something else, that it is actually a different relationship. Looking at it from a wider perspective, it becomes clear that it is a different matter altogether whether we allow the beech tree to grow and thrive in the cosmic sunlight, or whether we offer it the light that stems from primordial times and has become an ahrimanic light. And we will also remind ourselves that we have often heard how evolution progresses under normal conditions, or alternatively, what occurs if it is impacted by luciferic influences on the one side and ahrimanic ones on the other.

If we are able to see these things clearly enough, then we will not be so proud of our own cleverness, which has managed to overcome the cosmic stubbornness of the beech tree; instead, we would go much further. We would take a closer look at the sap of the beech tree and examine its effect on the human organism; we would examine the effect on the human organism of a beech tree that has been allowed to retain its stubbornness as well as the effect of a beech tree that has been robbed of its stubbornness by means of electric light. We may well learn something very special about the healing effect of the one beech tree as compared to that of the other. But then we must delve into the spiritual aspects!

And how do people deal with these things today? There certainly is much to be admired about the interests of the various fields of research. Researchers sit in classrooms, act as experimental psychologists, write down all kinds of notes to be remembered, test memory, carry out experiments on the children, and discover incredibly interesting things. Once people's interest in something has been aroused, then of course all things in the world are interesting—but all this only depends on the subjective point of view. Why should one not get to a point where a stamp collection becomes much more interesting than a botanical collection? And if that can be the case, why should something similar not happen in other fields? Why should one not be interested in what can be learnt from the torments inflicted upon children when experiments are carried out on them? In all these cases, however, the question is whether there are not higher obligations, or whether it is even advisable to experiment like this with children of a certain age. This gives rise to the question: What is being destroyed in the process? And then, an even more profound question arises: What is being ruined in the teachers themselves if, instead of asking them to develop a lively, warm-hearted connection to the children, it is demanded of them that they be interested in the speculative results of a psychology that carries out experiments? Consequently, the real question is whether one develops the right relationship to the sense-perceptible world with such research, and, if that is the case, whether one then also establishes the right relationship to the suprasensory world.

At this point, we may well hear loud objections from some people who speak of the necessary objectivity of research. They will say: "This man claims that there are certain minds who consider it immoral when Klebs removes the stubbornness from the beech tree in this way!" But this is not what I mean at all. This would not even occur to me in my dreams! Everything that is being done should be done, but we need a counterbalance, too. And in an age in which people are liberating themselves from a cosmic sensitivity in relation to the growth of beech trees, there must then also be—in a civilization that is absorbing such things—a sense of how spiritual progress occurs in the development of humanity. In an age such as ours, we must have a sense of these different epochs. I do not wish to restrict research, but we must develop a sense that something else must be there as a counterbalance. It must be countered by an open heart for the fact that, at specific times, certain things will always be revealed from the spiritual world. If, on the one hand, the materialistic sense becomes rampant and leads to strong and great results, then it becomes important, on the other hand, that precisely those people who have an interest in such results should also have an interest in the research findings about the spiritual world.

Moreover, this also is embedded in the innermost nature of Christianity. Christianity—understood correctly—perceives how the Christ-force, the Christ-impulse, continues to work in earthly existence, as the essential being of Christ, *after* the Mystery of Golgotha. This means that, even when the autumn mood sets in—when everything withers and becomes barren, when the sprouting and budding in the sense-perceptible natural world stops—we begin to perceive the sprouting and budding of the spirit, *if* we are able to sense in the leaf-shedding trees the glittering and glowing of those spiritual beings who are now accompanying human beings through the winter.

And, in the same way, we must learn—in an age which, from a certain point of view, rightfully goes about studying the details, and thus narrowing its view with respect to these details—we must learn to sense how our view must also include the greater, the all-encompassing perspective. This is the mood of St. John's in relation to Christianity. We must perceive and understand that the St. John's mood is the starting point for the event that is contained in the words: "He must increase, but I must decrease" (John 3:30).

This means that certain impressions must decrease—the impressions made on human beings from everything that is gained through research in the sensory world. And it is precisely when we penetrate more and more into the details of the sense world that the impression of the spiritual must increase and become ever stronger and stronger. The sun of the spirit must shine ever stronger into the human heart, the more the sun of the sensory world decreases.

We must experience the St. John's mood both as an entry into spiritual impulses and as an exit from sensory impulses. We must learn to perceive the St. John's mood as something in which there is a weaving and wafting—both in a spiritual and in a demon-like sense—from the sense-perceptible into the spiritual, and from the spiritual into the sense-perceptible. And we must learn, through the mood of St. John's, to make our spirit light and agile, so that it does not just cling in pitch-like fashion to the fixed contours of ideas but, instead, can find its way into weaving, wafting, living ideas. We must be able to notice the glowing of the sense-perceptible and the fading of the sense-perceptible; and we must be able to notice the glowing of the spiritual in the fading of the sense-perceptible. And we should actually feel that the symbol of the glowing of the fireflies at St. John's tide is something that also has meaning when the light is being dimmed again.

The little fireflies light up, and the little fireflies let the light fade away again. But as the light fades away, it leaves a living activity behind in us—the living weaving of the spiritual in the darkened sense-perceptible realm. And when we see, all around us in nature, the little spiritual waves glowing and fading, just as we symbolically see the glowing and fading of the fireflies in the sense world, then we will find the right St. John's mood for our age *if* we can do this with a full, light-filled, clear consciousness. And we need this right mood of St. John's tide; for, if we do not want to enter a state of complete decline, then we must go through our age in such a way that the spirit learns to glow and enliven itself and that we learn to follow this glowing, enlivened spiritual element in a meaningful way.

The mood of St. John's tide: Onward to the future of humanity and the earth! No longer the old mood, which only understands the sprouting and budding of the outer realm, which rejoices when it can actually imprison this sprouting and budding and when it can put under electric light what used to thrive in sunlight. Instead, we must learn to recognize the flashing-up and the springing-up of the spirit in such a way that the electric light becomes less important to us than it is at present, and that we thereby sharpen our vista, the St. John's view, sharpen it in order to perceive the old sunlight, which arises for us when we open ourselves to the great spiritual horizon—not just the narrow earthly horizon, but the great horizon extending all the way from Saturn to Vulcan.[†]

If we allow this light—the light that reveals itself to us on this great horizon—to work upon us in the right way, then all the trivial matters of our age can appear to us in this very light. Then we will be able to proceed in a forward and upward direction. Otherwise, if we do not resolve to do this, we will move only in a backward and downward direction.

Today, everything depends on human freedom and human will. Today, everything depends on human beings making a free, autonomous decision between forward and backward, between upward and downward.

Regaining the Living Source of Speech through the Christ-impulse

The Michael-thought as an Appeal to the Human Will

DORNACH, APRIL 13, 1923

IF YOU REMIND yourselves of some of the things that I have brought forward here in the course of recent lectures, then you will be able to call up a picture in your soul of the relationship between human language—that is, the faculty of human speech—and those beings in the spiritual world whom we have customarily identified as belonging to the hierarchy of the Archangeloi, the Archangels. You will remember that, in one of these earlier lectures, I outlined the significance of the way in which we shape our words when we are speaking. I described there that it makes a difference whether we shape our words in such a way that they only relate to purely material things, so that our speech takes on a materialistic character, or whether we shape our words in such a way that we develop a certain idealism in our speaking, so that in each word we speak, our use of language will let us sense that we belong to a spiritual world. For, what then resounds as words of our soul in our speaking must, precisely because it comes from the human soul, have some relation to spiritual beings. I described that, depending on whether the one or the other situation applies, the human being will, between falling asleep and awakening, come into either a right or a wrong relationship with the Archangels, with the beings we call Archangeloi; that, if we allow idealism to disappear from our speaking, we will gradually lose our all-important connection with these Archangeloi. I am reminding you of this fact because, today, I would like to single out one thing in particular that can place before your soul the inherent connection of human speech to the hierarchy of the Archangels.

Now, it is a fact that human speech, human language, has undergone a historical development in the course of the evolution of humanity—as has essentially all development insofar as it relates to human beings. We have already become familiar with this fact and its various manifestations within the development of the human being. What I would like to point out today is not related to any one language in particular. The time periods that we need to look at in relation to some of the most profound developments of language are so long that—in the context of what will be discussed today—even today's so-called primitive languages show largely the same character as more advanced languages. Accordingly, we will not point out the differences that exist between the various languages; instead, we will indicate the transformations, the metamorphoses, which human language in general has undergone in the course of humanity's evolution on earth.

If we consider the relationship that human beings have to language today, then we find that the words used in language are actually little more than designations for what exists outside of us and what is meant to be indicated by these words. You know that, in the course of our anthroposophical studies, we have also alluded to a more intimate relationship between a particular word and the object it describes. But this kind of intimate relationship is seldom experienced by people today. Words are more or less just external signs for what they intend to indicate. For instance, who is still capable today of sensing, when the word "lightning" [Blitz] is uttered, that something is contained in this word which, from its very sound, can be experienced by human beings in the same way as lightning is experienced when it actually flashes through space? Today, we are more or less inclined to feel that the sound-texture of this word "lightning" is simply the designation for the manifestation of the flashing light of lightning. But that was not always the case. For, if we go farther back—and we need only go back as far as the older part of Greek culture—then we find that people's relationship to language was not governed by thought in the same way, and that words were not just used as designations. We find, rather, that human beings were actively immersed in forming the sounds of the words, actively engaged in heart and soul. And, in the case of the languages of Northern Europe, we do not even need to go that far back.

Today, we no longer have a sense of the fact that the word "plough" [Pflug] could evoke the same inner experience as the actual activity carried out with this agricultural tool. Words have become mere signs, mere designations. But it was only relatively recently—and we need think here of maybe no more than fifteen hundred years ago—that, in the northern regions of Europe, people still experienced words in such a way that what they felt during the act of ploughing was actually similar to the inner feelings they had in response to the word that was used for "plough" in those days. This means that perceiving the meaning of a word did not so much involve a thought process in those days; instead, it was human feeling that was involved in this perceiving.

And if we go back into even more remote ages of humanity, then we find that it is not only feeling that was involved in the forming of words, but that the *will* took an intensive and active part in this as well. We must actually go back to the later Atlantean period if we want to look at a time when human beings, inasmuch as they lived in language, had a relationship to outer nature that was primarily one of will. For, we must bear in mind that the periods of time during which language develops in the way I have just indicated are very long indeed. And in language lives the language genius. After all, language and the development of language are not subject to human arbitrariness; rather, what lives in language is the language genius. And the genius of a language essentially belongs to the hierarchy of the Archangeloi. When the human being speaks, when, one could say, an atmosphere is prepared around the earth which is alive with the sounds of speech articulated by human beings, then this language-atmosphere is the element of the Archangeloi. This is why the Archangels are the spirits of the peoples, the folk spirits, as you may know from one of my lecture cycles.†

This means that what manifests in the evolution of human language here on earth is in fact intimately connected with the evolution of the Archangels. One could even say that what comes to expression in the evolution of language is an image of the evolution of the Archangels. For, even when we are studying something that only relates to the earth, we are by no means barred from learning about the evolution of the higher spiritual beings. We only need to know how to connect, in the right way, certain facts and phenomena with particular higher spiritual beings. We only need to develop a clear perception of how the continuous evolution of the Archangeloi is expressed and revealed in the metamorphoses of the human faculty of speech here on earth.

If we now go back to those very ancient times when human beings related to language through their will—that is, in the later part of the Atlantean evolution—then we find that language, or rather what lived in the language as a spiritual being from the hierarchy of the Archangeloi, was something different from what was there in that sense in more recent times.

Let us make clear to ourselves how language developed in humanity's earthly evolution in these ancient times. In those days, people were not really interested in the kind of feelings one might have when, for instance, flowers were blooming or when there were changes in weather. Such things interested them in connection with something else, but not in relation to the ability to let words spring up from the depths of their soul. When human beings were forming words, they were interested, for instance, in whether a particular outer situation posed a danger to them against which they would have to protect themselves, or whether something had a favorable effect on them so that they might want to incorporate it into their life situation; they were interested in whether something would be conducive or detrimental to their health. In short, how their forces of will were being activated toward a particular goal—this is what they were interested in. And what impelled them to act in response to certain outer realities—this is what interested them and what caused them to form their words accordingly. In those ancient times, words were expressions for the reactive processes of human beings; they were expressions for what human beings found themselves impelled to do in response to stimuli coming from the outer world. The expressions that were used in the very oldest languages of human evolution on earth, were almost exclusively expressions of will. How did that come about? This was an outcome of the fact that the Archangels came to language by way of *intuition.*

If you contemplate the descriptions about the nature of intuition, as they are given in some of my books, then you will find that, with these accounts of intuition, you also have a picture of the tasks which the Archangeloi had to carry out, say, in the later part of the Atlantean evolution, so that the will-based language of that time could be imparted to human beings. Later, these Archangels advanced further in their own evolution. In my booklet, *The Spiritual Guidance of the Individual and of Humanity*,[†] I already referred to the evolution of those beings, living in the spiritual world, who are the leaders and guides of individual human beings and humanity. Today, I would like to turn to a topic that was given less attention in this booklet, to the realm of language.

The evolutionary progress of the Archangels, with respect to language, may be described in the following way. Within this older faculty of intuition, the Archangels were primarily in the realms of still higher hierarchies, giving themselves up to the worlds of these higher hierarchies, so that, together with language, they absorbed something that was actually the very essence of those hierarchies that ranked higher than their own Archangel hierarchy. As long as this language-forming power in them was based in intuition, the Archangels surrendered themselves to the next higher hierarchy—the Kyriotetes, the Dynamis, and the Exusiai. They were inside this realm. And from what they experienced through their intuition-based presence within this higher hierarchy, they were able to infuse earthly life with the language-forming power.

In the subsequent era, the continuing progress of the Archangeloi occurred in such a way that their language-forming power no longer flowed from *intuition*, but rather from *inspiration*. They no longer surrendered themselves fully to the next higher hierarchy. Moreover, what they still received through their devotion to this higher hierarchy underwent a change; it became something else for them than what they had communicated to human beings as language. Now they were hearing and absorbing the inspirations of the first hierarchy—the Thrones, the Cherubim, and the Seraphim; and it was from this inspiration that they now infused the language-forming power into earthly life.

If we go back to the earliest times of post-Atlantean evolution, or even only back to the Egyptian-Chaldean cultural epoch, then we find that the source from which the Archangels drew—in order to impart language to human beings—was inspiration. That is when language underwent a metamorphosis and developed in such a way that words became primarily an expression of human sympathy and antipathy, of human feelings and emotions in general. The ancient *language of will* was replaced by a *language of feeling*; and a particular condition became the dominant one. What people now felt when they encountered events or beings in the outer world was the same as what was felt when sounds arising from the depths of the human being were articulated into words through the organs of speech.

We can say, then, that this is a significant event in the evolution of humanity. The hierarchy of the Archangels initially was subject to intuitions; and the language of will, brought down from out of these intuitions, was created by these hierarchical beings. The Archangels then advanced further and now were governed by inspiration. And, from what they received through the inspiration of the beings of the first hierarchy, the languages of feeling arose (see Plate 2 in the appendix and the endnote to page 167).[†]

It was actually out of a particularly deeply felt perception that Herman Grimm, the art historian,[†] drew a clear dividing line between the Greeks and the Romans. Herman Grimm stated that when we learn history today at school or at a university, we place our confidence in the fact that we understand what we are learning; but that, in learning history today, and in going over the evolution of humanity, we are only able to understand history as far back as Roman times. We can still understand Cicero and Caesar,[†] because to a certain extent they are quite similar to people today, although there is actually much that is unnatural in the way we tend to understand someone like Caesar, for example. If we were not so well trained in this kind of understanding, then Caesar would likely only be of interest to the pupils of military academies. It really is terrible how we are trained in this regard. Generally speaking, however, one can indeed trace a continuous stream going from our own time back to Roman times. For example, a certain pedantic element, which has gradually crept into humanity and is at its peak today, can already be found if we go back to Roman times. But, so says Herman Grimm, if we are honest with ourselves about our way of understanding the past, then we cannot claim to really comprehend, for example, Pericles or Alcibiades.† We understand them in the same way as we understand characters in fairy tales. It is really only through deepening our anthroposophical knowledge that we can gain a renewed understanding of the soul life of the Greeks, such as the figures mentioned. As you know, we have always attempted to find our way into how the ancient Greeks thought and formed ideas. This is also what Herman Grimm sensed. He felt that there is quite a distance between the soul life of an ancient Greek and the soul life of a modern human being; that we can still feel a certain closeness to the Romans, but that we then come to an abyss.

The way the Greeks are portrayed in the schools of today is really deplorable, for they are made out to be modern people. They were not like that at all; their whole soul life was of a different character altogether. We must use completely different tools if we want to characterize the Greeks. This situation was best illustrated by a striking case—namely, how the super-learned Wilamowitz† set about translating the Greek tragedians. The whole thing is actually an abomination, because there is nothing of the Greek tragedians left in it, absolutely nothing. And yet people today like it immensely; they are quite enchanted with Wilamowitz's translations. But the characters who appear in them are not those who appear in the Greek tragedies.

Accordingly, if we go back as far as Greece—and Herman Grimm sensed this with a reliable instinctive feeling—then we come into a completely different world; not to mention the Eastern elements in this respect. It is actually sheer mockery when people today imagine that, from reading the translations by Deussen,† they would be able to understand anything about what took place in the ancient Orient. To really understand this, one must be able to have insight into the full extent of the transformation and reconfiguration of the human soul at that time.

And if we now come to consider a particular element, the element of language, then we find that, right up to the time of ancient Greece, a language of feeling still prevailed, for example, among the philosophers up to Plato.† The first philosophical pedant is the great and universal spirit, Aristotle.† It will surprise you that I am mentioning these two attributes in succession, but one simply cannot understand Aristotle unless one sees him as the first philosophical pedant and simultaneously as a universal spirit. He is great in a certain respect, but in another respect, he is the first pedantic philosopher, for he extracted his thought-categories from the words. It would never have occurred to the Greeks of earlier times to pick out thought-categories from words, because they still had a sense that words are entities that work like inspirations into human beings. They felt the presence of higher spiritual beings when language came into being.

But the rest of humanity—which generally lags behind the philosophers in terms of certain things, but is often ahead with respect to spiritual things—retained this inspiration in terms of the language-forming power longer than the philosophers. Thus, we can really say that this element of inspiration within the language-forming power—an inspiration that actually lives in the soul of the Archangels—can still be perceived well into the Greek period and, as far as outer humanity is concerned, right up to the time of the Mystery of Golgotha. This is of course only approximate. In one region of the earth, it lasted longer, in another not as long. In certain regions of the earth, people still felt how words were pulsating in them just as the blood pulsates in the body; they felt this in the power of the breath. And it was in the breath flowing through the body, in the power of the breath surging all through the body, that they felt the Archangel who itself was governed by inspiration.

Then we come to the time period in which the Archangels, inasmuch as they are imparting language to humanity, are no longer subject to *inspiration*, but rather to *imagination* (see Plate 2 in the appendix and the endnote to page 167). And language becomes a *language of thought*. Human beings are now speaking more and more out of their thoughts; one could say that language begins to approach the abstract element in the human being.

A very significant fact lies at the root of this. The Archangels, who themselves belong to the third hierarchy, had received intuitions from the second hierarchy, and they had received inspirations from the Seraphim, Cherubim, and Thrones, that is, from the first hierarchy. And from whom do they receive imaginations? There is no hierarchy higher than the first! At first glance, the Archangels could not receive these imaginations from any of the hierarchies that are still chronicled in the writings of, for example, Dionysius the Areopagite.[†] For in these writings, there is no indication of a hierarchy beyond the first. Accordingly, certain Archangel-beings had to retrieve the imaginations, that is, the images of the language-forming power—for this is what these imaginations are—from the past, and thus continue what had been there before (see Plate 2 in the appendix and the endnote to page 167). The power to form language, which had welled up directly from a living source, had ceased. And because speech now was taken from an earlier stage, an ahrimanic element crept into it. This is a fact of tremendous significance. What the Archangels had felt in this upper realm—this is what then came to expression in the human world through the fact that language became more and more eroded, weakened, and no longer existed as something living, as it had been in earlier times.

Let us consider the tremendous significance of what is expressed through this fact! Something is entering the life of human beings, which, in reality, requires a higher hierarchy than what the first hierarchy represents. If we are able to feel this in its tremendous, all-encompassing significance, then we will realize that a time had arrived during which the gods had to grow beyond what is embodied in the first hierarchy.

Now, there is one thing which, until that time, had not yet been achieved by the gods, but which already existed in the form of an image [*im Abbilde*] here on earth. What the gods had not yet attained was the passage through death. I have already spoken about this fact on many occasions. The gods who, within the various hierarchies, stand above human beings, had only come to know transformations, metamorphoses from one form of life into another. Before the Mystery of Golgotha, the actual event of death—death in life—had not been an experience of the gods. Death had entered life through the luciferic and ahrimanic influences, that is, through divine beings who had either remained behind in evolution, or, in rushing ahead, had pressed forward too quickly. But death was not actually something that existed as a life experience for the higher hierarchies. Death entered as an experience for these higher hierarchies at the moment when Christ went through the Mystery of Golgotha, that is, when he went through death, when he united himself so deeply with the destiny of human beings on earth that he chose to have this experience in common with earthly humanity—the experience of going through death. This event of Golgotha, therefore, is not just an occurrence within life on earth; the event of Golgotha is an occurrence within the life of the gods.

The actual event that occurred on the earth, as well as the recognition that arises in the hearts and minds of human beings regarding this event of Golgotha—all this is an image of something infinitely more comprehensive, more magnificent, more powerful, more sublime that took place in the world of the gods themselves. And Christ's passing through death on Golgotha is an event that caused the first hierarchy to reach out beyond its own realm and into a still higher one. This is why I have always had to say to you that the realm of the trinity actually lies above the hierarchies. But it only developed into this in the course of evolution. Evolution is occurring in all realms.

And so, if we consider the hierarchies as specified by Dionysius the Areopagite, then we can say that the Archangels lost the possibility of forming imaginations out of the higher realm; that, as a result, human beings lost the possibility of continuing to develop language in a living way. In the world of the gods, something took place whose earthly reflection is the event of Golgotha. And it is for this reason that the event of Golgotha, among many other things, is also connected with the fact that, when human beings gradually grasp more and more of the Christ-impulse, they will again be able, through this Christ-impulse, to have access to the living source of language.

Today, we have a decline, one might say, of the purely natural languages. And if we are sufficiently impartial, then we can perceive in the declining natural languages—especially the further we go from the East toward the West—that these languages carry an element of death within them, that they are increasingly becoming empty husks. In the East, this is not yet occurring to that extent, but as we go further West, we find it to be increasingly the case that languages carry a dying element within them.

A renewed enlivening of the creative power of language in human beings can only arise if we increasingly embrace the Christ-impulse as something living again, so that the Christ-impulse may become the very element that gives creative power to speech. And among all the things that must be mentioned if one wants to explain the significance of the Christ-impulse for the evolution of humanity, there is also the fact that, at the very time when human beings were advancing toward freedom, humanity was also departing from the stage in which languages were thoroughly permeated by, and interwoven with, the divine-spiritual. If speech had remained just as it was in ancient Greece, then human beings would not have been able to develop toward freedom. This is why it became necessary for the absurdity, as I would call it, to occur that language served merely to designate things, and why it became necessary for the Archangeloi to lose the possibility of forming imaginations based on the present and to have to resort to the past for the forming of imaginations. However, during this time—at the beginning of which Christ had made himself known to humanity and had empowered [the evangelists] to record the mysteries of his being and his deeds in the gospels—throughout this time, the knowledge of Christ had not fully unfolded among human beings because this knowledge was not sufficiently spiritual, because it had often only been something traditional. Only when the word of the Gospel is enlivened based on an understanding of Christ—an understanding which, at the present time, comes directly from Christ, whose ongoing influence forever continues to work on human beings—only then will the language-forming power, too, emanate from this Christ-impulse, from the living Christ-impulse.

But let us now write down on the blackboard what I have indicated to you here (see Plate 2 in the appendix and the endnote to page 167). Let us be quite clear that something is happening up there in the higher regions, which causes the gods to grow more and more exalted; and that something is happening down here in the lower regions, through which human beings are increasingly taking up the Christ-impulse, but are also advancing ever more toward freedom. Now let us form the image that, inasmuch as the human being is elevated to a higher stage, this elevation of the human being also constitutes an elevation of the higher hierarchies. Let us be clear about the fact that, when the Archangels receive more and more of Christ into themselves, the imaginations of the Archangels will become quickened with immediately present life, because Christ—who will then have found a home in the hearts of human beings on earth—will enter, as an impulse, into the imaginations of the Archangels (see Plate 2 in the appendix and the endnote to page 167).

Then, there will be an altogether different kind of language-forming power. It will, in fact, be a very special kind of language-forming power that is coming. I have already mentioned this from certain other points of view in earlier lecture cycles, and now let us simply chronicle what I have explained to you there.

We can describe what transpired up above in the heavens during the developments that occurred up there, while the evolution of humanity took its course down below on earth. And we can also describe how this was reflected on the earth. We can describe how the language of will grew into the language of feeling and then into the languages of thought or symbol. And we can know that amidst all this, the Archangeloi were ascending—or one could also say descending—from *intuition* to *inspiration* and to *imagination*.

But, from the viewpoint of a human being, what is it that we must take into account if we want to interpret the evolution of the Archangeloi and everything that transpired in connection with it among the higher hierarchies? We must consider the development of language and of the word; we must fix our attention on this evolution; we must remember. As a human being, I want to concentrate on one particular stream in the evolution of humanity, and on what is interwoven into it—the stream of the gods. I go back to the original source, to the primordial beginning. "In the beginning was the Word." Where was the Word when, as humanity, we had a language of will? The Word was with God and had to be sought in God by means of intuition. "And the Word was with God." The Archangeloi had to immerse themselves, by means of intuition, into the essential being of the second hierarchy. And this essential being, which they then let flow into themselves, was the Word: "And the Word was a God."

> In the beginning was the Word,
> And the Word was with God,
> And the Word was a God (John 1:1).

We can see from this how intimate the connection was between that which had been in continual flow all through its development—and had found its culmination in the Mystery of Golgotha—and the Logos, the Word. And this whole development is, of course, also connected with the great cosmic event of Christ's becoming a human being and passing through death. The time in which these great words were spoken: "In the beginning was the Word, and the Word was with God, and the Word was a God," was a time when human beings perceived the Word's weaving, above all else, in the realm of the soul. But then a time came, with the Mystery of Golgotha, when Christ was present in a human body and people perceived Christ through the Word—a time when the Word had entered the physical human being: "And the Word became flesh" (John 1:14).

Deep truths about evolution are contained in these ancient writings; but it requires steadfast, intense work to rediscover these truths again, work that consists in observing the spiritual world. However, we must be clear about the fact that these ancient writings must be approached with reverence—the kind of reverence that leads us to realize that we will only be able to penetrate ever deeper into these things if we first learn to investigate them ourselves. Then we can enter into the deeper meaning of these ancient writings. And as we enter into their deeper meaning, we also enter into spiritual life itself.

And in this connection, imagine how good it would be for our present age to have a Michael civilization, a culture that would let itself be inspired by what I have referred to in previous lectures as the Michael-thought! The Michael-thought should become alive for us preferably through an autumn festival. The leaves have withered and are falling from the trees; the plants are wilting and fading away; life becomes mineralized. Everything we saw in the earlier part of the year as sprouting, springing life—all this is now receiving death into itself, death and disintegration, and is undergoing mineralization. This is the time when the Michael-force, the force of will, must spring up in human beings, a force through which we recognize that the spiritual must enter wherever the physical-material element loses its strength and is fading away. The autumnal festival of Michaelmas, at the end of September, should become a festival filled with active impulses. It should be an image of how the human being, while standing within the withering processes of nature, grows correspondingly stronger and more active in soul. And if this festival takes on this character, then all human activity will be fructified through it.

Just think of all the things we experience nowadays! We do not even need to go very far back in time to find an abundance of experiences that people have encountered. In all fields of study, for example that of language, one can hear people saying that they are eager to pursue their studies, but that it will not lead anywhere; that things are simply placed side by side, but are completely lacking in anything spiritual.

It really is the case, especially for young people coming straight out of high school, that, even though they have not yet fully awakened to life, they are now supposed to be able to think and go to university to study languages, for example. Then they reflect on what they have learned so far in their language studies and how this is likely to continue in university, and they will become dizzy imagining what is in store for them. And yet, all the preliminary principles already exist, which could guide them to recognize the wonders that unfold before us when we look upward from today's language of thought, through the language of feeling, and up to the language of will, and behold there the divine element, the archangelic working and weaving, and then realize that these elements can still be seen today in what might be called the corpses of the languages. And if the life of the Primal Beginnings [the Archai] were to flow into the languages again, then this would result in something magnificent!

The Michael-thought is not something that simply becomes a reality when a few people decide to have an autumn festival, thinking how nice that would be and how it would put them in the very forefront of progress. The Michael-thought is something that must take into account the innermost and strongest impulses of the human will. And a festival of Michael must really be something that gives a powerful impulse to human life, much like in earlier times, when human beings still had the forces to create festivals, when the institution of Christmas or Easter gave a new urge and impetus to the life of human beings.

Creating a Michael Festival out of the Spirit

The Mystery of the Inner Human Being

BERLIN, MAY 23, 1923

What I would like to present to you today will have to be said—as has everything that I have had to say about anthroposophy recently—with a particular undertone elicited by the painful event[†] that befell our work and our Society last New Year's Eve; by the fact that, for the time being, the Goetheanum in Dornach is no longer there. It was consumed by flames on last New Year's Eve. And all those who witnessed the work of ten long years destroyed in just one night, work that had been carried out by so many of our friends who had dedicated themselves to it, as well as those who, because of this work and because of what this Goetheanum meant to us, had loved it very much—all those will feel weighed down by the realization that we no longer have this outer sign of anthroposophical activity. For, even when some other building suitable for our purposes will rise again on the same site—and this should certainly occur—it would of course never become the old Goetheanum again because of the impact of the difficult circumstances of the present time. And so, behind everything that I have had to say since those days, there actually stands the fearful glow of the flames that interfered, in such a heart-wrenching way, in the continuing development of all our work. Now that this outer hallmark is gone, we must dedicate ourselves all the more to taking hold of the inner forces and the inner essence of the anthroposophical movement and what is connected with it for the whole evolution of humanity.

Let me begin, then, with a contemplation of sorts regarding the nature of the human being. I have made many such contemplations here in your midst and would like to make another one today from a specific point of view.

I would like to take my start from a consideration of the human being entering this world, the human being who has descended from pre-earthly existence and is taking his or her first steps here in earthly life. We know that at the time of this entrance into earthly life, the soul is governed by a condition that actually has a certain similarity to the ever-recurring condition of the human being's life of sleep. And, just as ordinary consciousness has, upon awakening, no memory of what the human soul and spirit experienced from the time of falling asleep to that of waking up—with the exception of the colorful variety of dreams, which, however, in reality also float away when we sink into sleep or when we awaken, and which, for our ordinary consciousness, do not rise beyond the state of deep sleep—just as ordinary consciousness does not remember these states, so does, for this same consciousness, the memory of the whole of earthly life extend only back to a certain point in childhood. For some, this point lies somewhat earlier, for others a little later. And what exists in earthly life before this point in time is, in reality, just as hidden from ordinary consciousness as what takes place in the sleep state. It is true, of course, that a small child is not in a real state of sleep but, rather, lives in a sort of dreamy, indefinable inner activity. In comparison to the whole of later life, however, this state is, to begin with, not entirely unlike that of dream-filled sleep.

Now, there are three activities that begin to take effect during this time, three things that the child is learning—the activity that is usually summarized in the expression *learning to walk*, then that which is connected with *learning to speak*, and that which, for the child, is connected with *learning to think*. However, with the expression "learning to walk" we are actually describing something that is extraordinarily complex; and it is only because of a certain convenience on our part that we describe this activity in an exceedingly condensed way. We only have to think of how the child initially enters life in a state of complete ineptitude; how it gradually gains the ability to adjust its own position of balance to the surrounding space—a condition in which it will have to move throughout its whole life. What we observe in the child is not just "learning to walk"; rather, it is a quest for the state of equilibrium in earthly life. And connected with this learning to walk is the use of the limbs in general. To those who have the ability to observe such things in the right way, the most remarkable, most magnificent riddles of life are expressed in this learning to walk. A whole world is expressed in the very manner in which the child progresses from crawling to standing upright, to moving its little feet, but also to other things—to raising its head, to making use of its arms and legs. And if we then look into this in a more intimate way, one might say, if we observe how one child tends to place its little feet down on the heels, while another is more inclined to put its toes down first, then we will perhaps get an inkling of what I shall have to speak about today with regard to the three activities mentioned and their connection with the spiritual world. But I would first like to characterize these three activities from their outer aspects.

It is on the basis of this seeking for balance—or, if I may express myself in a somewhat more learned, perhaps even slightly pompous way—it is on the basis of this search for the dynamics, for the mobility in human life, that the faculty of speech then develops. For, anyone capable of observing knows quite well that the normal development of a child proceeds in such a way that learning to speak develops on the basis of learning to walk and learning to grasp things with the hands. With regard to this learning to speak, it can be noticed right from the start how the child's walking—whether it be with a firm or a light step—also comes to expression in the rhythms of its speaking, in its accenting of the syllables, in the forcefulness of its speech. And, continuing these observations, one will also notice how the modulation of the words, how the shaping of the words shows a certain parallel in how the child is learning to bend its little fingers or hold them straight—whether this is done in a skillful or in a clumsy way.

If we are able to observe the whole inner configuration of the human organism, then we are also able to know—and the present-day theory of evolution also recognizes this—that right-handed people have the speech center in the posterior third left frontal convolution, in the so-called Broca's convolution[†] (which simply represents physiologically the characteristic connection between language and the ability to grasp objects or, if I am allowed to use a more pleonastic phrasing, the whole scope of the ability to perform functions with one's arms and hands); and if we recognize this, then we will also know how intimately the movement of the vocal cords, the entire functioning of the speech organism, takes on the exact same character as the movements used in walking and in grasping objects. But in the normal development of the child, speech—which is developed by imitating the surroundings—cannot develop at all unless its foundation has first been laid through the quest for the state of equilibrium in life.

And then we come to thinking. Here we see that the more delicate organs of the brain, which form the basis of thinking, develop in turn out of the speech organism. No one should suppose that, in the normal development of the child, thinking could develop before speaking. Anyone observing these things, will find that for the child, speech is not initially an expression of "thinking." Not at all! It would be silly to believe that. For the child, speech is an expression of feelings, sensations, and the life of the soul. This is why you will find that what the child initially expresses through language are all the things connected with feelings, words related to feelings. When the child says "Mama" or "Papa," it wants to express its feelings for Mama or Papa, not any particular concepts or thoughts. Thinking only develops out of speaking. It is true that this sequence may deviate in some cases, and people might then say: "This child learned to speak before it learned to walk." But this is not the normal development, and it is important in raising children to see to it that the normal course of development is actually observed—that is, the sequence of walking, speaking, thinking.

However, the true nature of these faculties of the child can only be perceived when we observe the other side of human life, that is to say, when we observe what part these activities play during sleep in later life; for these activities arise from sleep or, at any rate, from the dreamlike sleep of the child, as I have indicated. But what form do these faculties assume during later life on earth?

In general, it is not possible for present-day science to enter into these matters. Today's scientific practice actually only knows the external side of the essential human being and does not know of the inner relationships between the human being and the being of the cosmos, insofar as this being of the cosmos is spiritual. In all areas of life, humanity's civilization—if I may use the expression—or one could also say, human culture, has developed into a certain materialism or naturalism. Do not think that it is my intention to rail against materialism here; for, if materialism had not come into humanity's civilization, then human beings would not have become free. Materialism, therefore, constitutes a necessary epoch in the evolution of humanity. Today, however, we must clarify for ourselves which paths we have to take, both now and further into the future. And we have to be clear about this in relation to all realms. In order for you to visualize more clearly what I have to speak about today, I would like to illustrate this by means of an example.

You all know, and can also learn from my writings, that earthly humanity, before it passed through the cultural epochs that are still somewhat similar to the present one—the ancient Indian, the ancient Persian, the Egyptian-Chaldean, the Greco-Latin, and now our own—that, prior to this, humanity went through the so-called Atlantean catastrophe. And at the time of this Atlantean catastrophe, humanity—which, broadly speaking, is today's European, Asian, and American humanity—lived for the most part on a continent that is now covered by water, namely the Atlantic Ocean. At that time—a long time ago—this area was mostly land, and humanity had evolved for a very long time on this Atlantean continent. You can, of course, also read about all the things that humanity went through in my books and lecture cycles.

It is not my intention at this time to speak about what humanity experienced in the ancient Atlantean era, other than specifically about their musical experiences. The whole musical experience of the ancient Atlanteans would have to appear very strange, even grotesque, to us modern human beings—*if* we could hear it, which we cannot do, of course. For, what the ancient Atlanteans sought out in music was, for example, the musical intervals of the seventh. In the Atlantean time, these seventh chords had the peculiarity of affecting the souls of these ancient people—whose bodies we all inhabited, of course, because we ourselves also went through that era in previous lives on earth—affecting them in such a way that they were immediately transported out of their bodies when they lived in their music, which primarily embraced intervals of the seventh. They knew no other soul-mood in music than a state of rapture, of enthusiasm, of being permeated by God. And, as soon as they heard the sounds of their extraordinarily simple instruments—which, incidentally, were intended only to accompany singing—then these Atlanteans actually felt themselves as though weaving and living in the spiritual world surrounding them.

Then came the Atlantean catastrophe. All post-Atlantean people initially developed a preference for sequences of fifths. You probably know that, for a long time, the interval of the fifth was the most comprehensive element in musical development; in ancient Greece, for example, intervals of fifths played a very broad role. And this preference for sequences of fifths had the special consequence that, when people experienced music, they actually no longer experienced themselves outside their bodies, but instead felt themselves to be soul-spiritually within their bodies. While living in this musical experience, they completely forgot any experiences related to the physical. They still felt that they were inside their skin, as it were, but that their skin was entirely filled with soul and spirit.

The effect of music was such—and very few people will believe this—that almost until the tenth and eleventh centuries AD, the inherently natural music was as I have described it. For, it was not until then that human beings developed the ability to experience the intervals of the thirds, both the major and minor thirds, as well as the qualities characteristic of the major and minor keys.[†] This came relatively late. But together with this late entry, the inner experience of music was formed as well. Human beings now remained within themselves during the musical experience. Just as all other realms of culture at that time sought to transition from the spiritual down to the material, so did the human perception of music. It transitioned from an experience of the spiritual—for this is what music in general had brought about for human beings in ancient times—down to an experience of the musical element inside the human being. It no longer extended as far outward as to the skin, but stayed entirely within the human being. This is also the reason that the moods of the major and minor keys only emerged at that time, for these moods can essentially only arise when the human being experiences the musical element inwardly.

In this way, one can observe in all other domains how human beings have evolved from the spiritual down into the material, but also down into their own being. This is why one should not always say, in a narrow-minded way, that materialism is something so inferior, something from which human beings must break away. We would not have become true human beings at all if we had not come down in order to embrace life in the material world. It was precisely by taking hold of the spiritual in the material realm that the human being became a self-conscious, free I-being. And today, with the help of anthroposophic spiritual science, we must once again find the way back into the spiritual world; we must find it in all realms. This is why it is so painful that the artistic attempt that was made in this direction with the Goetheanum in Dornach has now been wiped out! For it is in all domains that the path into the spiritual world must be sought.

Let us now first look at one faculty that the child acquires—namely, the faculty of speech—in its relation to the overall development of the human being. We really have to say that what the child learns is something magnificent. And it was Jean Paul,[†] the German poet, who said that the human being learns far more in the first three years of life—when the child essentially learns to walk, speak, and think—than in three academic years. In the meantime, these "three" academic years have, of course, become many years, but one still does not learn more in all these academic years than one learns in the first three years of life as a child. Let us look, then, at the faculty of speech! When we speak, this initially involves the external physical-physiological factor; that is, the larynx and the other speech organs are set in motion. They move the air, and sound is transmitted. But this is where we also approach the outer limits of the physical-physiological aspect, one could say, because the soul is of course also involved in our speaking; the soul weaves and shines through everything that we utter in sounds.

Certainly, to the extent that speech is something physical, the physical body and the etheric body of the human being are participating in it. They are of course silent from the time of falling asleep to that of waking up, meaning that, as a rule, the human being does not speak between falling asleep and waking up. However, to the extent that the soul and the I are involved in speaking, when they leave the physical body and the etheric body at the time of falling asleep, they—the soul and the I, the astral body and the I—take with them the soul's ability to speak, and with it, they actually take everything of a soul nature that the person has put into his or her speech during the whole day. In reality, we are different beings each evening, for we have been busy speaking all day long—some a lot, others less, some far too much, others not nearly enough—but at any rate, we have spent the whole day speaking and putting our souls into what we have said. And what we have put into our speech we take with us into sleep, and this remains our essential being between falling asleep and waking up.

Now, it can certainly be the case today, especially in our materialistic age, that people no longer have an inkling about the fact that idealism or spirituality can be expressed in language. Today, many people are simply of the opinion that language is intended to express only the external, only what is tangible and touchable. The feeling that ideals can be expressed in speech has in many cases been completely lost. It is also for this reason that people often are not able to understand what is said to them about the spirit. For what do people say to themselves when the spirit is mentioned? They say to themselves that the other person is just speaking "words." And all they know about "words" is that they indicate things that can be touched or seen. People no longer like the idea at all that words can also indicate something suprasensory or invisible. This can be the one way in which people relate to language. But there is another way. We can endeavor to find idealism again, even in words, even in language, so that human beings will know again that a soul-spiritual experience can resonate, as it were, through every word.

Now, it is worthy of note that someone who lives entirely in the materialism of language will carry some of this over into the spiritual world upon falling asleep, and that this then brings that person into a difficult relationship with the world of the Archangels, the world of the Archangeloi—the world into which we are meant to enter each night between going to sleep and awakening. On the other hand, someone who retains the idealism of speech, and who knows that the genius of language lives in speech, will enter into the necessary relationship with the hierarchy of the Archangels, and specifically with the one Archangel to whom that particular person belongs in the world that lies between falling asleep and awakening. And this is expressed even in the outer manifestations of the world.

For, why are people today so desperately seeking an outer relationship to their national languages? Why did this terrible misfortune come over Europe, which Woodrow Wilson,[†] who was really just an odd illusionist, considered a "good fortune"? Why did this great misfortune come over Europe—the notion that freedom is linked to the desperate desire to grab hold of the national languages, even of the smallest nations? Because, in reality, people are desperately seeking a relationship in an outer sense, a relationship they no longer have in the spiritual sense; for, in going to sleep they no longer have their natural connection to language, and therefore also not to the hierarchy of the Archangeloi. Humanity will have to find its way back again to permeating everything that pertains to language with idealism—if it does not want to lose the path into the spiritual world.

How does humanity today actually look at what happens with the individual human being between falling asleep and waking up? People do not take the state of sleep into account at all. When we think back about our life, we believe that what we have before us is a complete picture of life. But that is not true! The times spent in sleep are always left out; the whole picture is continuously interrupted. We always link the morning to the previous evening; but there is a night in between! And what occurs during sleep at night constitutes, firstly, at least a third of human life in external terms—this, at any rate, is the case for the average person—and, secondly, what occurs during sleep is much more important for the inner human being than the external activities undertaken during the entire day. Certainly, outer activity is more important for external civilization. But our whole inner constitution, as it is formed during life, is brought about by our entering in the right way into a relationship with the spiritual world during the night while we are sleeping.

And this is equally true for what forms the basis of the other faculties. If we put idealism into our actions, that is, into the whole range of our movements—which is, of course, also the first thing we learn when we begin our life on earth—if we put idealism into the totality of our actions, that is, if the shaping of our life contains idealism, then we will find the right relationship with the hierarchy of the Archai again. And through our thinking—that is, if our thoughts contain idealism and are not materialistic thoughts—the human being finds, while asleep at night, the connection with the hierarchy of the Angeloi, the Angels. This is what we discover when we investigate the connection between the state of sleep at night and these three faculties, acquired during childhood, from an anthroposophic and spiritual-scientific perspective.

But this connection can also be revealed in a much more comprehensive sense if we look at the whole life of the human being within the cosmos. You are familiar with the descriptions in my book *Theosophy*. When we pass through the portal of death, we first experience—for a few days—the state during which our thoughts and our mental images dissipate. One could express this by saying that the etheric body expands out into the distances of the cosmos, that the human being "loses" the etheric body. But this is actually the same as saying that the human being's mental images and thoughts are dissipating. But what does it really mean that our mental images, concepts, and thoughts are dissipating? This actually means a great deal. For it means that our entire waking life is departing from us. Our whole waking life withdraws from us in the course of two or three days, and there would be nothing left of our life, *if* we did not then experience the things that remain unconscious during our earthly life, *if* we did not then begin to relive in full consciousness what we experienced during our life of sleep. For, this life of sleep is spiritually infinitely richer and more intense than the waking life. Regardless of whether we are asleep for a short or a long period, our sleep life is always a repetition (in reverse order) of our daily waking life, but with a spiritual impact.

The *actions* you have undertaken during the day bring you into a relationship with the Archai, with the Primal Powers, during the night. What you have gone through as a *speaking* human being during the day brings you into a relationship with the Archangeloi, the Archangel beings, at night. And, similarly, what you have gone through as a *thinking* person brings you into a relationship with your Angel being, with the realm of the Angeloi. What a human being experiences during sleep is quite independent of time. There is no need to say: "Very well, but it is also possible that my sleep is interrupted, that there is a noise in the night, that something wakes me up; is it not true that I will then be unable to complete this process of living-through-my-day-in-reverse?" In fact, you will be able to finish it nevertheless, because these time relationships are completely different. What otherwise might continue for hours, if sleep proceeds regularly, can also be passed through in an instant. The conditions related to time are completely different during sleep. This is why it can certainly be said—and must, in fact, be said—that each time we sleep, we live once more, in reverse order, through everything that we experienced here in the physical world between the last time of waking up and falling asleep; but that we now live through it in its spiritual form, character, and essence.

And when, in the first few days after death, all the concepts we had formed during our waking life have dissipated into the cosmos, then we live through everything that we experienced during the third of our life spent in sleep. This is why I have always had to describe that human beings require a period amounting to a third of their earthly life in order to live through what they experienced during the nights. It is, of course, essentially the same as our daytime life, but is experienced in a different way. This is the period during which human beings, as the second condition after death,† live through everything in reverse order and actually experience once more, in a third of the time, their entire life back to birth. At that point, the human being has arrived at birth again, and enters into the state that I have already described to you in another context, that is to say, one enters into the state in which one's whole view of the world becomes essentially very different.

You see, here on earth we stand at a particular spot on this earth. The world is all around us. We know very little about ourselves with our ordinary consciousness. We observe the world with our outer senses; we know that world. Perhaps you will say that the anatomists know the inside of the human being very well. Not at all! They know only the outer aspect of what is inside us. Our real inside is something entirely different. When you remember something today that you went through ten years ago, then you actually have something in your memory that exists inside your soul. It is a compressed, shortened memory—possibly of a very, very extensive experience. Moreover, it provides merely a soul picture of something that you went through in your earthly life. But if you now look deeper into yourself—not into your memories, but into your physical organism, that is, the apparently physical organism—and take note of your wonderfully constructed brain, your wonderfully constructed lungs and so on, then you will *not* find the experiences of this earthly life living there, coiled up, as it were, but rather the whole cosmos, the entire universe, rolled up together. The human being is really a small universe, a microcosm. The whole world is rolled up in our organism. But we do not know this with our ordinary consciousness. When we stand here on earth, we have a memory of our experiences. But we do not realize that, within our physical nature, we ourselves are in a certain sense the embodied memory of the whole cosmos.

And so, when our reverse journey through life, which I have just specified here, has been completed, then we enter—between death and a new birth—into a cosmic life where we are no longer surrounded by the world with its mountains, clouds, stars, seas, and so on, but where our surroundings instead consist of the riddles of the inner human being, where everything that eludes us in earthly life concerning the mysteries of the inner human being now constitutes our environment. Here on this earth, we live within our skin and know about the world of the stars, clouds, mountains, stones, animals, and plants. Between death and a new birth, we know about the human being. All the mysteries of the human being are then all around us. And do not suppose that this is a less interesting environment than the one that surrounds us on earth! Certainly, the starry sky is magnificent; the mountains and the oceans are grandiose. But what the inside of the human being really *is*, even in just one tiny single vessel, is more magnificent and more powerful, when we have it around us in its majestic vastness between death and a new birth, than what surrounds us in our earthly environment. The human being *is* the world between death and a new birth, and must be this world, because we are preparing our next earthly life. We must be within it in order to prepare, together with the beings of the higher hierarchies, the future earthly human being.

And, just as we attend to our outer culture and civilization here—just as we make boots, sew coats, operate telephones, cut people's hair, give lectures, do something artistic, or anything else that is part of civilization today—so do we, between death and a new birth, create, together with the beings of the higher hierarchies, what constitutes the human being and what we ourselves shall be again in a physical body in our next earthly life. This is the spiritual goal of all culture, and it is mightier, infinitely grander and more magnificent than the earthly goal of culture. It is not by chance, after all, that the ancients called the physical human body *the temple of the gods*, because it is together with the gods, with the beings of the higher hierarchies, that this human physical body is formed between death and a new birth. This is what we are engaged in, this is where we are with our I—among the beings of the higher hierarchies, working on humanity together with the beings of the higher hierarchies. In a sense, we are then walking among the beings of the higher hierarchies; we are spirits among spirits.

What we are doing there, however, we can only do in a measure proportionate to what we have accomplished in our earthly life; and this, too, manifests in a particular way in the relationship of the state of sleep to that of being awake. Just think how chaotic dreams are! I do not undervalue the wonderfully multi-colored variety and grandeur of dreams, but we must be clear about the fact that—compared to earthly life, from which dreams derive their images—dreams are chaotic. You only need to remember a particular dream which I have used before as an illustration.† Volkelt† recounts this dream, according to a report from Württemberg—and we are all familiar with such dreams, of course—in which a lady from the city went to visit her sister, the wife of a pastor, in the country. She dreamt that she went to church with her sister to hear a sermon. But things became quite peculiar for her because, after the Gospel had been read and the pastor went up to the pulpit, he did not begin to preach. Instead, he lifted *not* his arms, but rather his wings, and eventually began to crow like a rooster! Or think of another dream, in which a lady described that in her dream she was thinking about what she should cook for her husband, and that nothing had occurred to her until, eventually, she remembered that she still had an old pickled grandmother upstairs in the loft, who was, however, still too tough. This is how chaotic dreams can be—strangely chaotic. But what does it actually mean to say that dreams seem so chaotic? What does that really mean?

While we sleep, we are with our I and astral body outside the physical body and the etheric body. And during that time, we experience again in reverse order—specifically with regard to its moral significance—everything that we have done, said, and thought during the day. We live through all this in reverse. We are preparing our karma for our next life on earth, and this is what already appears in images between the time of falling asleep and that of waking up. But these images are still very clumsy; for, when we then want to enter into the physical body again upon awakening, these images do not yet fit into it in the right way. We cannot form images that align with macrocosmic conditions. Instead, we conceive something entirely different—perhaps a "pickled" grandmother. This occurs because we are not able to understand the process of adjusting that which we have already formed [during sleep] to the human physical body; and this process of adapting to the human physical body is exceedingly difficult. We acquire this ability during our working together—in the way I have described it—with the beings of the higher hierarchies between death and new birth. At that time, our inner soul-spiritual being—which otherwise often inserts itself so awkwardly into our dreaming—must then first reconcile this condition once this whole sleep consciousness, no longer active, has been overcome once again and we have descended again into our existing physical body.

Between death and a new birth, this soul-spiritual being must penetrate all the mysteries of the physical body, so that the body may be built up in the right way. For it is really not true that the body is formed by the parents and ancestors alone. To believe this is one of the veritable follies of science—and it should be possible to make such a statement. For how does science view this process of becoming human? Today, science says approximately the following: At the base of material substances, we have molecules, which are made up of atoms in a very complicated way. The albumin molecule, contained in the embryonic cell, is the most complex molecule of all—of course, no scientist can actually describe it, but only point out its immense complexity—and because it is so complicated, a human being can emerge from it. This surely is the simplest way of explaining the human being! It is simply asserted that the entire human being is already contained in it; that it is just a molecule with a very complicated structure. But the truth is that the albumin molecule must totally revert back to chaos, must turn into the dust of disorganized matter, if a human being is to arise from it. In the outer world, we have organized matter, in crystals, in plants, and so on. If something is to come into existence, including even a plant or an animal, then matter must first completely return to dust. And it is only when matter no longer carries a defined form within itself, that the entire cosmos works upon the tiniest bit of matter and creates an image of itself within it.

How is it, then, with the human being? Between death and a new birth, we form this human image, with all its mysteries, into which we now weave our karma; then we send it down ahead of us into the body of the mother. We have, therefore, first formed the spiritual germ, which is large in comparison with the physical germ, and this then descends into matter that has become chaotic. This is the truth—not what modern physiology dreams up.

During this time, which I have just described, the I lives as a soul-spiritual being among soul-spiritual divine beings; it lives in the activity of getting to know the full extent of the real inner human being for the next life on earth. What is thus experienced spiritually in tremendous majesty and grandeur finds a reflection in the child, in what emerges in such a wonderful way in the individually formed movements of its search for balance. It is very interesting to see how the Primal Powers, the Archai, are now working from the realm of the life between death and a new birth into the whole realm of the child's searching for balance, into what we trivially refer to as "learning to walk." Anyone able to see a reflection of the spiritual in all earthly things can see how the soul-spiritual actions that we undertake between death and a new birth, as an I among higher I-beings in the search for a spiritual balance, are reflected in the activities related to walking, to grasping things with the hands, and so on—how all this finds a reflection in learning to walk on the earth.

At some point, we will have passed through these conditions, during which we are a spirit among spirits and are preparing what will then emerge in our earthly life in our body, in our limbs—all of which will then, in turn, determine what kind of human being we will become and how we will experience our karma. Once we have passed through these conditions in yonder world between death and a new birth, the following occurs. We enter a particular stage in our pre-earthly life in which we can no longer distinguish the individual spiritual beings with whom we have worked together for such a long time, a stage in which we only have a general perception of the spirit. It is true that, during this stage, we still know that we live in a spiritual world; but, because we are now already approaching earthly life, the impression made on us by the spiritual world becomes one of a unified whole and is no longer an impression of an individualized perception of the specific spiritual beings. I would like to describe this by means of a trivial comparison in order to make it understandable, but please be quite clear about the fact that, in doing so, I am pointing to something very sublime. If you see a small cloud appearing somewhere in the distance, then you will say that it is a little cloud. But when you come closer, you become aware that it is actually a swarm of insects! Then you are distinguishing the individual entities. However, in the spiritual world between death and new birth, the situation is the other way round. There, you first distinguish the single individualities of the spiritual beings and then it becomes a generalized impression. One could say that the *manifestation* of the spiritual takes the place of the *experience* of the spiritual.

And indeed, this condition—which leads us away from the spiritual world in a certain sense, because we are already seeking our way down to the earth again—this condition is mirrored inside the human being, in what forms the basis of human speech. Suppose we are speaking. It starts in a sense with the larynx—this is not quite correct, but approximately—and then the other organs of speech are set in motion. The essential part, however, lies behind all this. The essential part lies in the heart, behind the larynx; it lies in the whole breathing process and in everything connected with it. What actually lies at the basis of speech is just as much an earthly image of the state of manifestation (in which we perceive the divine-spiritual only in a blurred way) as learning to walk—searching for balance—is an earthly image of our movements in the spiritual world. And so, as the child learns to speak, it is again experiencing a state which it also went through between death and a new birth.

And, when we have sent down the spiritual germ of our physical body and it has, through the process of conception, gradually united with the body of the mother—then we still remain up above. It is the last phase before earthly incarnation. There, we draw together our etheric body from all the regions of the universe, and what occurs in the suprasensory world in this contracting process of the etheric body is what comes to expression in the child's learning to think.

We now have here the three successive conditions: Perceiving within the spiritual world, which is reflected in learning to walk; manifestation of the spiritual world, which is reflected in learning to speak. (This, incidentally, is why we call the cosmic word, which forms the basis of speech, the World Logos, the inner word. It is the manifestation of the universal Logos, in which the spiritual expresses itself—like the insect in a swarm of insects; it is what lies at the foundation of speech.) And thirdly, what we then do in order to form our etheric body—which actually thinks in us, for we think all night long, even though we are not present with our I and astral body—this process of collecting our etheric body (the last thing we do before we descend to earth) is what then extends into our thinking. Accordingly, in learning to walk, speak, and think, the little child incorporates into its physical body what it brings down from pre-earthly existence.

What leads us to real knowledge of the spiritual—and therefore also to an artistic comprehension of the world and a religious understanding of the world—is the fact that we are able to relate each single phenomenon in our physical, sense-perceptible existence to the spiritual. I have often compared someone who prefers to speak about the divine-spiritual only "in general terms," to a person who goes out into a meadow, is shown some flowers, and then is told: "Look, there are daisies, there are dandelions, there is wild chicory," whereupon this person replies: "I am not really interested in all these details! All I need to know is that they are flowers." It is so convenient to say that these are all just flowers. But surely, there are differences in what makes a flower into a particular flower! And the same is true with respect to the spiritual world. It is, of course, also convenient to say that something spiritual lies at the base of all physical, sense-perceptible things. But what matters is that we increasingly learn to know *which* spiritual element underlies each single physical-sensory phenomenon; for only in this way can we actually intercede again, out of the spirit, in the physical-sensory course of life.

And it is through this principle that, for example, our Waldorf pedagogy[†] becomes a unique way of educating children, as it considers the real human being. This will become even more evident once this pedagogy will have been able to apply these principles to the child's first years as well. We cannot do this yet. Up until now we have always had to add more at the upper level, and this year, we have established the highest grade. There is a lot to do if one wants to give shape to an entire school in terms of its teaching objectives. This is why, up to now, it has not been possible to consider making things more complete at the lower end as well, and adding some form of kindergarten to it. This year [1923], the first Waldorf students will be taking their high school exams. Then, further additions in the upper levels will no longer be needed, but, given the extraordinary "abundance of financial shortages" that we are dealing with, particularly with respect to the Waldorf school, I fear that additions at the lower levels will have to be halted for now. At any rate, in the same way as we would configure the kindergarten toward the child's learning to walk, learning to speak, learning to think and the further development of these faculties, so are we momentarily adapting these pedagogical principles toward the early grade school—starting from the sixth, seventh years of life and then continuing with the next ones—in such a way that we consider questions such as: What is incarnating in the child at this time? What comes to expression in the child's life, with each week, with each month, of what existed before birth? This is how a pedagogy is actually developed from the spirit.

This is one of these moments in time—and there shall have to be many more—that must be rediscovered if humanity is not to remain on a downward path but, instead, is to begin the ascent again. We must find the paths into the spiritual world again. But we can only do this if we learn, in full consciousness, to find ways and means to act and speak out of the spirit.

In the time immediately following the great Atlantean catastrophe, human beings—every single one—lived out of the spirit, because each one could be told, based on the time of that person's birth, what his or her karma was. At that time, astrology did not imply the kind of amateurism that it often represents today; rather, astrology meant livingly co-experiencing the deeds of the stars. And as an outcome of this living experience, the mysteries revealed to each individual human being how he or she had to live. In those days, astrology had a living significance for the individual human experience.

Then came the time—around the sixth, fifth, and fourth millennium before Christ—during which human beings no longer experienced the mysteries of the starry heavens, but instead experienced the course of the year. What do I mean when I say that people experienced the course of the year? It means that they knew from direct perception that the earth is not the coarse chunk that modern geology imagines it to be. On an earth such as geology pictures it, plants could never grow and live, much less animals or human beings. This could never be the case, because the geologists' earth is a stone, and things can only grow directly in a stone if the entire cosmos works upon it, if it has a connection to the whole universe. In these ancient times, people simply knew that the earth is an organism, that it has a soul—something we must learn again today.

And it is even the case that this earth-soul also has its own special destiny. Suppose it is winter, Christmas time, the time of the winter solstice. This is the time when the earth-soul is fully united with the earth; for, when a blanket of snow covers the earth, when there is something like a mantle of cold surrounding the earth, then the earth-soul is united with the earth, rests in the interior of the earth. Then it is even the case that the earth-soul, which is resting in the earth, sustains the life of a multitude of elemental spirits. If a naturalistic worldview today believes that the seeds, which I plant in the soil in the autumn, merely lie there until the following spring, then this is not true. The seeds must be preserved and protected throughout the winter by the elemental spirits of the earth. And all this is connected with the fact that during the winter time the earth-soul is united with the earth-body.

Now let us take the opposite season, the time of St. John's. Just as we human beings inhale and exhale the air, meaning that sometimes it is inside us and sometimes outside us, so does the earth breathe in its soul. That is the case during the winter. And at the height of summer, at St. Johns tide, the earth-soul is completely exhaled, transported out into the far reaches of the cosmos. At that time, the earth-body has been emptied, as it were, of the earth-soul. The earth accompanies, with its soul, the events of the cosmos, the movement of the stars, and so on. This is why in ancient times, human beings had winter mysteries, in which they experienced the union of the earth-soul with the earth, and they had summer mysteries, in which they could perceive the secrets of the universe. They were able to do this by perceiving what the earth-soul experienced in its togetherness with the stars; for the human souls living in the initiates were able to follow the earth-soul out into the cosmic spaces.

That people had an awareness of these things can be seen from old remnants of certain traditions that still exist today. It is quite a while back now that I often sat together, right here in Berlin, with an astronomer who was very famous here,[†] and who strongly advocated for having Easter fall on, say, the first Sunday in April every year. He mentioned how disturbing it would be if this were not implemented and how terrible it was that Easter had to fall on the first Sunday after the first full moon after the spring equinox. Of course, it was no use citing reasons against his argument, because everything always came down to the fear that when Easter falls at a different time each year, it causes a dreadful disorder in the debit and credit columns of the bookkeepers' ledgers. This movement had already become quite prevalent. (By the way, I once mentioned the fact here that on the first page of the bookkeepers' books there is typically written "with God," but that, on the whole, what is in these books is not exactly "with God.")

Back in the times when the date of the Easter festival was determined according to the course of the stars—when the first Sunday after the first full moon after the spring equinox was consecrated to the sun—there was still an awareness of the fact that in wintertime, the earth-soul is in the earth; that in the St. John's season, the earth-soul is wholly outside in cosmic spaces; and that in the spring, the earth-soul is on its way to the cosmic spaces. And it is for this reason that the spring festival, Easter, cannot be set on a specific day based on the earth alone, but must instead conform with the constellations of the stars. There is a deep wisdom in this, a wisdom that stems from the times when human beings could, by means of an ancient instinctive clairvoyance, still perceive the spiritual nature of the course of the year. We must find our way to this again, and we can do this in a certain sense if we take up the tasks of the present time by linking them specifically to contemplations such as the ones we have undertaken here together.

I have already mentioned on occasion, including here, that some of the spiritual beings with whom human beings are united every night, in the way I have told you—for instance, with the Archangels through speech—that some of these beings are the reigning spiritual powers for a particular period of time. I have also mentioned that in the last third of the nineteenth century, the Michael age began—the age in which the spiritual being who is usually referred to as Michael in various records became the leading spirit for all matters related to human civilization—and that these things are repeated in cycles.

In ancient times, people still had some knowledge of all these spiritual events. The ancient Hebrews spoke of Yahweh, but they always spoke of the *countenance of Yahweh*, and in saying the word "countenance" they meant the Archangels who are the actual mediators between Yahweh and the earth. And when the Jewish people anticipated the Messiah's coming to the earth, they knew that it was the time of Michael, the time when Michael mediates Christ's activity on earth; but they did not recognize the significance of this fact within its deeper context. And now, since the 1870s, a time has come again for the earth, when the Michael power is the ruling spiritual power in the world, and when we must understand how to bring the spiritual into our actions, how to organize our lives out of the spirit—in service to Michael. Serving Michael means that we organize our lives not merely from the perspective of the material world, but that we have an awareness of the fact that the one whose mission it is to overcome the base ahrimanic powers—Michael—must become, one might say, the genius for the evolution of civilization. How can he do this? In point of fact, he can become our guiding spirit if we remember how we can connect, in a spiritual sense, with the course of the year again.

The great wisdom embodied in the whole cosmic cycle can truly be seen in the fact that we are able to connect the spring festival with the festival of the resurrection of Christ Jesus. The way this connection was determined historically is absolutely correct, as I have often explained, and was based on the knowledge that the spring festival—Easter—*can* only fall on a different day every year because it is viewed from the perspective of the other world. Only we, human beings living on the earth, have the short-sighted conception that time runs continuously, that one hour is always as long as the next. We calculate time only with our earthly tools, with mathematics; whereas, for the actual spiritual world, a cosmic hour is something living. In that world, no cosmic hour is the same as another, but is either longer or shorter. This means that there is always the possibility of error when we establish something from the perspective of the earth that should be determined from the perspective of the heavens. The festival of Easter is rightfully determined according to the heavens.

What kind of a festival is it? It is the festival that is meant to remind us, as it had once reminded people most vividly, that a God descended to earth and took up residence in the human being Jesus of

Nazareth, in order that humanity, at a time when it was approaching the development of the I, would be able in an appropriate manner to find the way back again through death into a spiritual life. I have often spoken about this here. Accordingly, the Easter festival is the festival in which the human being, through the Mystery of Golgotha, contemplates death and the immortality that follows it. We look at this spring festival in the right sense if we say to ourselves: Christ has confirmed the immortality of human beings in that he himself has conquered death. But we human beings can only understand the immortality of Christ Jesus properly if we embrace this understanding and make it our own during our earthly life, that is to say, if we enliven our relationship to the Mystery of Golgotha in our souls and if we can break free from the materialistic notion that seeks to disassociate anything spiritual from the Mystery of Golgotha. Today, people no longer want to acknowledge Christ at all, but only Jesus as "the simple man from Nazareth." People actually feel somewhat ashamed if, with their supposed scientific methods, they were to admit that the Mystery of Golgotha might contain a spiritual mystery in the middle of earthly existence, namely, the death and resurrection of a God.

If we experience this in a spiritual sense, however, then we are also preparing ourselves to experience other things spiritually. This is why it is so important that we, as human beings of the present time, first acquire the possibility of experiencing the Mystery of Golgotha as something purely spiritual. Then we will experience other things spiritually as well, and we will find the entry to the spiritual worlds, the paths to the spiritual worlds, through the Mystery of Golgotha. But then we must, starting from the Mystery of Golgotha, understand the resurrection while we are still living. And if we develop a perceptive understanding of the resurrection while we are alive, then this understanding will also enable us to go through death in the right way. In other words, death and resurrection in the Mystery of Golgotha are meant to instruct the human being to reverse the way these things interrelate—that is, to experience the resurrection inwardly within one's soul during life, so that, after this inner soul-resurrection, one can go through death in the right way. This is the experience that is the opposite of the Easter experience.

At Easter we should be able to immerse ourselves in the death and resurrection of Christ. But as human beings we also need the possibility to immerse ourselves in what is for us the resurrection of the soul, so that the resurrected soul of the human being may go through death in the right way. We acquire the right Easter mood in spring when we see how the plants germinate and sprout, how nature rises again, how nature overcomes the death of winter. And, if we then have experienced summer in the right way, then we can develop a feeling of certainty that the soul has ascended into cosmic expanses, that we are now approaching autumn, that September is coming, that the autumnal equinox is approaching. We see that the leaves, which in the spring had sprouted and turned green, are now becoming brownish, yellowish, and are dropping off; that the trees stand there, already partially bare of leaves; that nature is dying. And we will understand this dying nature if we see inside this process of decay, inside the approaching snow cover of the earth and then say to ourselves: The earth-soul is returning to the earth again, and it will be fully within the earth when the winter solstice will have arrived.

There is a way to experience this autumnal season with the same intensity as we experience the spring season. If we feel and perceive the death and resurrection of God in the spring and Easter season, then we can feel and perceive the resurrection and death of the human soul in the autumn—in other words, experience the resurrection during earthly life so that we may go through death in the right way. But then we must also understand what it signifies for us, for our present time, that the earth-soul is breathed out into the cosmic expanses during the St. John's season in the summer, unites there with the stars, and then comes back again. Those who have insight into the mysteries of this earthly cycle of the seasons over the course of the year, know that the Michael-power, which in earlier centuries did not come down to earth, is now coming down again through the forces of nature, meaning that we are now able to meet the approaching autumn, with its falling leaves, by perceiving in it the Michael-power as it comes down from the clouds to the earth.

It is true that one can find "Michael" written in calendars for this day [September 29], and that Michaelmas is considered a festival day among farmers. But we will only be able to experience the present time spiritually—meaning, in such a way that earthly human events are closely joined to natural events—if we become capable again of understanding the course of the year broadly enough to be able to give shape to annual festivals over the course of the year, as earlier peoples had given shape to them out of their ancient dreamlike clairvoyance. The ancients understood the year and established—based on these mysteries, which I could only describe briefly here today—the festivals of Christmas, Easter, St. John's. Today, people give each other presents at Christmas, and do some other things as well, but—and I have often explained this here when presenting Christmas or Easter lectures—very little remains of these old festival practices; everything has become traditional and superficial for people today. But if we shall once again come to understand the festivals, which we merely celebrate today but do not understand, then we will also have the strength to establish, out of a spiritual knowledge of the course of the year, a festival that will be right and meaningful for present-day humanity. This will become the Michael festival at the end of September, when autumn approaches, when the leaves wither, when the trees become bare, when nature moves toward decay (in the same way as it moves toward sprouting in the Easter festival), when we become aware, precisely from the wilting processes in nature, how the earth-soul unites with the earth, how it brings Michael with it from the clouds.

If we have the strength to create, out of the spirit, a festival that brings a sense of community into our social life again, then we shall have done it from the spirit; for then we shall have initiated something among us that has its origin in the spirit. It would indeed be more important than all other social musings and the like—which, in the current confused circumstances, can only lead to something meaningful if the spirit is present in them—it would be more important if, initially, a number of discerning people were to come together in order to establish, out of the cosmos, something like a Michaelmas festival on the earth again, a festival that would be worthy of the Easter festival, but, as an autumn festival, would be the counterpart to the Easter Festival. If people could commit to something like this—something for which the motivating impulse lies only in the spiritual world, but which could bring a communal feeling among people through festivals that would have been created in the immediate present, out of full, joyous human hearts—then this would result in something that unites people again socially. For in ancient times, the festivals created strong bonds and united human beings socially. Just think of what has been done, said, and thought for the sake of the festivals and during these festivals for the whole culture! This is what has permeated the physical world in a living way as a result of determining the times of these festivals directly out of the spirit.

If people today could decide to establish a Michaelmas festival at the end of September in a worthy manner, then that would be a deed of the greatest significance. For this to transpire, however, people would have to find the courage to do more than merely talk about outer social organizations and the like; instead, they would have to create something that unites the earth with the heavens, that connects physical conditions again to spiritual conditions. Then, because the spirit would be brought back into earthly conditions as a result of this, something would actually arise among human beings that would be a powerful impulse for the continuation of our civilization and of our whole life.

There is of course not enough time to describe for you what all this would engender in regard to scientific, religious, and artistic experiences—what would be brought about through such a grand-scale new festival created out of the spirit, just as through the ancient festivals—or to describe for you how much more important such a creation out of the spiritual world would be than all the social diatribes that are generated today. For what would be the significance of such a creation? It would mean a great deal for a true observation of the inner human being if I were able to discern, from observing someone, what that person really means, or whether I understand his or her words correctly. If, today, we can learn from observation how the whole cosmic cycle unfolds as autumn approaches, if we can unravel and decipher the whole physiognomy of the universe and then work creatively out of this insight—then we shall unveil not only the will of human beings engaged in creating such a festival, but also the will of gods and spiritual beings. Then, spirit will be among human beings again!

But what is really happening today is that the spiritual is taken up in a peculiar way in the world. In conclusion, I may perhaps be permitted to say a few words in connection with what I said at the start. I have already had to point out several times how a certain phrase was injected into the world. It originated from a very subordinate Masonic division, was then repeated in a variety of astrological writings, and was then taken up by all our opponents for quite some time. It stated that "more than enough spiritual fire-sparks have flown though the Goetheanum in Dornach; the time will come when a physical spark of fire will fly into this Goetheanum."† People have been writing this already for two years. This is how the things that are truly created out of the spirit are received in the world today!

At the other end of the spectrum there must be people who are able to become entirely earnest about how they take up the spiritual. One cannot be fully in earnest by speaking about the spirit alone, but rather by speaking about the spirit in a way that can actually spread the spirit among us human beings. We would be able to spread the spirit in this way if we were to work creatively out of the spirit, just as in ancient times people created out of the spirit. I have often had the opportunity to speak with you about Christmas and Easter, that is, about the old festivals. And it is beautiful to derive the spirit of the old festivals from the course of time! However, what I would prefer is that people not only understand when anthroposophy brings to the surface what ancient wisdom knew, but I would wish that people could also understand what speaks to us as an appeal from the spirit of our own time, our immediate present. It is not enough to simply view the gospels as an expression of Christianity, because Christ said: "I am with you always, even unto the end of the earth's cycles of time" (Matthew 28:20). He is here! If we understand his spirit, his words, then we will be able to speak out of this spirit every day.

The very quality that enabled the ancients to work creatively out of a cosmic wisdom and also makes it possible for us today to reveal the profound meaning of the festivals—this certainly still lives among us. After all, we aspire to be complete human beings. But then we must also be able to work and create spiritually as complete human beings. Then we must be able not just to reflect on the meaning of the old festivals, but rather become socially creative ourselves, by becoming human beings who can create festivals out of an awareness of the course of the year.

This, however, demands more of human beings than simply interpreting the old, long-established festivals; for this is actually a real anthroposophy, a higher anthroposophy. And the true value of the Anthroposophical Society can only be assessed by verifying whether it understands not only dead anthroposophy, which concerns itself with what is past, but whether it also understands living anthroposophy. Living anthroposophy can also be a sum of flaming sparks! But these sparks of fire will be inside a temple that is not made of external material. Physical flames consume temples that consist of outer materials. The flames of genuine spiritual enthusiasm, of true spiritual life—which must permeate the temple because they must illuminate it with what lights up in the spirit—these flames cannot destroy the temple; they can only give an ever more glorious form to this temple. Let us think of what living anthroposophy is; let us think of it as the fiery flame that will lead us ever further, like the living spirit of anthroposophy itself—which shall lead us to the further evolution of humanity and to the rebuilding of what is now in such an evident decline.

This is what I wanted to tell you during my present visit to Berlin,[†] my dear friends, because it is good to discuss such serious matters now, especially since we are so rarely able to be together. I hope that these contemplations will also lead us to a true togetherness in thought. For, anthroposophy should work in the spirit, not just in physical space. And so, let me express my farewell greetings to you with the hope that we may remain together in spirit, even though we must now be separated spatially again for a longer period of time.

EDITORIAL AND REFERENCE NOTES

On this edition

On the structure of the volume: The present volume is structured thematically rather than chronologically. In the present order, the Bern lecture of April 6, 1923, the four Stuttgart lectures of May 2, June 21, July 4 and 11, 1923, and the first of the two Prague lectures, held on April 28, 1923, are more closely related. Their central theme consists in the various ways in which the life of the soul is connected with the spiritual world and its beings. Although they also take up this theme, the lectures in the second part of the volume culminate in explanations of the necessity of a spiritual deepening of the seasonal festivals. Thus the second of the Prague lectures on April 29 ends with an Easter reflection. The subsequent Dornach lecture of May 7, 1923, opens up new aspects of the Ascension and the Pentecost event. This is followed by the Dornach St. John's lecture of June 24, 1923. The Dornach lecture of April 13, 1923, which is also included in the second part of the volume, has the strongest correspondences to the first three lectures in terms of content, but was placed here because it contains fundamental statements on the prerequisites of a Michael festival. This is followed by the lecture of May 23, 1923, the last that Rudolf Steiner ever gave in Berlin, in which he sheds light on the origin of the traditional yearly festivals and the establishment of a Michaelmas autumn festival as a counterpart to the movable Easter spring festival out of cosmic-earthly contexts.

Text documents: The lectures from Bern, Dornach, and Berlin were stenographically recorded by Helene Finckh (1883–1960) and transcribed into plain text. The printed text is based on this transcription. For the 2nd edition in 1986, questionable passages were compared with the original stenogram. There are no original stenograms for the lectures in Prague and Stuttgart, and the stenographers are not known.

Although the transcript of the Stuttgart lecture of July 11, 1923, is inadequate, it has been included in this volume because of its importance for the overall context. Rudolf Steiner gave it on the evening of the same day on which he had opened a cycle of four lectures for theologians of The Christian Community.

The introduction to the lecture in Prague on April 28, 1923, and the conclusion of the lecture in Dornach on May 7, 1923, appear in GA 259.

Anna-Maria Balaster and Michel Schweizer were responsible for reviewing the 2nd edition of 1983 and for compiling the notes.

The titles of the lectures were mostly borrowed from Marie Steiner's earlier editions.

On the blackboard drawings: Beginning in 1919, Rudolf Steiner's blackboard drawings, which he often made during his lectures, were recorded using sheets of black paper that were then rolled up and saved. Roughly 1,100 such drawings were preserved in this way. Rudolf Steiner's original blackboard drawings and inscriptions from the lectures in Dornach on May 7 and April 13, 1923, are reproduced in reduced size at the end of this volume.

Notes on the text

Works by Rudolf Steiner within the Collected Works (CW) are indicated in the notes with the bibliographic number. See also the overview at the end of the volume.

1 **yesterday's public lecture**
The Aims of Anthroposophy and the Purpose of the Goetheanum, Bern, April 5, 1923. This lecture was not published. But a parallel lecture, given in Basel on April 9, 1923, is included in the lecture cycle with the same name (CW 84).

7 ***Esoteric Science***
Rudolf Steiner, *An Outline of Esoteric Science* (CW 13).

the Archangeloi, the Archangels
In his books and lectures, Rudolf Steiner frequently refers to the nine hierarchies of spiritual, angelic beings. These were already described by Dionysius the Areopagite, a disciple of Paul, in his book, *Celestial Hierarchies*. There, the nine hierarchies are designated, in descending order: the Seraphim (Spirits of Love), Cherubim (Spirits of Harmony), Thrones (Spirits of Will), Kyriotetes (Spirits of Wisdom), Dynamis (Spirits of Movement), Exusiai (Spirits of Form), Archai (Spirits of Personality), Archangeloi, Archangels (Spirits of Fire), and Angeloi, Angels (Sons of Life). Rudolf Steiner sometimes uses these Greek and Hebrew names and at other times his own designations here given in parentheses.

in earlier lecture courses
Particularly in *The Mission of Folk Souls* (CW 121), also in *Cosmosophy, Volume I* (CW 207), and in *The Driving Force of Spiritual Powers in World History* (CW 222).

8 **arise**
Here, Rudolf Steiner uses a forceful word (*herausringen*): to struggle, to wrestle out of (the human soul).

10 **karma or destiny**
"Karma" is a Sanskrit word that refers to the laws of human destiny as it unfolds over many incarnations. *Karma* and *reincarnation* are two fundamental concepts in anthroposophy.

13 **construct**
Here, Rudolf Steiner uses a metaphor related to carpentry (*zimmern*); so, literally: "how we 'hammer/carpenter' our next life."

in previous lectures
Especially in *Manifestations of Karma* (CW 120) and *Reincarnation and Karma: Two Fundamental Truths of Human Existence* (CW 135).

17 **Logos**
The Logos (Greek for "Word") is the creative word-power which, according to the Gospel of St. John (1:1), gave rise to the whole creation ("In the beginning was the Word"). Additional aspects of the Logos are described in some of the other lectures contained in the present volume.

the Exusiai and the Kyriotetes
See first two notes to page 7.

19 **Jupiter phase of evolution**
Rudolf Steiner describes three earlier embodiments of the Earth: (old) Saturn, (old) Sun, and (old) Moon; and that the Earth incarnation itself will then be followed by the future evolutionary phases of Jupiter, Venus, and Vulcan. The "Jupiter phase of evolution," therefore, refers to the next, future, embodiment of the Earth. See *An Outline of Esoteric Science* (CW 13), chapter 4.

20 ***Philosophy of Freedom***
Rudolf Steiner, *The Philosophy of Freedom* (CW 4).

21 **described yesterday**
See note to page 1.

first stage of suprasensory cognition
Rudolf Steiner refers to *imagination*, *inspiration*, and *intuition* as three progressive stages of higher spiritual consciousness that can be achieved by pursuing the path described in *Knowledge of the Higher Worlds* (CW 10) and in the fifth chapter of *An Outline of Esoteric Science* (CW 13).

29 **Exusiai**
See second note to page 7.

32 **in the periodical *Lucifer-Gnosis***
See *Lucifer-Gnosis, Grundlegende Aufsätze zur Anthroposophie und Berichte aus den Zeitschriften "Luzifer" und "Lucifer-Gnosis" 1903–1908* [Lucifer-Gnosis: Foundational essays on anthroposophy and reports from the periodicals "Lucifer" and "Lucifer-Gnosis" 1903–1908] (GA 34).

34 **my book *Theosophy***
Rudolf Steiner, *Theosophy* (CW 9).

35 Raphael
Raffaello Sanzio da Urbino (1483–1520), Italian painter; one of the great masters of the Renaissance.

38 Leibnitz and Giordano Bruno
Gottfried Wilhelm Leibniz (1646–1716), mathematician, philosopher, scientist, and diplomat. His *Monadologia* was published in 1714. According to Leibniz, the universe contains only God and non-composite, immaterial, soul-like entities called *monads*, which have no causal relation with other monads, but are perfectly synchronized with each other by God in a "pre-established harmony."

Giordano Bruno (1548–1600), Italian Dominican friar, philosopher, mathematician, and astronomer. His *De Monade, Numero et Figura Liber* was published in 1591. There, he described three fundamental types: God, souls, and atoms. According to Bruno, there are innumerable "Minima" or "Monads," right up to "the Monad of all Monads"—God.

44 the German philosopher Hegel
Georg Wilhelm Friedrich Hegel (1770–1831), German philosopher, one of the most influential figures of German idealism and nineteenth century philosophy. In his *Lectures on the History of Philosophy*, Hegel states: "What the human being has that is nobler than being an animal, he has because of the faculty of thinking; everything that is human, no matter how it appears, is only human because thinking is at work and has worked in it" (*Friedr. Wilh. Hegels Vorlesungen über die Geschichte der Philosophie* [Friedr. Wilh. Hegel's lectures on the history of philosophy], ed. G. J. P. J. Bolland [Leiden, 1908], p. 7).

55 characterized in Dornach
See *The Anthroposophic Movement: The History and Conditions of the Anthroposophical Movement in Relation to the Anthroposophical Society: An Encouragement for Self-Examination* (CW 258).

59 continually transfused
Literally, "bubbled/fizzled through" (*durchsprudelt*).

63 Mauthner wrote his *Critique of Language*
Fritz Mauthner (1849–1923), German author, journalist, novelist, philosopher, and literary critic. In his *Beiträge zu einer Kritik der Sprache* [Contributions to a critique of language], vol. II, 3rd. ed., (Leipzig, 1923), p. 77, it states: "We cannot imagine it any other way than that language, as an expression of the speech organ, is inherited—just as life, as an expression of the individual animal organism, is inherited." And further on (vol. III, p. 223): "One of the most important points in the science of language-criticism is that we recognize the connection, or rather the lack of connection,

between the world of reality and the sounds of speech. There has never, ever, been anything originally in the sounds of speech that has a direct or indirect relationship to an object in the world of reality."

64 still utter the word "soul"
See Mauthner, *Beiträge zu einer Kritik der Sprache* [Contributions to a critique of language] vol. I, 3rd. ed. (Leipzig, 1923), p. 253: "From the philosophy of Descartes to that of today's ministers and cooks, it has been assumed that only human beings have a soul; we will have to get used to realizing that the soul is an exclusively human attribute only to the extent that human beings possess a concept of a soul only in their language." Ibid., p. 259: "We should not at all believe that the notion 'soul' is the only one with which we play a merry-go-round, carousel-like game with an intangible substance. Such fantastical creations are always used whenever the material carrier of a particular appearance cannot be perceived. And no one takes offense at the very common words 'seeing,' 'hearing,' and 'feeling,' which are, in my opinion, relatively new formations. In like manner, one should speak of a 'soul-ing.'"

66 Professor Kuno Fischer
Kuno Fischer (1824–1907), German philosopher, critic, and historian of philosophy, considered a brilliant lecturer with a remarkable gift for clear presentation. He introduced the philosophical-aesthetic analysis of classical poetry.

71 Max Rubner
Max Rubner (1854–1932), known for his research in metabolism, energy physiology, hygiene, and dietary thermogenesis.

74 Albert Schweitzer
Albert Schweitzer (1875–1965), theologian, organist, musicologist, writer, humanitarian, philosopher, and physician. His book *Decline and Reconstruction of Culture* was published in 1923. Rudolf Steiner uses a number of quotes from this book throughout this lecture.

75 Kant-Laplace theory
The "nebular hypothesis"—first put forward in general terms by Immanuel Kant (1724–1804) in 1775, and then elaborated more specifically by the French astronomer and mathematician, Pierre Simon Laplace (1749–1827) in 1796—is the idea that the solar system was formed through condensation out of matter orbiting the early sun. Hence the term "Kant-Laplace."

85 square of the distance
This refers to Newton's *law of universal gravitation*, which states that "every particle attracts every other particle in the universe with a force that is proportional to the product of their masses and inversely proportional to the

square of the distance between their centers"; Isaac Newton (1642–1727), English mathematician, physicist, astronomer, alchemist, theologian.

92 in such a bad way
In this section of the text, the stenography is incomplete.

96 applied to the soul
Here, Rudolf Steiner uses a poignant word (*hineinschieben*), literally, "pushed into" the soul.

"souling"
See notes to pages 63 and 64.

is also vain
I Corinthians 15:14 (Updated King James Version).

98 Goethe
Johann Wolfgang von Goethe (1749–1832), German poet, playwright, scientist, and statesman.

100 contemporary philosopher
This refers to Wincenty Lutoslawski (1863–1954), Polish philosopher, scholar, publicist, social activist. He had written an article in 1910/11 about Rudolf Steiner's "so-called Esoteric Science" in *Hochland - Monatsschrift für alle Gebiete des Wissens, der Literatur und Kunst* [Highland - Magazine for all fields of knowledge, literature, and art].

102 Anthroposophical Society and the Free Anthroposophical Society
In February 1923, Rudolf Steiner had inaugurated the Free Anthroposophical Society, as a separate society; see CW 259, as well as the Introduction to the present volume.

103 yesterday's public lecture
This refers to the lecture given in Prague on April 27, 1923, on "The Eternity of the Soul in the Light of Anthroposophy," included in *The Aims of Anthroposophy and the Purpose of the Goetheanum* (CW 84).

105 as Angeloi, Angels
See second note to page 7.

109 Schiller
Friedrich Schiller (1759–1805), German playwright, poet, philosopher, and historian.

111 Jupiter existence
See note to page 19.

123 Gnostic
Gnosticism developed in the late first century AD among Jewish and early Christian sects. According to Rudolf Steiner, the Gnostics viewed Christ primarily as a cosmic being.

124 **Augustine**
Aurelius Augustinus Hipponensis (AD 354–430), theologian and philosopher. His writings influenced the development of Western philosophy and Western Christianity. His many important works include *The City of God* and *On Christian Doctrine*. He speaks of his inner development in his book *Confessions*.

Manichaean
Manichaeism, formerly a major religion, teaches a dualistic cosmology, describing the struggle between a good, spiritual world of light, and an evil, material world of darkness. Manichaeism was founded in the third century AD by the Persian, Mani (216–277).

Scholastics
Scholasticism was a medieval school of philosophy that employed a critical, organic method of philosophical analysis based on Aristotelian logic and the writings of the early Church Fathers. Its aim was a synthesis of learning. Principal figures in early Scholasticism were Peter Abelard, Anselm of Canterbury, and Albertus Magnus. The movement flourished in the thirteenth century, drawing on the writings and doctrines of Thomas Aquinas.

125 **simple man from Nazareth**
See, for example, Heinrich Weinel (1874–1936), *Jesus im neunzehnten Jahrhundert* [Jesus in the Nineteenth Century], and *Die Gleichnisse Jesu* [The Parables of Jesus].

historian Ranke
Leopold von Ranke (1795–1886), German historian and founder of modern source-based history. As a researcher, he focused on the importance of primary sources and narrative history. See Herman Grimm, *Fragmente* [Fragments], vol. II (Berlin and Stuttgart, 1902), p. 174f.: "Someone who highly respected Ranke is said to have demanded of him that Christ be included in world history as the originator of all human destinies. This request, it is reported, caused the historian to have a fierce inner struggle, but was finally rejected with the explanation that it must suffice that Christ stands before us in world history in two forms: as the founder of Christianity and as the superhuman all-powerful Son of God, as the Church teaches."

128 **Kingdom of God has come down to earth**
Mark 1:15: "And saying, the time is fulfilled, and the kingdom of God is at hand: repent all of you, and believe the gospel"; Luke 10:9: "And heal the sick that are therein, and say unto them, The kingdom of God has come nigh unto you" (Updated King James Version).

Eduard Suess
Eduard Suess (1831–1914), Austrian geologist who helped lay the foundations for paleogeography and tectonics; he was professor of geology in Vienna, president of the Vienna Academy of Sciences. The reference is

taken from *Das Antlitz der Erde* [The face of the earth], vol. III, (Prague and Leipzig, 1885–1909).

130 "Not I, but Christ in me"
For this important quote, Rudolf Steiner always uses a more concentrated version of the passage from Galatians 2:20, "I am crucified with Christ: nevertheless, I live; yet not I, but Christ lives in me: and the life which I now live in the flesh I live by the faith of the Son of God, who loved me, and gave himself for me" (Updated King James Version).

132 content and meaning of the gospels
Between 1907 and 1912 Rudolf Steiner had already presented several lecture cycles on the gospels:

1907: *True Knowledge of the Christ: Theosophy and Rosicrucianism—The Gospel of John* (CW 100)

1908: *The Gospel of John* (CW 103)

1908: *The Apocalypse of John* (CW 104)

1909: *The Gospel of John in Relation to the Three Other Gospels, Especially the Gospel of Luke* (CW 112)

1909: *The Gospel of Luke* (CW 114)

1909: *Deeper Secrets of Human Evolution in Light of the Gospels* (CW 117)

1910: *The Gospel of John and the Other Three Gospels* (CW 117a)

1910: *The Gospel of Matthew* (CW 123)

1910: *Background to the Gospel of Mark* (CW 124)

1912: *The Gospel of Mark* (CW 139)

133 *An Outline of Esoteric Science*
See note to page 19.

135 Eduard Suess
See second note to page 128.

136 *From Jesus to Christ*
From Jesus to Christ, course of eleven lectures held in Karlsruhe, Germany, from October 4–14, 1911 (CW 131).

146 this afternoon
This refers to the lecture titled "The Mood of St. John's and Experiencing the Festival Seasons" (Dornach, June 24, 1923) included in *The Birth and Development of Eurythmy* (CW 277).

147 around the world
The phrase "the fiery ride of the sun around the world" is taken from

the German poem "Sternenballade" [Ballad of the stars] by Ernst Moritz Arndt.

148 Fritz Mauthner
See notes to pages 63 and 64.

Klopstock
Friedrich Gottlieb Klopstock (1724–1803), German epic and lyric poet. His best-known epic poem is *The Messiah*, written between 1748 and 1773.

154 Klebs
Georg Klebs (1857–1918), German botanist and professor of botany; wrote *Über das Treiben der einheimischen Bäume speziell der Buche* [Regarding the forcing of native trees, specifically the beech tree] in 1914.

160 from Saturn to Vulcan
See note to page 19.

164 one of my lecture cycles
This refers to Rudolf Steiner's lecture cycle *The Mission of Folk Souls* (CW 121).

166 humanity
The Spiritual Guidance of the Individual and of Humanity (CW 15).

167 see Plate 2 in the appendix
The following is a rendering in English of the diagram in Plate 2:

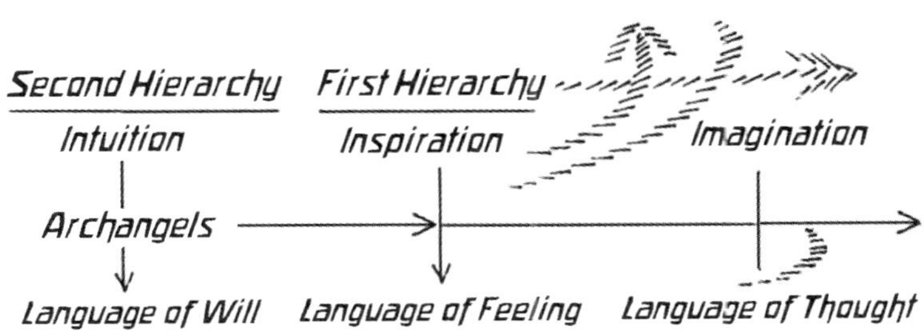

Herman Grimm, the art historian
Herman Grimm (1828–1901), German author, art historian, philosopher, and Goethe biographer. See Herman Grimm, *Goethe*, vol. II, lecture 16, 7th ed. (1903), p. 4f.: "It is only with the advent of Roman politics that people and things begin to become understandable to us. That is when we are in a position to measure events with the same yardstick as is still used today. Everything Greek, right up into the most solidly historical times, retains something fairytale-like to us. Alcibiades is purely a fairytale prince, compared to Caesar, who, despite having so much blackness, does not

show a single obscured spot. . . We will never be able to get beyond this alien aspect in the Greek character. . . Therefore, no matter how familiar Homer and Plato, even Aristotle and Thucydides, or Phidias and Pindar may seem to us, there is always a small halfmoon in their nails reminding us of something like Ichor, the blood of the gods, a last drop of which was still streaming into the veins of the Greeks. In the case of the Romans, this fairytale element is completely lacking. In them, there is no trace left of mythical origins, and they can, from the very first moment, be understood as politicians, legal scholars, soldiers, officials, merchants."

167 Cicero and Caesar
Marcus Tullius Cicero (106–43 BC), Roman statesman, lawyer, scholar, and writer. Gaius Julius Caesar (100–44 BC), Roman general, politician, and statesman.

168 Pericles or Alcibiades
Pericles (c. 500–429 BC), Athenian general and statesman. Alcibiades (c. 450–404 BC), Athenian statesman and military commander.

Wilamowitz
Ulrich von Wilamowitz-Moellendorff (1848–1931), German classical scholar and philologist; wrote *The Greek Tragedies Translated*, 4 volumes.

translations by Deussen
Paul Deussen (1845–1919), German Orientalist and Sanskrit scholar; wrote *System of the Vedanta*, 1887; *Sixty Upanisads of the Veda* (2 Volumes), 1897; *Outlines of Indian Philosophy*, 1907.

169 Plato
Plato (427–347 BC), Greek philosopher, born in Athens during the classical period in ancient Greece; pupil of Socrates and teacher of Aristotle. He founded the Academy, the first institution of higher learning in the Western world.

Aristotle
Aristotle (384–322 BC), Greek philosopher. His writings span a wide range of disciplines, from metaphysics, logic to ethics, politics, rhetoric and more.

170 Dionysius the Areopagite
Dionysius the Areopagite, an Athenian judge at the Areopagus Court in Athens, lived in the first century. He is referred to in Acts 17:34 as a disciple of Paul. The books *On the Celestial Hierarchy* and *On the Ecclesiastical Hierarchy* were published under his name at the end of the fifth century. They were translated into Latin by Scotus Erigena in the ninth century. See second note to page 7.

177 painful event
The first Goetheanum, built entirely out of wood as an artistic expression of the whole of anthroposophy, burned down on New Year's Eve 1922/23.

Rudolf Steiner describes this building in *Paths to a New Style of Architecture* (CW 286) and *Toward a New Theory of Architecture: The First Goetheanum in Pictures* (CW 290).

179 **Broca's convolution**
Pierre Paul Broca (1824–1880), French physician, anatomist, and anthropologist. He identified the posterior third left frontal convolution of the human brain as a critical area for speech production.

182 **major and minor keys**
Rudolf Steiner goes into more detail regarding the various musical intervals, and how they were experienced both during the Atlantean and the post-Atlantean times, in lectures given two months before this one—particularly the lectures of March 7, 8, and 16, 1923; see *The Inner Nature of Music and the Experience of Tone* (CW 283).

183 **Jean Paul**
Jean Paul, born Johann Paul Friedrich Richter (1763–1825), German writer, best known for his humorous novels and stories. The quote is taken from *Levana: Or the Doctrine of Education*, a philosophical treatise on the subject of education.

185 **Woodrow Wilson**
Woodrow Wilson (1856–1924), president of the United States from 1912–1920. In his speech, "A Program for World Peace: Speeches to the U.S Congress," on January 8, 1918, he presented fourteen points that were to form the principles for a general world peace. In later speeches to Congress, he expanded these fourteen points to a total of twenty-seven principles of peace, among which "the right of peoples to self-determination" occupied a special place.

187 **second condition after death**
Rudolf Steiner also refers to this second condition as *Kamaloka*. It is the period during which the soul frees itself from all inclinations toward physical existence, and experiences its whole life once again, but this time *not* from the personal perspective but from the perspective of those affected by one's actions. See *Theosophy* (CW 9), chapter 3, and *An Outline of Esoteric Science* (CW 13), chapter 3.

189 **as an illustration**
Rudolf Steiner spoke about this particular dream, for instance, in the public lecture of March 21, 1918, in Berlin (CW 67); in the public lecture of March 7, 1904, in Berlin (CW 52); and on November 23, 1911 (CW 61).

Volkelt
In the lecture of March 21, 1918 (see the previous note), Rudolf Steiner discusses two sources of this dream: one by Johannes Volkelt (1848–1930), and the other by Friedrich Theodor Vischer (1807–1887). The example

cited in the present lecture can, however, only be found in the study by Vischer and not in the study by Volkelt.

194 Waldorf School pedagogy
This pedagogy, based on the anthroposophical understanding of the growing child, has now developed into one of the largest independent school movements in the world. With Rudolf Steiner's help, the first Waldorf school opened in Stuttgart, Germany, in 1919. Rudolf Steiner's remarks in this section of the lecture refer to this first school.

196 astronomer who was very famous here
This refers to Wilhelm Foerster (1832–1921), director of the Berlin Observatory, co-founder of the Urania in Berlin, an institution for astronomical education that reached out to the wider public.

203 into this Goetheanum
This refers to a magazine article in *Der Leuchtturm*, Lorch (Württemberg), of October 1920, as quoted by Elsbeth Ebertin in the yearbook *Ein Blick in die Zukunft? Den Freunden der wissenschaftlichen Astrologie* [A look into the future? For the friends of scientific astrology] (Freiburg [Baden], 1921]. There, it states on page 63: "Spiritual sparks of fire, hissing in lightning-like fashion at the wooden mousetrap [meaning the Goetheanum], are therefore available in sufficient quantities, and it will require some cleverness on Steiner's part to work in a conciliatory manner lest, one day, a real spark of fire will bring an inglorious end to the glory of Dornach."

204 my present visit to Berlin
This lecture was the last one Rudolf Steiner gave in Berlin.

RUDOLF STEINER'S COLLECTED WORKS

The German Edition of Rudolf Steiner's Collected Works (the *Gesamtausgabe* [GA], published by Rudolf Steiner Verlag, Dornach, Switzerland) will be completed in the year 2025. The works are organized either by type of work (written, spoken, artistic creations), chronology, audience (public or other), or subject (education, art, etc.). For ease of comparison, the Collected Works in English (CW), listed below, follows the German organization and numbering.

The volumes that have so far been published in the English Collected Works edition appear *in italics with their published titles*; all other volumes, including those that have appeared in editions other than the CW, are set in Roman type with *literal translations* of the German titles. Published English titles are not necessarily the same as the German.

This list is current as of the date of this volume's publication.

A. Written Works

I. Writings 1884–1925

CW 1	Introductions and Selected Commentary on Goethe's Natural-scientific Writings
CW 1a–e	Goethe's Natural-scientific Writings
CW 1f	Editorial Afterwords to Goethe's Natural-scientific Writings in the Weimar Edition (1891–1896)
CW 2	*Goethe's Theory of Knowledge: An Outline of the Epistemology of His Worldview*
CW 3	Truth and Science
CW 4	The Philosophy of Freedom
CW 4a	Documents to "The Philosophy of Freedom"
CW 5	Friedrich Nietzsche, A Fighter against His Own Time
CW 6	Goethe's Worldview
CW 7	Mysticism at the Dawn of Modern Spiritual Life and Its Relationship with Modern Worldviews
CW 8	*Christianity as Mystical Fact and the Mysteries of Antiquity*
CW 9	Theosophy: An Introduction into Supersensible World Knowledge and Human Purpose
CW 10	How Does One Attain Knowledge of Higher Worlds?
CW 11	From the Akasha-Chronicle
CW 12	Levels of Higher Knowledge
CW 13	Occult Science in Outline
CW 14	*Four Modern Mystery Dramas*
CW 15	The Spiritual Guidance of the Individual and Humanity
CW 16/17	*A Way of Self-Knowledge & The Threshold of the Spiritual World*

CW 18 The Riddles of Philosophy in Their History, Presented as an Outline
CW 18a Views of the World and of Life in the Nineteenth Century
CW 19 Thoughts during the Time of War (1915) and Further Texts on the Events of the World War (1917–1921)
CW 20 The Riddles of the Human Being: Articulated and Unarticulated in the Thinking, Views and Opinions of a Series of German and Austrian Personalities
CW 21 The Riddles of the Soul
CW 22 Goethe's Spiritual Nature and Its Revelation in "Faust" and through the "Fairy Tale of the Snake and the Lily"
CW 23 The Central Points of the Social Question in the Necessities of Life in the Present and the Future
CW 24 Essays Concerning the Threefold Division of the Social Organism and the Period 1915–1921
CW 25 Three Steps of Anthroposophy. Philosophy – Cosmology – Religion
CW 26 Anthroposophical Leading Thoughts
CW 27 Fundamentals for Expansion of the Art of Healing according to Spiritual-Scientific Insights
CW 28 *Autobiography: Chapters in the Course of My Life: 1861–1907*

II. Collected Essays

CW 29 Collected Essays on Dramaturgy, 1889–1900
CW 30 Methodical Foundations of Anthroposophy: Collected Essays on Philosophy, Natural Science, Aesthetics and Psychology, 1884–1901
CW 31 Collected Essays on Culture and Current Events, 1887–1901
CW 32 Collected Essays on Literature, 1884–1902
CW 33 Biographies and Biographical Sketches, 1894–1905
CW 34 Lucifer-Gnosis: Foundational Essays on Anthroposophy and Reports from the Periodicals "Luzifer" and "Lucifer-Gnosis," 1903–1908
CW 35 Philosophy and Anthroposophy: Collected Essays, 1904–1923
CW 36 The Goetheanum-Idea in the Middle of the Cultural Crisis of the Present: Collected Essays from the Periodical "Das Goetheanum," 1921–1925
CW 37 Writings on the History of the Anthroposophical Movement and Society 1902–1925

III. Publications from the Literary Estate

CW 38/1 Complete Letters, Vol. 1: Weimar Period 1879–1890

CW 38/2 Complete Letters, Vol. 2: Weimar Period 1890–1897
CW 38/3 Complete Letters, Vol. 3: Early Berlin Period 1897–1905 [forthcoming]
CW 38/4 Complete Letters, Vol. 4: Activity within the Theosophical Society 1905–1912 [forthcoming]
CW 38/5 Complete Letters, Vol. 5: From the Founding of the Anthroposophical Society to the Opening of the Goetheanum 1913–1920 [forthcoming]
CW 38/6 Complete Letters, Vol. 6: The Last Years 1920–1925 [forthcoming]
CW 40 Truth-Wrought Words
CW 40a Sayings, Poems and Mantras; Supplementary Volume
CW 41a Translations and Free Renderings from the Old and New Testaments
CW 41b Translations and Free Renderings of Various Works
CW 42 Stage Adaptations I: Dramas by Edouard Schuré
CW 43 Stage Adaptations II: The Oberufer Christmas Plays
CW 44 Sketches, Fragments and Paralipomena on the Four Mystery Dramas
CW 45 Anthroposophy: A Fragment from the Year 1910
CW 46 Posthumous Essays and Fragments 1879–1924
CW 47/48 Notebooks and Notepads (digital edition)
CW 49 Notes for and about Helmuth and Eliza von Moltke and Relatives, 1904–1924 [forthcoming]
CW 50 [Blank number]

B. Lectures

I. Public Lectures

CW 51 *On Philosophy, History, and Literature: Lectures at the Worker Education School and the Independent College, Berlin, 1901–1905*
CW 52 Spiritual Teachings Concerning the Soul and Observation of the World
CW 53 The Origin and Goal of the Human Being
CW 54 The Riddles of the World and Anthroposophy
CW 55 Knowledge of the Supersensible in Our Times and Its Meaning for Life Today
CW 56 Knowledge of the Soul and of the Spirit
CW 57 Where and How Does One Find the Spirit?
CW 58 The Metamorphoses of the Soul Life. Paths of Soul Experiences: Part One
CW 59 The Metamorphoses of the Soul Life. Paths of Soul Experiences: Part Two

CW 60 The Answers of Spiritual Science to the Biggest Questions of Existence
CW 61 Human History in the Light of Spiritual Research
CW 62 *Results of Spiritual Research*
CW 63 Spiritual Science as a Treasure for Life
CW 64 Out of Destiny-Burdened Times
CW 65 Out of Central European Spiritual Life
CW 66 Spirit and Matter, Life and Death
CW 67 The Eternal in the Human Soul. Immortality and Freedom
CW 68a On the Being of Christianity
CW 68b The Cycle of the Human Being within the Sense-, Soul-, and Spirit-World
CW 68c Goethe and the Present
CW 68d The Being of Man in the Light of Spiritual Science
CW 69a Truths and Errors of Spiritual Research. Spiritual Science and the Future of Mankind
CW 69b Knowledge and Immortality
CW 69c New Christ-Experience
CW 69d Death and Immortality in the Light of Spiritual Science
CW 69e Spiritual Science and the Spiritual Goals of Our Time
CW 70a Human Soul, Destiny and Death
CW 70b Paths to the Knowledge of the Eternal Powers of the Human Soul
CW 71a Soul Immortality [forthcoming]
CW 71b The Human Being as a Soul and Spirit Being
CW 72 Freedom – Immortality – Social Life
CW 73 The Supplementing of the Modern Sciences through Anthroposophy
CW 73a Specialized Fields of Knowledge and Anthroposophy
CW 74 The Philosophy of Thomas Aquinas
CW 75 *Anthroposophy and the Natural Sciences: Foundations and Methods*
CW 76 The Fructifying Effect of Anthroposophy on Specialized Fields
CW 77a The Task of Anthroposophy in Relation to Science and Life: The Darmstadt College Course
CW 77b Art and Anthroposophy. The Goetheanum-Impulse
CW 78 Anthroposophy, Its Roots of Knowledge and Fruits for Life
CW 79 The Reality of the Higher Worlds
CW 80a The Being of Anthroposophy
CW 80b The Inner Realm of Nature and the Being of the Human Soul
CW 80c Anthroposophical Spiritual Science and the Great Civilizational Questions of the Present
CW 81 *Reimagining Academic Studies: Science, Philosophy, Education, Social Science, Theology, Theory of Language*

CW 82 *Becoming Fully Human: The Significance of Anthroposophy in Contemporary Spiritual Life*
CW 83 *The Tension between East and West*
CW 84 *The Aims of Anthroposophy and the Purpose of the Goetheanum*
CW 85 Supplementary Volume: Individual Public Lectures I [forthcoming]
CW 86 Supplementary Volume: Individual Public Lectures II [forthcoming]

II. Lectures to the Members of the Anthroposophical Society

CW 87 Ancient Mysteries and Christianity
CW 88 *Concerning the Astral World and Devachan*
CW 89 Consciousness – Life – Form. Fundamental Principles of a Spiritual-Scientific Cosmology
CW 90a Self-knowledge and Knowledge of the Divine, Vol. I. Theosophy, Christology, and Mythology
CW 90b Self-knowledge and Knowledge of the Divine, Vol. II. Theosophy, Christology, and Mythology
CW 90c Theosophy and Occultism
CW 91 Cosmology and Human Evolution. Introduction to Theosophy – Theory of Colors
CW 92 *The Occult Truths of Myths and Legends: Greek and Germanic Mythology: Richard Wagner in the Light of Spiritual Science*
CW 93 The Temple Legend and the Golden Legend as a Symbolic Expression of Past and Future Secrets of Human Development. From the Contents of the Esoteric School
CW 93a Fundamentals of Esotericism
CW 94 Cosmogony. Popular Occultism. The Gospel of John. Theosophy Based on the Gospel of John
CW 95 *Founding a Science of the Spirit*
CW 96 Origin-Impulses of Spiritual Science. Christian Esotericism in the Light of New Spirit-knowledge
CW 97 The Christian Mystery
CW 98 *Nature Beings and Spirit Beings: Their Activity in Our Visible World*
CW 99 The Theosophy of the Rosicrucians
CW 100 *True Knowledge of the Christ: Theosophy and Rosicucianism—The Gospel of John*
CW 101 Myths and Legends. Occult Signs and Symbols
CW 102 *Good and Evil Spirits and Their Influence on Humanity*
CW 103 *The Gospel of John*
CW 104 The Apocalypse of John
CW 104a From the Picture-Script of the Apocalypse of John
CW 105 *Universe, Earth, Human Being: Their Relationship to Egyptian Myths and Modern Civilization*

CW 106	Egyptian Myths and Mysteries in Relation to the Active Spiritual Forces of the Present
CW 107	*Disease, Karma, and Healing: Spiritual-scientific Enquiries into the Nature of the Human Being*
CW 108	Answering the Questions of Life and the World through Anthroposophy
CW 109	The Principle of Spiritual Economy in Connection with the Question of Reincarnation. An Aspect of the Spiritual Guidance of Humanity
CW 110	*The Spiritual Hierarchies and the Physical World: Zodiac, Planets, and Cosmos*
CW 111	Introduction to the Foundations of Theosophy
CW 112	The Gospel of John in Relation to the Three Other Gospels, Especially the Gospel of Luke
CW 113	The Orient in the Light of the Occident. The Children of Lucifer and the Brothers of Christ
CW 114	The Gospel of Luke
CW 115	Anthroposophy – Psychosophy – Pneumatosophy
CW 116	*The Christ-Impulse and the Development of Ego-Consciousness*
CW 117	*Deeper Secrets of Human Evolution in Light of the Gospels*
CW 117a	*The Gospel of John and the Other Three Gospels*
CW 118	The Event of the Christ-Appearance in the Etheric World
CW 119	*Macrocosm and Microcosm: The Greater and the Lesser World: Questions Concerning the Soul, Life and the Spirit*
CW 120	The Revelations of Karma
CW 121	*The Mission of Folk Souls*
CW 122	The Secrets of the Biblical Creation-Story. The Six-Day Work in the First Book of Moses
CW 123	The Gospel of Matthew
CW 124	*Background to the Gospel of St. Mark*
CW 125	*Paths and Goals of the Spiritual Human Being: Life Questions in the Light of Spiritual Science*
CW 126	Occult History. Esoteric Observations of the Karmic Relationships of Personalities and Events of World History
CW 127	*The Mission of the New Spiritual Revelation: The Pivotal Nature of the Christ Event in Earth Evolution*
CW 128	An Occult Physiology
CW 129	*Wonders of the World: Trials of the Soul, Revelations of the Spirit*
CW 130	Esoteric Christianity and the Spiritual Guidance of Humanity
CW 131	*From Jesus to Christ*
CW 132	*Inner Experiences of Evolution*
CW 133	*Earthly and Cosmic Man*

CW 134 *The World of the Senses and the World of the Spirit*
CW 135 Reincarnation and Karma and Their Meaning for the Culture of the Present
CW 136 *Spiritual Beings in the Heavenly Bodies and in the Kingdoms of Nature*
CW 137 The Human Being in the Light of Occultism, Theosophy and Philosophy
CW 138 On Initiation. On Eternity and the Passing Moment. On the Light of the Spirit and the Darkness of Life
CW 139 The Gospel of Mark
CW 140 Occult Investigation into the Life between Death and New Birth. The Living Interaction between Life and Death
CW 141 *Between Death and Rebirth: In Relation to Cosmic Facts*
CW 142/46 *The Bhagavad Gita and the West: The Esoteric Significance of the Bhagavad Gita and Its Relation to the Epistles of Paul*
CW 143 *Three Paths to Christ: Experiencing the Supersensible*
CW 144 *The Mysteries of Initiation: From Isis to the Holy Grail*
CW 145 What Significance Does Occult Development of the Human Being Have for the Sheaths – Physical Body, Etheric Body, Astral Body, and Self?
CW 146 [See CW 142/46]
CW 147 The Secrets of the Threshold
CW 148 The Fifth Gospel
CW 149 *Christ and the Spiritual World: The Quest for the Holy Grail*
CW 150 *How the Spiritual World Projects into Physical Existence: The Influence of the Dead*
CW 151 *Human and Cosmic Thought*
CW 152 *Approaching the Mystery of Golgotha*
CW 153 The Inner Being of Man and Life Between Death and New Birth
CW 154 How Does One Gain an Understanding of the Spiritual World? The Flowing in of Spiritual Impulses from out of the World of the Deceased
CW 155 *Christ and the Human Soul: The Meaning of Life – The Spiritual Foundation of Morality – Anthroposophy and Christianity*
CW 156 *Inner Reading and Inner Hearing: And How to Achieve Existence in the World of Ideas*
CW 157 Human Destinies and the Destiny of Peoples
CW 157a The Formation of Destiny and the Life after Death
CW 158 *Our Connection with the Elemental World: Kalevala – Olaf Åsteson – the Russian People: The World as the Result of Balancing Influences*
CW 159 *The Mystery of Death: The Nature and Significance of Central Europe and the European Folk-Spirits*
CW 160 [Blank number]

CW 161	*Artistic Sensitivity as a Spiritual Approach to Knowing Life and the World*
CW 162	Questions of Art and Life in Light of Spiritual Science
CW 163	Coincidence, Necessity and Providence. Imaginative Knowledge and the Processes after Death
CW 164	*The Value of Thinking for a Cognition that Satisfies the Human Being: The Relationship between Spiritual Science and Natural Science*
CW 165	*Unifying Humanity Spiritually through the Christ Impulse*
CW 166	*Necessity and Freedom*
CW 167	*The Human Spirit Past and Present: Occult Fraternities and the Mystery of Golgotha*
CW 168	*The Connection between the Living and the Dead*
CW 169	World-being and Selfhood
CW 170	The Riddle of the Human Being. The Spiritual Background of Human History
CW 171	Inner Development-Impulses of Humanity. Goethe and the Crisis of the 19th Century.
CW 172	The Karma of the Vocation of the Human Being in Connection with Goethe's Life.
CW 173a	Observations of Modern History, Vol. I: Paths to an Objective Judgment
CW 173b	Observations of Modern History, Vol. II: The Karma of Untruthfulness
CW 173c	Observations of Modern History, Vol. III: The Reality of Occult Impulses
CW 174a	*Europe Between East and West in Cosmic and Human History*
CW 174b	*The Spiritual Background to the First World War*
CW 175	*Building Stones for an Understanding of the Mystery of Golgotha: Human Life in a Cosmic Context*
CW 176	*The Karma of Materialism: Aspects of Human Evolution*
CW 177	*The Fall of the Spirits of Darkness: The Spiritual Background to the Outer World: Spiritual Beings and Their Effects*
CW 178	Individual Spiritual Beings and Their Influence in the Soul of the Human Being
CW 179	*The Influence of the Dead on Destiny*
CW 180	Mystery Truths and Christmas Impulses. Ancient Myths and their Meaning.
CW 181	*Dying Earth and Living Cosmos: The Living Gifts of Anthroposophy: The Need for New Forms of Consciousness*
CW 182	Death as Transformation of Life
CW 183	*Human Evolution: A Spiritual-Scientific Quest*
CW 184	*Eternal and Transient Elements in Human Life: The Cosmic Past of Humanity and the Mystery of Evil*

CW 185 Historical Symptomology
CW 185a Historical-Developmental Foundations for Forming a Social Judgment
CW 186 The Fundamental Social Demands of Our Time. In Changed Times
CW 187 How Can Humanity Find the Christ Again? The Threefold Shadow-Existence of our Time and the New Christ-Light
CW 188 *Goetheanism: An Impulse of Transformation and Resurrection*
CW 189 *Conscious Society: Anthroposophy and the Social Question*
CW 190 *Past and Future Impulses in Societal Events*
CW 191 *Understanding Society through Spiritual-Scientific Knowledge: Social Threefolding, Christ, Lucifer, and Ahriman*
CW 192 Spiritual-Scientific Treatment of Social and Pedagogical Questions
CW 193 *Problems of Society: An Esoteric View, from Luciferic Past to Ahrimanic Future*
CW 194 *Michael's Mission: Revealing the Essential Secrets of Human Nature*
CW 195 *Cosmic New Year: Thoughts for New Year 1920*
CW 196 *What Is Necessary in These Urgent Times*
CW 197 *Polarities in the Evolution of Humanity: West and East – Materialism and Mysticism – Knowledge and Belief*
CW 198 *Healing the Social Organism*
CW 199 Spiritual Science as Knowledge of the Foundational Impulses of Social Formation
CW 200 The New Spirituality and the Christ-Experience of the 20th Century
CW 201 The Correspondences Between Microcosm and Macrocosm. The Human Being – A Hieroglyph of the Universe.
CW 202 *Universal Spirituality and Human Physicality: Bridging the Divide: The Search for the New Isis and the Divine Sophia*
CW 203 *The Hour of Decision: Human Responsibility for World Development through Our Spiritual Connection with the Earth and the World of the Stars.*
CW 204 Perspectives of the Development of Humanity. The Materialistic Knowledge-Impulse and the Task of Anthroposophy
CW 205 *The Human Being as Body and Soul in Relation to the Cosmos: Human Evolution and the Soul and Spirit of the Universe, Part I*
CW 206 *The Human Being as Spiritual Being Evolving Through the Course of History: Human Evolution and the Soul and Spirit of the Universe. Part II*
CW 207 Anthroposophy as Cosmosophy. Part One: Characteristic Features of the Human Being in the Earthly and the Cosmic Realms
CW 208 Anthroposophy as Cosmosophy. Part Two: The Forming of the Human Being as the Result of Cosmic Influence

CW 209 *The Language of the Cosmos: Cosmic Influences and the Spiritual Task of Northern Europe*
CW 210 *Old and New Methods of Initiation: Drama and Poetry in the Change of Consciousness in Modern Times*
CW 211 *The Sun Mystery and the Mystery of Death and Resurrection: Exoteric and Esoteric Christianity*
CW 212 *Life of the Human Soul: And Its Relation to World Evolution*
CW 213 *Human Questions and Cosmic Answers*
CW 214 The Mystery of the Trinity: The Human Being in Relationship with the Spiritual World in the Course of Time
CW 215 Philosophy, Cosmology, and Religion in Anthroposophy
CW 216 *Supersensible Impulses in the Historical Development of Humanity*
CW 217 *Becoming the Archangel Michael's Companions: Rudolf Steiner's Challenge to the Younger Generation*
CW 217a *Youth and the Etheric Heart: Rudolf Steiner Speaks to the Younger Generation*
CW 218 *Spirit as Sculptor of the Human Organism*
CW 219 The Relationship of the World of the Stars to the Human Being, and of the Human Being to the World of the Stars. The Spiritual Communion of Humanity
CW 220 *Awake! For the Sake of the Future*
CW 221 Earth-Knowing and Heaven-Insight
CW 222 *The Driving Force of Spiritual Powers in World History*
CW 223 The Cycle of the Year as Breathing Process of the Earth and the Four Great Festival-Seasons. Anthroposophy and the Human Heart (*Gemüt*)
CW 224 *The Seasonal Festivals as Soul Experience: The Human Being in Relation to Individual Spiritual Beings*
CW 225 *Three Perspectives of Anthroposophy: Cultural Phenomena from the Point of View of Spiritual Science*
CW 226 Human Being, Human Destiny, and World Development
CW 227 Initiation-Knowledge
CW 228 *Initiation Science: And the Development of the Human Mind*
CW 229 The Experiencing of the Course of the Year in Four Cosmic Imaginations
CW 230 The Human Being as Harmony of the Creative, Building, and Formative World-Word
CW 231 The Supersensible Human Being, Understood Anthroposophically
CW 232 The Forming of the Mysteries
CW 233 *World History and the Mysteries in the Light of Anthroposophy*
CW 233a *Rosicrucianism and Modern Initiation: Mystery Centres of the Middle Ages: The Easter Festival and the History of the Mysteries*
CW 234 Anthroposophy. A Summary after 21 Years

CW 235 Esoteric Observations of Karmic Relationships in 6 Volumes, Vol. 1
CW 236 Esoteric Observations of Karmic Relationships in 6 Volumes, Vol. 2
CW 237 Esoteric Observations of Karmic Relationships in 6 Volumes, Vol. 3: The Karmic Relationships of the Anthroposophical Movement
CW 238 Esoteric Observations of Karmic Relationships in 6 Volumes, Vol. 4: The Spiritual Life of the Present in Relationship to the Anthroposophical Movement
CW 239 Esoteric Observations of Karmic Relationships in 6 Volumes, Vol. 5
CW 240 Esoteric Observations of Karmic Relationships in 6 Volumes, Vol. 6
CW 241 [Blank number]
CW 242 [Blank number]
CW 243 *True and False Paths of Spiritual Research*
CW 244 Answers to Questions, and Interviews
CW 245 [Blank number]
CW 246 Supplementary Volume I: Individual Members Lectures
CW 247 Supplementary Volume II: Individual Members Lectures
CW 248 [Blank number]
CW 249 [Blank number]
CW 250 On the History of the German Section of the Theosophical Society 1902–1913. Lectures, Speeches, Reports, and Minutes
CW 251 On the History of the Anthroposophical Society 1913–1922
CW 252 On the History of the Building Association and the Goetheanum Association 1911–1924
CW 253 *Sexuality, Inner Development, and Community Life: Ethical and Spiritual Dimensions of the Crisis in the Anthroposophical Society in Dornach, 1915*
CW 254 The Occult Movement in the 19th Century and Its Relationship to World Culture. Significant Points from the Exoteric Cultural Life around the Middle of the 19th Century
CW 255b Anthroposophy and Its Opponents
CW 256 [Blank number]
CW 257 Anthroposophical Community-Building
CW 258 *The Anthroposophic Movement: The History and Conditions of the Anthroposophical Movement in Relation to the Anthroposophical Society: An Encouragement for Self-Examination*
CW 259 The Year of Destiny 1923 in the History of the Anthroposophical Society. From the Burning of the Goetheanum to the Christmas Conference

CW 260 The Christmas Conference for the Founding of the General Anthroposophical Society 1923/24
CW 260a The Constitution of the General Anthroposophical Society and the School for Spiritual Science. The Rebuilding of the Goetheanum
CW 261 *Our Dead: Memorial, Funeral, and Cremation Addresses 1906–1924*
CW 262 Rudolf Steiner and Marie Steiner-von Sivers: Correspondence and Documents, 1901–1925
CW 263/1 Rudolf Steiner and Edith Maryon: Correspondence: Letters, Verses, Sketches, 1912–1924
CW 264 *From the History and Contents of the First Section of the Esoteric School: Letters, Documents, and Lectures: 1904–1914*
CW 265 *Freemasonry and Ritual Work: The Misraim Service*
CW 265a Teaching and Instruction Lessons for Members of the Knowledge-Cultic Section of the Esoteric School 1904–1914 [forthcoming]
CW 266/1 *From the Esoteric School: Esoteric Lessons 1904–1909*
CW 266/2 *From the Esoteric School: Esoteric Lessons 1910–1912*
CW 266/3 *From the Esoteric School: Esoteric Lessons 1913–1923*
CW 267 *Soul Exercises: Word and Symbol Meditations*
CW 268 *Mantric Sayings: Meditations 1903–1925*
CW 269 Ritual Texts for the Celebration of the Free Christian Religious Instruction. The Collected Verses for Teachers and Students of the Waldorf School
CW 270 Esoteric Instructions for the First Class of the School for Spiritual Science at the Goetheanum 1924, 4 Volumes

III. Lectures and Courses on Specific Realms of Life

Lectures on Art

CW 271 *Art and Theory of Art: Foundations of a New Aesthetics*
CW 272 *Anthroposophy in the Light of Goethe's* Faust*: Volume One of Spiritual-Scientific Commentaries on Goethe's* Faust
CW 273 *Goethe's* Faust *in the Light of Anthroposophy: Volume Two of Spiritual-Scientific Commentaries on Goethe's* Faust
CW 274 Addresses for the Christmas Plays from the Old Folk Traditions
CW 275 Art in the Light of Mystery Wisdom
CW 276 *The Arts and Their Mission*
CW 277a The Origin and Development of Eurythmy 1912–1918
CW 277b The Origin and Development of Eurythmy 1918–1920
CW 277c The Origin and Development of Eurythmy 1920–1922 [forthcoming]
CW 277d The Origin and Development of Eurythmy 1923–1924 [forthcoming]

CW 278 Eurythmy as Visible Song
CW 279 *Eurythmy as Speech Made Visible: Speech Eurythmy Course*
CW 280 The Method and Nature of Speech Formation
CW 281 The Art of Recitation and Declamation
CW 282 Speech Formation and Dramatic Art
CW 283 *The Inner Nature of Music and the Experience of Tone*
CW 284 *Rosicrucianism Renewed: The Unity of Art, Science & Religion: The Theosophical Congress of Whitsun 1907*
CW 285 [Blank number]
CW 286 Paths to a New Style of Architecture. "And the Building Becomes Man"
CW 287 *Architecture as Peacework: The First Goetheanum, Dornach, 1914*
CW 288 *Architecture, Sculpture, and Painting of the First Goetheanum*
CW 289 The Building-Idea of the Goetheanum: Lectures with Slides from the Years 1920–1921
CW 290 *Toward a New Theory of Architecture: The First Goetheanum in Pictures* [no longer in the German GA]
CW 291 The Being of Colors
CW 291a Knowledge of Colors. Supplementary Volume to "The Being of Colors"
CW 292 *Art History as a Reflection of Inner Spiritual Impulses*

Lectures on Education

CW 293 General Knowledge of the Human Being as the Foundation of Pedagogy
CW 294 The Art of Education: Methodology and Didactics
CW 295 The Art of Education: Seminar Discussions and Lectures on Lesson Planning
CW 296 The Question of Education as a Social Question
CW 297 The Idea and Practice of the Waldorf School
CW 297a Education for Life: Self-Education and the Practice of Pedagogy
CW 298 Rudolf Steiner in the Waldorf School
CW 299 Spiritual-Scientific Observations on Speech
CW 300a Conferences with the Teachers of the Free Waldorf School in Stuttgart, 1919 to 1924, in 3 Volumes, Vol. 1
CW 300b Conferences with the Teachers of the Free Waldorf School in Stuttgart, 1919 to 1924, in 3 Volumes, Vol. 2
CW 300c Conferences with the Teachers of the Free Waldorf School in Stuttgart, 1919 to 1924, in 3 Volumes, Vol. 3
CW 301 The Renewal of Pedagogical-Didactical Art through Spiritual Science
CW 302 Knowledge of the Human Being and the Forming of Class Lessons
CW 302a Education and Teaching from a Knowledge of the Human Being

CW 303 The Healthy Development of the Human Being
CW 304 Methods of Education and Teaching Based on Anthroposophy
CW 304a Anthroposophical Knowledge of the Human Being and Pedagogy
CW 305 The Soul-Spiritual Foundational Forces of the Art of Education. Spiritual Values in Education and Social Life
CW 306 Pedagogical Praxis from the Viewpoint of a Spiritual-Scientific Knowledge of the Human Being. The Education of the Child and Young Human Beings
CW 307 The Spiritual Life of the Present and Education
CW 308 The Method of Teaching and the Life-Requirements for Teaching
CW 309 Anthroposophical Pedagogy and Its Prerequisites
CW 310 The Pedagogical Value of a Knowledge of the Human Being and the Cultural Value of Pedagogy
CW 311 The Art of Education from an Understanding of the Being of Humanity

Lectures on Medicine

CW 312 *Introducing Anthroposophical Medicine*
CW 313 *Illness and Therapy: Spiritual-Scientific Aspects of Healing*
CW 314 *Physiology and Healing: Treatment, Therapy, and Hygiene*
CW 315 Curative Eurythmy
CW 316 *Understanding Healing: Meditative Reflections on Deepening Medicine through Spiritual Science*
CW 317 *Education for Special Needs: The Curative Education Course*
CW 318 The Working Together of Doctors and Pastors
CW 319 *The Healing Process: Spirit, Nature & Our Bodies*

Lectures on Natural Science

CW 320 Spiritual-Scientific Impulses for the Development of Physics 1: The First Natural-Scientific Course: Light, Color, Tone, Mass, Electricity, Magnetism
CW 321 Spiritual-Scientific Impulses for the Development of Physics 2: The Second Natural-Scientific Course: Warmth at the Border of Positive and Negative Materiality
CW 322 The Borders of the Knowledge of Nature
CW 323 *Interdisciplinary Astronomy: Third Scientific Course*
CW 324 Nature Observation, Mathematics, and Scientific Experimentation and Results from the Viewpoint of Anthroposophy
CW 324a The Fourth Dimension in Mathematics and Reality
CW 325 Natural Science and the World-Historical Development of Humanity since Ancient Times

CW 326 The Moment of the Coming Into Being of Natural Science in World History and Its Development Since Then
CW 327 *Agriculture: Spiritual-Scientific Foundations for Agricultural Renewal*

Lectures on Social Life and the Threefold Arrangement of the Social Organism

CW 328 The Social Question
CW 329 The Liberation of the Human Being as the Foundation for a New Social Form
CW 330 The Renewal of the Social Organism
CW 331 Work-Council and Socialization
CW 332a The Social Future
CW 332b Lectures and Speeches on Social and Economic Issues
CW 333 *Freedom of Thought and Societal Forces: Implementing the Demands of Modern Society*
CW 334 From the Unified State to the Threefold Social Organism
CW 335 The Crisis of the Present and the Path to Healthy Thinking
CW 336 The Great Questions of the Times and Anthroposophical Spiritual Knowledge
CW 337a Social Ideas, Social Realities, Social Practice, Vol. 1: Question-and-Answer Evenings and Study Evenings of the Alliance for the Threefold Social Organism in Stuttgart, 1919–1920
CW 337b Social Ideas, Social Realities, Social Practice, Vol. 2: Discussion Evenings of the Swiss Alliance for the Threefold Social Organism
CW 338 *Communicating Anthroposophy: The Course for Speakers to Promote the Idea of Threefolding*
CW 339 Anthroposophy, Threefold Social Organism, and the Art of Public Speaking
CW 340/41 *Rethinking Economics: Lectures and Seminars on World Economics*

Lectures and Courses on Christian Religious Work

CW 342 *First Steps in Christian Religious Renewal: Preparing the Ground for The Christian Community*
CW 343 Lectures and Courses on Christian Religious Work, Vol. 2: Spiritual Knowledge – Religious Feeling – Cultic Doing
CW 344 Lectures and Courses on Christian Religious Work, Vol. 3: Lectures at the Founding of the Christian Community
CW 345 Lectures and Courses on Christian Religious Work, Vol. 4: Concerning the Nature of the Working Word
CW 346 Lectures and Courses on Christian Religious Work, Vol. 5: The Apocalypse and the Work of the Priest

Lectures for Workers at the Goetheanum

CW 347 The Knowledge of the Nature of the Human Being According to Body, Soul and Spirit. On Earlier Conditions of the Earth
CW 348 On Health and Illness. Foundations of a Spiritual-Scientific Doctrine of the Senses
CW 349 On the Life of the Human Being and of the Earth. On the Nature of Christianity
CW 350 Rhythms in the Cosmos and in the Human Being. How Does One Come To See the Spiritual World?
CW 351 The Human Being and the World. The Influence of the Spirit in Nature. On the Nature of Bees
CW 352 Nature and the Human Being Observed Spiritual-Scientifically
CW 353 The History of Humanity and the World-Views of the Folk Cultures
CW 354 The Creation of the World and the Human Being. Life on Earth and the Influence of the Stars

C. Artistic Works

CW A 1–10; 57 The Architectural Work I: The Goetheanum and Its Predecessors
CW A 11 The Sculptural Work
CW A 12 The Goetheanum Windows. The Speech of Light. Sketches and Studies
CW A 13–16; 52–56 The Painting Work
CW A 14 Sketches for the Painting of the Small Dome of the First Goetheanum
CW A 27–43 The Architectural Work II: Commercial and Residential Buildings in Dornach and Other Places [forthcoming]
CW A 45 The Graphic Work
CW A 48 The Drawing Work
CW A 51 The Art of Jewelry as a Goethean Language of Form
CW A 54.0 A Path of Training in Painting. Pastel Sketches and Watercolors
CW A 54.1 Nature Moods. Nine Training Sketches for Painters

Eurythmy Figures

CW A 26 Skectches of the Eurythmy Figures
CW A 26a The Eurythmy Figures of Rudolf Steiner, Artistically Executed by Annemarie Bäschlin
CW A 26b Eurythmy Figures from the Time When They Were Created

Eurythmy Forms

CW A 23/1 Volume I: Eurythmy Forms for Poems by Rudolf Steiner

CW A 23/2	Volume II: Eurythmy Forms for the Calender of the Soul by Rudolf Steiner
CW A 23/3	Volume III: Euythmy Forms for Poems by J. W. von Goethe
CW A 23/4	Volume IV: Eurythmy Forms for Poems by Christian Morgenstern
CW A 23/5	Volume V: Eurythmy Forms for Poems by Albert Steffen
CW A 23/6	Volume VI: Eurythmy Forms for German Poems by Fercher von Steinwand, Hamerling, Hebbel, C. F. Meyer, Nietzsche, among others
CW A 23/7	Volume VII: Eurythmy Forms for English Poems
CW A 23/8	Volume VIII: Eurythmy Forms for French and Russian Poems
CW A 24	Volume IX: Eurythmy Forms for Tone Eurythmy

Blackboard Drawings from Lectures

CW A 58/1	Volume I: 20 Plates from Public Lectures 1920–1924 in CWs 73a, 74, 76, and 84
CW A 58/2	Volume II: 38 Plates from Lectures in 1919 in CWs 191 and 194
CW A 58/3	Volume III: 34 Plates from Lectures in 1920 in CWs 196 and 198
CW A 58/4	Volume IV: 33 Plates from Lectures in 1920 in CWs 199 and 200
CW A 58/5	Volume V: 31 Plates from Lectures in 1920 in CW 201
CW A 58/6	Volume VI: 46 Plates from Lectures 1920–1921 in CWs 202–204
CW A 58/7	Volume VII: 38 Plates from Lectures in 1921 in CWs 205 and 206
CW A 58/8	Volume VIII: 42 Plates from Lectures in 1921 in CWs 207–209
CW A 58/9	Volume IX: 40 Plates from Lectures in 1922 in CWs 210–212
CW A 58/10	Volume X: 35 Plates from Lectures in 1922 in CWs 213–215
CW A 58/11	Volume XI: 41 Plates from Lectures 1922–1923 in CWs 216, 218–220
CW A 58/12	Volume XII: 37 Plates from Lectures in 1923 in CWs 221–225
CW A 58/13	Volume XIII: 38 Plates from Lectures in 1923 in CWs 227–230
CW A 58/14	Volume XIV: 36 Plates from Lectures in 1923 in CWs 232 and 233
CW A 58/15	Volume XV: 37 Plates from Lectures in 1924 in CWs 233a, 234, and 243
CW A 58/16	Volume XVI: 56 Plates from the "Karma Lectures" in CWs 235–238 and 240
CW A 58/17	Volume XVII: 21 Plates from Lectures on the History of the Anthroposophical Society in CWs 257, 258, 260, and 260a
CW A 58/18	Volume XVIII: 33 Plates from Lectures on Art in CWs 271, 276, 283, 288–290, and 291
CW A 58/19	Volume XIX: 41 Plates from Lectures on Eurythmy in CWs 278, 279, and 315

CW A 58/20 Volume XX: 27 Plates from Lectures on Speech Formation in CWs 281 and 282

CW A 58/21 Volume XXI: 42 Plates from Lectures on Education in CWs 296, 303, 304, 306, and 311

CW A 58/22 Volume XXII: 46 Plates from Lectures on Medicine in CWs 312–315

CW A 58/23 Volume XXIII: 48 Plates from Lectures in 1924 in CWs 316–318

CW A 58/24 Volume XXIV: 39 Plates from Lectures on Natural Science and the Social Question in CWs 322, 326, 327, 339, and 340

CW A 58/25 Volume XXV: 33 Plates from the "Workers Lectures" (Volumes 1 and 2) in CWs 347 and 348

CW A 58/26 Volume XXVI: 51 Plates from the "Workers Lectures" (Volumes 3 and 4) in CWs 349 and 350

CW A 58/27 Volume XXVII: 35 Plates from the "Workers Lectures" (Volumes 5 and 6) in CWs 351 and 352

CW A 58/28 Volume XXVIII: 42 Plates from the "Workers Lectures" (Volumes 7 and 8) in CWs 353 and 354

CW A 58/29 Volume XXIX: 43 Plates from Lectures and Courses on Christian Religious Activity in CWs 342–344 and 346

CW A 58/30 Volume XXX: 27 Plates from CWs 255b, 324a, 337b, and 340, Corrigenda, Plates without CW Assignment, Copies

SIGNIFICANT EVENTS IN THE LIFE OF RUDOLF STEINER

1829: June 23: birth of Johann Steiner (1829–1910)—Rudolf Steiner's father—in Geras, Lower Austria.

1834: May 8: birth of Franciska Blie (1834–1918)—Rudolf Steiner's mother—in Horn, Lower Austria. "My father and mother were both children of the glorious Lower Austrian forest district north of the Danube."

1860: May 16: marriage of Johann Steiner and Franciska Blie.

1861: February 25: birth of *Rudolf Joseph Lorenz Steiner* in Kraljevec, Croatia, near the border with Hungary, where Johann Steiner works as a telegrapher for the South Austria Railroad. Rudolf Steiner is baptized two days later, February 27, the date usually given as his birthday.

1862: Summer: the family moves to Mödling, Lower Austria.

1863: The family moves to Pottschach, Lower Austria, near the Styrian border, where Johann Steiner becomes stationmaster. "The view stretched to the mountains...majestic peaks in the distance and the sweet charm of nature in the immediate surroundings."

1864: November 15: birth of Rudolf Steiner's sister, Leopoldine (d. November 1, 1927). She will become a seamstress and live with her parents for the rest of her life.

1866: July 28: birth of Rudolf Steiner's deaf-mute brother, Gustav (d. May 1, 1941).

1867: Rudolf Steiner enters the village school. Following a disagreement between his father and the schoolmaster, whose wife falsely accused the boy of causing a commotion, Rudolf Steiner is taken out of school and taught at home.

1868: A critical experience. Unknown to the family, an aunt dies in a distant town. Sitting in the station waiting room, Rudolf Steiner sees her "form," which speaks to him, asking for help. "Beginning with this experience, a new soul life began in the boy, one in which not only the outer trees and mountains spoke to him, but also the worlds that lay behind them. From this moment on, the boy began to live with the spirits of nature...."

1869: The family moves to the peaceful, rural village of Neudorfl, near Wiener-Neustadt in present-day Austria. Rudolf Steiner attends the village school. Because of the "unorthodoxy" of his writing and spelling, he has to do "extra lessons."

1870: Through a book lent to him by his tutor, he discovers geometry: "To grasp something purely in the spirit brought me inner happiness. I know that I first learned happiness through geometry." The same tutor allows him to draw, while other students still struggle with their reading and writing. "An artistic element" thus enters his education.

1871: Though his parents are not religious, Rudolf Steiner becomes a "church child," a favorite of the priest, who was "an exceptional character." "Up to the age of ten or eleven, among those I came to know, he was far and away the most significant." Among other things, he introduces Steiner to Copernican, heliocentric cosmology. As an altar boy, Rudolf Steiner serves at Masses, funerals, and Corpus Christi processions. At year's end, after an incident in which he escapes a thrashing, his father forbids him to go to church.

1872: Rudolf Steiner transfers to grammar school in Wiener-Neustadt, a five-mile walk from home, which must be done in all weathers.

1873–75: Through his teachers and on his own, Rudolf Steiner has many wonderful experiences with science and mathematics. Outside school, he teaches himself analytic geometry, trigonometry, differential equations, and calculus.

1876: Rudolf Steiner begins tutoring other students. He learns bookbinding from his father. He also teaches himself stenography.

1877: Rudolf Steiner discovers Kant's *Critique of Pure Reason*, which he reads and rereads. He also discovers and reads von Rotteck's *World History*.

1878: He studies extensively in contemporary psychology and philosophy.

1879: Rudolf Steiner graduates from high school with honors. His father is transferred to Inzersdorf, near Vienna. He uses his first visit to Vienna "to purchase a great number of philosophy books"—Kant, Fichte, Schelling, and Hegel, as well as numerous histories of philosophy. His aim: to find a path from the "I" to nature.

October 1879–1883: Rudolf Steiner attends the Technical College in Vienna—to study mathematics, chemistry, physics, mineralogy, botany, zoology, biology, geology, and mechanics—with a scholarship. He also attends lectures in history and literature, while avidly reading philosophy on his own. His two favorite professors are Karl Julius Schröer (German language and literature) and Edmund Reitlinger (physics). He also audits lectures by Robert Zimmerman on aesthetics and Franz Brentano on philosophy. During this year he begins his friendship with Moritz Zitter (1861–1921), who will help support him financially when he is in Berlin.

1880: Rudolf Steiner attends lectures on Schiller and Goethe by Karl Julius Schröer, who becomes his mentor. Also "through a remarkable combination of circumstances," he meets Felix Koguzki, an "herb gatherer" and healer, who could "see deeply into the secrets of nature." Rudolf Steiner will meet and study with this "emissary of the Master" throughout his time in Vienna.

1881: January: "… I didn't sleep a wink. I was busy with philosophical problems until about 12:30 a.m. Then, finally, I threw myself down on my couch. All my striving during the previous year had been to research whether the following statement by Schelling was true or not: *Within everyone dwells a secret, marvelous capacity to draw back from the stream of time—out of the self clothed in all that comes to us from outside—into our innermost being and there, in the immutable form of the Eternal, to look into ourselves.* I believe, and I am still quite certain of it, that I discovered this capacity in myself; I had long had an inkling of it. Now the whole of idealist philosophy stood before me in modified form. What's a sleepless night compared to that!"

Rudolf Steiner begins communicating with leading thinkers of the day, who send him books in return, which he reads eagerly.

July: "I am not one of those who dives into the day like an animal in human form. I pursue a quite specific goal, an idealistic aim—knowledge of the truth! This cannot be done offhandedly. It requires the greatest striving in the world, free of all egotism, and equally of all resignation."

August: Steiner puts down on paper for the first time thoughts for a "Philosophy of Freedom." "The striving for the absolute: this human yearning is freedom." He also seeks to outline a "peasant philosophy," describing what the worldview of a "peasant"—one who lives close to the earth and the old ways—really is.

1881–1882: Felix Koguzki, the herb gatherer, reveals himself to be the envoy of another, higher initiatory personality, who instructs Rudolf Steiner to penetrate Fichte's philosophy and to master modern scientific thinking as a preparation for right entry into the spirit. This "Master" also teaches him the double (evolutionary and involutionary) nature of time.

1882: Through the offices of Karl Julius Schröer, Rudolf Steiner is asked by Joseph Kurschner to edit Goethe's scientific writings for the *Deutschen National-Literatur* edition. He writes "A Possible Critique of Atomistic Concepts" and sends it to Friedrich Theodor Vischer.

1883: Rudolf Steiner completes his college studies and begins work on the Goethe project.

1884: First volume of Goethe's *Scientific Writings* (CW 1) appears (March). He lectures on Goethe and Lessing, and Goethe's approach to science. In July, he enters the household of Ladislaus and Pauline Specht as tutor to the four Specht boys. He will live there until 1890. At this time, he meets Josef Breuer (1842–1925), the coauthor with Sigmund Freud of *Studies in Hysteria*, who is the Specht family doctor.

1885: While continuing to edit Goethe's writings, Rudolf Steiner reads deeply in contemporary philosophy (Edouard von Hartmann, Johannes Volkelt, and Richard Wahle, among others).

1886: May: Rudolf Steiner sends Kurschner the manuscript of *Outlines of Goethe's Theory of Knowledge* (CW 2), which appears in October, and which he sends out widely. He also meets the poet Marie Eugenie Delle Grazie and writes "Nature and Our Ideals" for her. He attends her salon, where he meets many priests, theologians, and philosophers, who will become his friends. Meanwhile, the director of the Goethe Archive in Weimar requests his collaboration with the *Sophien* edition of Goethe's works, particularly the writings on color.

1887: At the beginning of the year, Rudolf Steiner is very sick. As the year progresses and his health improves, he becomes increasingly "a man of letters," lecturing, writing essays, and taking part in Austrian cultural life. In August–September, the second volume of Goethe's *Scientific Writings* appears.

1888: January–July: Rudolf Steiner assumes editorship of the "German Weekly" (*Deutsche Wochenschrift*). He begins lecturing more intensively, giving, for example, a lecture titled "Goethe as Father of a New Aesthetics." He meets and becomes soul friends with Friedrich Eckstein (1861–1939), a vegetarian, philosopher of symbolism, alchemist, and musician, who will introduce him to various spiritual currents (including Theosophy) and with whom he will meditate and interpret esoteric and alchemical texts.

1889: Rudolf Steiner first reads Nietzsche (*Beyond Good and Evil*). He encounters Theosophy again and learns of Madame Blavatsky in the Theosophical circle around Marie Lang (1858–1934). Here he also meets well-known figures of Austrian life, as well as esoteric figures like the occultist Franz Hartman and Karl Leinigen-Billigen (translator of C.G. Harrison's *The Transcendental Universe*). During this period, Steiner first reads A.P. Sinnett's *Esoteric Buddhism* and Mabel Collins's *Light on the Path*. He also begins traveling, visiting Budapest, Weimar, and Berlin (where he meets philosopher Edouard von Hartman).

1890: Rudolf Steiner finishes volume 3 of Goethe's scientific writings. He begins his doctoral dissertation, which will become *Truth and Science* (CW 3). He also meets the poet and feminist Rosa Mayreder (1858–1938), with whom he can exchange his most intimate thoughts. In September, Rudolf Steiner moves to Weimar to work in the Goethe-Schiller Archive.

1891: Volume 3 of the Kurschner edition of Goethe appears. Meanwhile, Rudolf Steiner edits Goethe's studies in mineralogy and scientific writings for the *Sophien* edition. He meets Ludwig Laistner of the Cotta Publishing Company, who asks for a book on the basic question of metaphysics. From this will result, ultimately, *The Philosophy of Freedom* (CW 4), which will be published not by Cotta but by Emil Felber. In October, Rudolf Steiner takes the oral exam for a doctorate in philosophy, mathematics, and mechanics at Rostock University, receiving his doctorate on the twenty-sixth. In November, he gives his first lecture on Goethe's "Fairy Tale" in Vienna.

1892: Rudolf Steiner continues work at the Goethe-Schiller Archive and on his *Philosophy of Freedom*. *Truth and Science*, his doctoral dissertation, is published. Steiner undertakes to write introductions to books on Schopenhauer and Jean Paul for Cotta. At year's end, he finds lodging with Anna Eunike, née Schulz (1853–1911), a widow with four daughters and a son. He also develops a friendship with Otto Erich Hartleben (1864–1905) with whom he shares literary interests.

1893: Rudolf Steiner begins his habit of producing many reviews and articles. In March, he gives a lecture titled "Hypnotism, with Reference to Spiritism." In September, volume 4 of the Kurschner edition is completed. In November, *The Philosophy of Freedom* appears. This year, too, he meets John Henry Mackay (1864–1933), the anarchist, and Max Stirner, a scholar and biographer.

1894: Rudolf Steiner meets Elisabeth Förster Nietzsche, the philosopher's sister, and begins to read Nietzsche in earnest, beginning with the as yet unpublished *Antichrist.* He also meets Ernst Haeckel (1834–1919). In the fall, he begins to write *Nietzsche, A Fighter against His Time* (CW 5).

1895: May: *Nietzsche, A Fighter against His Time* appears.

1896: January 22: Rudolf Steiner sees Friedrich Nietzsche for the first and only time. Moves between the Nietzsche and the Goethe-Schiller Archives, where he completes his work before year's end. He falls out with Elisabeth Förster Nietzsche, thus ending his association with the Nietzsche Archive.

1897: Rudolf Steiner finishes the manuscript of *Goethe's Worldview* (CW 6). He moves to Berlin with Anna Eunike and begins editorship of the *Magazin fur Literatur.* From now on, Steiner will write countless reviews, literary and philosophical articles, and so on. He begins lecturing at the "Free Literary Society." In September, he attends the Zionist Congress in Basel. He sides with Dreyfus in the Dreyfus affair.

1898: Rudolf Steiner is very active as an editor in the political, artistic, and theatrical life of Berlin. He becomes friendly with John Henry Mackay and poet Ludwig Jacobowski (1868–1900). He joins Jacobowski's circle of writers, artists, and scientists—"The Coming Ones" (*Die Kommenden*)—and contributes lectures to the group until 1903. He also lectures at the "League for College Pedagogy." He writes an article for Goethe's sesquicentennial, "Goethe's Secret Revelation," on the "Fairy Tale of the Green Snake and the Beautiful Lily."

1898–99: "This was a trying time for my soul as I looked at Christianity. . . . I was able to progress only by contemplating, by means of spiritual perception, the evolution of Christianity. . . . Conscious knowledge of real Christianity began to dawn in me around the turn of the century. This seed continued to develop. My soul trial occurred shortly before the beginning of the twentieth century. It was decisive for my soul's development that I stood spiritually before the Mystery of Golgotha in a deep and solemn celebration of knowledge."

1899: Rudolf Steiner begins teaching and giving lectures and lecture cycles at the Workers' College, founded by Wilhelm Liebknecht (1826–1900). He will continue to do so until 1904. Writes: *Literature and Spiritual Life in the Nineteenth Century; Individualism in Philosophy*; *Haeckel and His Opponents; Poetry in the Present;* and begins what will become (fifteen years later) *The Riddles of Philosophy* (CW 18). He also meets many artists and writers, including Käthe Kollwitz, Stefan Zweig, and Rainer Maria Rilke. On October 31, he marries Anna Eunike.

1900: "I thought that the turn of the century must bring humanity a new light. It seemed to me that the separation of human thinking and willing from the spirit had peaked. A turn or reversal of direction in human evolution seemed to me a necessity." Rudolf Steiner finishes *World and Life Views in the Nineteenth Century* (the second part of what will become *The Riddles of Philosophy*) and dedicates it to Ernst Haeckel.

It is published in March. He continues lecturing at *Die Kommenden*, whose leadership he assumes after the death of Jacobowski. Also, he gives the Gutenberg Jubilee lecture before 7,000 typesetters and printers. In September, Rudolf Steiner is invited by Count and Countess Brockdorff to lecture in the Theosophical Library. His first lecture is on Nietzsche. His second lecture is titled "Goethe's Secret Revelation." October 6, he begins a lecture cycle on the mystics that will become *Mystics after Modernism* (CW 7). November–December: "Marie von Sivers appears in the audience…." Also in November, Steiner gives his first lecture at the Giordano Bruno Bund (where he will continue to lecture until May, 1905). He speaks on Bruno and modern Rome, focusing on the importance of the philosophy of Thomas Aquinas as monism.

1901: In continual financial straits, Rudolf Steiner's early friends Moritz Zitter and Rosa Mayreder help support him. In October, he begins the lecture cycle *Christianity as Mystical Fact* (CW 8) at the Theosophical Library. In November, he gives his first "Theosophical lecture" on Goethe's "Fairy Tale" in Hamburg at the invitation of Wilhelm Hubbe-Schleiden. He also attends a tea to celebrate the founding of the Theosophical Society at Count and Countess Brockdorff's. He gives a lecture cycle, "From Buddha to Christ," for the circle of the *Kommenden*. November 17, Marie von Sivers asks Rudolf Steiner if Theosophy does not need a Western-Christian spiritual movement (to complement Theosophy's Eastern emphasis). "The question was posed. Now, following spiritual laws, I could begin to give an answer…." In December, Rudolf Steiner writes his first article for a Theosophical publication. At year's end, the Brockdorffs and possibly Wilhelm Hubbe-Schleiden ask Rudolf Steiner to join the Theosophical Society and undertake the leadership of the German section. Rudolf Steiner agrees, on the condition that Marie von Sivers (then in Italy) work with him.

1902: Beginning in January, Rudolf Steiner attends the opening of the Workers' School in Spandau with Rosa Luxemberg (1870–1919). January 17, Rudolf Steiner joins the Theosophical Society. In April, he is asked to become general secretary of the German Section of the Theosophical Society, and works on preparations for its founding. In July, he visits London for a Theosophical congress. He meets Bertram Keightly, G.R.S. Mead, A.P. Sinnett, and Annie Besant, among others. In September, *Christianity as Mystical Fact* appears. In October, Rudolf Steiner gives his first public lecture on Theosophy ("Monism and Theosophy") to about three hundred people at the Giordano Bruno Bund. From October 19–21, the German Section of the Theosophical Society has its first meeting; Rudolf Steiner is the general secretary, and Annie Besant attends. Steiner lectures on practical karma studies. On October 23, Annie Besant inducts Rudolf Steiner into the Esoteric School of the Theosophical Society. On October 25, Steiner begins a weekly series of lectures: "The Field of Theosophy." During this year, Rudolf Steiner also first meets Ita Wegman (1876–1943), who will become his close collaborator in his final years.

1903: Rudolf Steiner holds about 300 lectures and seminars. In May, the first issue of the periodical *Luzifer* appears. In June, Rudolf Steiner visits London for the first meeting of the Federation of the European Sections of the Theosophical Society, where he meets Colonel Olcott. He begins to write *Theosophy* (CW 9).

1904: Rudolf Steiner continues lecturing at the Workers' College and elsewhere (about 90 lectures), while lecturing intensively all over Germany among Theosophists (about 140 lectures). In February, he meets Carl Unger (1878–1929), who will become a member of the board of the Anthroposophical Society (1913). In March, he meets Michael Bauer (1871–1929), a Christian mystic, who will also be on the board. In May, *Theosophy* appears, with the dedication: "To the spirit of Giordano Bruno." Rudolf Steiner and Marie von Sivers visit London for meetings with Annie Besant. In June, Rudolf Steiner and Marie von Sivers attend the meeting of the Federation of European Sections of the Theosophical Society in Amsterdam. In July, Steiner begins the articles in *Lucifer-Gnosis* that will become *How to Know Higher Worlds* (CW 10) and *Cosmic Memory* (CW 11). In September, Annie Besant visits Germany. In December, Steiner lectures on Freemasonry. He mentions the High Grade Masonry derived from John Yarker and represented by Theodore Reuss and Karl Kellner as a blank slate "into which a good image could be placed."

1905: This year, Steiner ends his non-Theosophical lecturing activity. Supported by Marie von Sivers, his Theosophical lecturing—both in public and in the Theosophical Society—increases significantly: "The German Theosophical Movement is of exceptional importance." Steiner recommends reading, among others, Fichte, Jacob Boehme, and Angelus Silesius. He begins to introduce Christian themes into Theosophy. He also begins to work with doctors (Felix Peipers and Ludwig Noll). In July, he is in London for the Federation of European Sections, where he attends a lecture by Annie Besant: "I have seldom seen Mrs. Besant speak in so inward and heartfelt a manner...." "Through Mrs. Besant I have found the way to H.P. Blavatsky." September to October, he gives a course of thirty-one lectures for a small group of esoteric students. In October, the annual meeting of the German Section of the Theosophical Society, which still remains very small, takes place. Rudolf Steiner reports membership has risen from 121 to 377 members. In November, seeking to establish esoteric "continuity," Rudolf Steiner and Marie von Sivers participate in a "Memphis-Misraim" Masonic ceremony. They pay forty-five marks for membership. "Yesterday, you saw how little remains of former esoteric institutions." "We are dealing only with a 'framework'... for the present, nothing lies behind it. The occult powers have completely withdrawn."

1906: Expansion of Theosophical work. Rudolf Steiner gives about 245 lectures, only 44 of which take place in Berlin. Cycles are given in Paris, Leipzig, Stuttgart, and Munich. Esoteric work also intensifies. Rudolf Steiner begins writing *An Outline of Esoteric Science* (CW 13). In January, Rudolf Steiner receives permission (a patent) from the Great Orient of the Scottish A & A Thirty-Three Degree Rite of the Order of the Ancient Freemasons of the Memphis-Misraim Rite to direct a chapter under the name "Mystica Aeterna." This will become the "Cognitive Cultic Section" (also called "Misraim Service") of the Esoteric School. (See: *From the History and Contents of the Cognitive Cultic Section* [CW 264].) During this time, Steiner also meets Albert Schweitzer. In May, he is in Paris, where he visits Edouard Schuré. Many Russians attend his lectures (including Konstantin Balmont, Dimitri Mereszkovski, Zinaida Hippius, and Maximilian Woloshin). He attends the General Meeting of the European Federation of the Theosophical Society, at which Col. Olcott is present for the last time. He spends the year's end in Venice and Rome, where he writes and works on his translation of H. P. Blavatsky's *Key to Theosophy*.

1907: Further expansion of the German Theosophical Movement according to the Rosicrucian directive to "introduce spirit into the world"—in education, in social questions, in art, and in science. In February, Col. Olcott dies in Adyar. Before he dies, Olcott indicates that "the Masters" wish Annie Besant to succeed him: much politicking ensues. Rudolf Steiner supports Besant's candidacy. April–May: preparations for the Congress of the Federation of European Sections of the Theosophical Society—the great, watershed Whitsun "Munich Congress," attended by Annie Besant and others. Steiner decides to separate Eastern and Western (Christian-Rosicrucian) esoteric schools. He takes his esoteric school out of the Theosophical Society (Besant and Rudolf Steiner are "in harmony" on this). Steiner makes his first lecture tours to Austria and Hungary. That summer, he is in Italy. In September, he visits Edouard Schuré, who will write the introduction to the French edition of *Christianity as Mystical Fact* in Barr, Alsace. Rudolf Steiner writes the autobiographical statement known as the "Barr Document." In *Luzifer–Gnosis*, "The Education of the Child" appears.

1908: The movement grows (membership: 1150). Lecturing expands. Steiner makes his first extended lecture tour to Holland and Scandinavia, as well as visits to Naples and Sicily. Themes: St. John's Gospel, the Apocalypse, Egypt, science, philosophy, and logic. *Lucifer-Gnosis* ceases publication. In Berlin, Marie von Sivers (with Johanna Mücke [1864–1949]) forms the *Philosophisch-Theosophisch* (after 1915 *Philosophisch-Anthroposophisch*) *Verlag* to publish Steiner's work. Steiner gives lecture cycles titled *The Gospel of St. John* (CW 103) and *The Apocalypse* (104).

1909: *An Outline of Esoteric Science* appears. Lecturing and travel continue. Rudolf Steiner's spiritual research expands to include the polarity of Lucifer and Ahriman; the work of great individualities in history; the

Maitreya Buddha and the Bodhisattvas; spiritual economy (CW 109); the work of the spiritual hierarchies in heaven and on Earth (CW 110). He also deepens and intensifies his research into the Gospels, giving lectures on the Gospel of St. Luke (CW 114) with the first mention of two Jesus children. Meets and becomes friends with Christian Morgenstern (1871–1914). In April, he lays the foundation stone for the Malsch model—the building that will lead to the first Goetheanum. In May, the International Congress of the Federation of European Sections of the Theosophical Society takes place in Budapest. Rudolf Steiner receives the Subba Row medal for *How to Know Higher Worlds*. During this time, Charles W. Leadbeater discovers Jiddu Krishnamurti (1895–1986) and proclaims him the future "world teacher," the bearer of the Maitreya Buddha and the "reappearing Christ." In October, Steiner delivers seminal lectures on "anthroposophy," which he will try, unsuccessfully, to rework over the next years into the unfinished work, *Anthroposophy (A Fragment)* (CW 45).

1910: New themes: *The Reappearance of Christ in the Etheric* (CW 118); *The Fifth Gospel* (CW 148); *The Mission of Folk Souls* (CW 121); *Occult History* (CW 126); the evolving development of etheric cognitive capacities. Rudolf Steiner continues his Gospel research with *The Gospel of St. Matthew* (CW 123). In January, his father dies. In April, he takes a month-long trip to Italy, including Rome, Monte Cassino, and Sicily. He also visits Scandinavia again. July–August, he writes the first mystery drama, *The Portal of Initiation* (CW 14). In November, he gives "psychosophy" lectures. In December, he submits "On the Psychological Foundations and Epistemological Framework of Theosophy" to the International Philosophical Congress in Bologna.

1911: The crisis in the Theosophical Society deepens. In January, "The Order of the Rising Sun," which will soon become "The Order of the Star in the East," is founded for the coming world teacher, Krishnamurti. At the same time, Marie von Sivers, Rudolf Steiner's coworker, falls ill. Fewer lectures are given, but important new ground is broken. In Prague, in March, Steiner meets Franz Kafka (1883–1924) and Hugo Bergmann (1883–1975). In April, he delivers his paper to the Philosophical Congress. He writes the second mystery drama, *The Soul's Probation* (CW 14). Also, while Marie von Sivers is convalescing, Rudolf Steiner begins work on *Calendar 1912/1913*, which will contain the "Calendar of the Soul" meditations. On March 19, Anna (Eunike) Steiner dies. In September, Rudolf Steiner visits Einsiedeln, birthplace of Paracelsus. In December, Friedrich Rittelmeyer, future founder of the Christian Community, meets Rudolf Steiner. The *Johannes-Bauverein*, the "building committee," which would lead to the first Goetheanum (first planned for Munich), is also founded, and a preliminary committee for the founding of an independent association is created that, in the following year, will become the Anthroposophical Society. Important lecture cycles include *Occult Physiology* (CW 128);

Wonders of the World (CW 129); *From Jesus to Christ* (CW 131). Other themes: esoteric Christianity; Christian Rosenkreutz; the spiritual guidance of humanity; the sense world and the world of the spirit.

1912: Despite the ongoing, now increasing crisis in the Theosophical Society, much is accomplished: *Calendar 1912/1913* is published; eurythmy is created; both the third mystery drama, *The Guardian of the Threshold* (CW 14) and *A Way of Self-Knowledge* (CW 16) are written. New (or renewed) themes include life between death and rebirth and karma and reincarnation. Other lecture cycles: *Spiritual Beings in the Heavenly Bodies and the Kingdoms of Nature* (CW 136); *The Human Being in the Light of Occultism, Theosophy, and Philosophy* (CW 137); *The Gospel of St. Mark* (CW 139); and *The Bhagavad Gita and the Epistles of Paul* (CW 142). On May 8, Rudolf Steiner celebrates White Lotus Day, H.P. Blavatsky's death day, which he had faithfully observed for the past decade, for the last time. In August, Rudolf Steiner suggests the "independent association" be called the "Anthroposophical Society." In September, the first eurythmy course takes place. Also, with Marie von Sivers, he first visits Dornach, near Basel, Switzerland, and they stand on the hill where the Goetheanum will be. In November, a Theosophical Society lodge is opened by direct mandate from Adyar (Annie Besant). In December, a meeting of the German section occurs at which it is decided that belonging to the Order of the Star of the East is incompatible with membership in the Theosophical Society. December 28: informal founding of the Anthroposophical Society in Berlin.

1913: Expulsion of the German section from the Theosophical Society. February 2–3: Foundation meeting of the Anthroposophical Society. Board members include: Marie von Sivers, Michael Bauer, and Carl Unger. September 20: Laying of the foundation stone for the *Johannes Bau* (Goetheanum) in Dornach. Building begins immediately. The third mystery drama, *The Soul's Awakening* (CW 14), is completed. Also: *The Threshold of the Spiritual World* (CW 147). Lecture cycles include: *The Bhagavad Gita and the Epistles of Paul* and *The Esoteric Meaning of the Bhagavad Gita* (CW 146), which the Russian philosopher Nikolai Berdyaev attends; *The Mysteries of the East and of Christianity* (CW 144); *The Effects of Esoteric Development* (CW 145); and *The Fifth Gospel* (CW 148). In May, Rudolf Steiner is in London and Paris, where anthroposophical work continues.

1914: Building continues on the *Johannes Bau* (Goetheanum) in Dornach, with artists and coworkers from seventeen nations. The general assembly of the Anthroposophical Society takes place. In May, Rudolf Steiner visits Paris, as well as Chartres Cathedral. June 28: assassination in Sarajevo ("Now the catastrophe has happened!"). August 1: War is declared. Rudolf Steiner returns to Germany from Dornach—he will travel back and forth. He writes the last chapter of *The Riddles of Philosophy*. Lecture cycles include: *Human and Cosmic Thought* (CW 151); *Inner Being of*

Humanity between Death and a New Birth (CW 153); *Occult Reading and Occult Hearing* (CW 156). December 24: marriage of Rudolf Steiner and Marie von Sivers.

1915: Building continues. Life after death becomes a major theme, also art. Writes: *Thoughts during a Time of War* (CW 24). Lectures include: *The Secret of Death* (CW 159); *The Uniting of Humanity through the Christ Impulse* (CW 165).

1916: Rudolf Steiner begins work with Edith Maryon (1872–1924) on the sculpture "The Representative of Humanity" ("The Group"—Christ, Lucifer, and Ahriman). He also works with the alchemist Alexander von Bernus on the quarterly *Das Reich*. He writes *The Riddle of Humanity* (CW 20). Lectures include: *Necessity and Freedom in World History and Human Action* (CW 166); *Past and Present in the Human Spirit* (CW 167); *The Karma of Vocation* (CW 172); *The Karma of Untruthfulness* (CW 173).

1917: Russian Revolution. The U.S. enters the war. Building continues. Rudolf Steiner delineates the idea of the "threefold nature of the human being" (in a public lecture March 15) and the "threefold nature of the social organism" (hammered out in May–June with the help of Otto von Lerchenfeld and Ludwig Polzer-Hoditz in the form of two documents titled *Memoranda*, which were distributed in high places). August–September: Rudolf Steiner writes *The Riddles of the Soul* (CW 20). Also: commentary on "The Chemical Wedding of Christian Rosenkreutz" for Alexander Bernus (*Das Reich*). Lectures include: *The Karma of Materialism* (CW 176); *The Spiritual Background of the Outer World: The Fall of the Spirits of Darkness* (CW 177).

1918: March 18: peace treaty of Brest-Litovsk—"Now everything will truly enter chaos! What is needed is cultural renewal." June: Rudolf Steiner visits Karlstein (Grail) Castle outside Prague. Lecture cycle: *From Symptom to Reality in Modern History* (CW 185). In mid-November, Emil Molt, of the Waldorf-Astoria Cigarette Company, has the idea of founding a school for his workers' children.

1919: Focus on the threefold social organism: tireless travel, countless lectures, meetings, and publications. At the same time, a new public stage of Anthroposophy emerges as cultural renewal begins. The coming years will see initiatives in pedagogy, medicine, pharmacology, and agriculture. January 27: threefold meeting: " We must first of all, with the money we have, found free schools that can bring people what they need." February: first public eurythmy performance in Zurich. Also: "Appeal to the German People" (CW 24), circulated March 6 as a newspaper insert. In April, *Toward Social Renewal* (CW 23)—"perhaps the most widely read of all books on politics appearing since the war"—appears. Rudolf Steiner is asked to undertake the "direction and leadership" of the school founded by the Waldorf-Astoria Company. Rudolf Steiner begins to talk about the "renewal" of education. May 30: a building is selected and purchased for the future Waldorf School.

August–September: Rudolf Steiner gives a lecture course for Waldorf teachers, *The Foundations of Human Experience (Study of Man)* (CW 293). September 7: Opening of the first Waldorf School. December (into January): first science course, the *Light Course* (CW 320).

1920: The Waldorf School flourishes. New threefold initiatives. Founding of limited companies *Der Kommenden Tag* and *Futurum A.G.* to infuse spiritual values into the economic realm. Rudolf Steiner also focuses on the sciences. Lectures: *Introducing Anthroposophical Medicine* (CW 312); *The Warmth Course* (CW 321); *The Boundaries of Natural Science* (CW 322); *The Redemption of Thinking* (CW 74). February: Johannes Werner Klein—later a cofounder of the Christian Community—asks Rudolf Steiner about the possibility of a "religious renewal," a "Johannine church." In March, Rudolf Steiner gives the first course for doctors and medical students. In April, a divinity student asks Rudolf Steiner a second time about the possibility of religious renewal. September 27–October 16: anthroposophical "college course." December: lectures titled *The Search for the New Isis* (CW 202).

1921: Rudolf Steiner continues his intensive work on cultural renewal, including the uphill battle for the threefold social order. "College" arts, scientific, theological, and medical courses include: *The Astronomy Course* (CW 323); *Observation, Mathematics, and Scientific Experiment* (CW 324); the *Second Medical Course* (CW 313); *Color* (CW 291). In June and September–October, Rudolf Steiner also gives the first two "priests' courses" (CW 342 and 343). The "youth movement" gains momentum. Magazines are founded: *Die Drei* (January), and—under the editorship of Albert Steffen (1884–1963)—the weekly, *Das Goetheanum* (August). In February–March, Rudolf Steiner takes his first trip outside Germany since the war (Holland). On April 7, Steiner receives a letter regarding "religious renewal," and May 22–23, he agrees to address the question in a practical way. In June, the Clinical-Therapeutic Institute opens in Arlesheim under the direction of Dr. Ita Wegman. In August, the Chemical-Pharmaceutical Laboratory opens in Arlesheim (Oskar Schmiedel and Ita Wegman, directors). The Clinical-Therapeutic Institute is inaugurated in Stuttgart (Dr. Ludwig Noll, director); also the Research Laboratory in Dornach (Ehrenfried Pfeiffer and Gunther Wachsmuth, directors). In November–December, Rudolf Steiner visits Norway.

1922: The first half of the year involves very active public lecturing (thousands attend); in the second half, Rudolf Steiner begins to withdraw and turn toward the Society—"The Society is asleep." It is "too weak" to do what is asked of it. The businesses—*Die Kommenden Tag* and *Futura A.G.*—fail. In January, with the help of an agent, Steiner undertakes a twelve-city German tour, accompanied by eurythmy performances. In two weeks he speaks to more than 2,000 people. In April, he gives a "college course" in The Hague. He also visits England. In June, he is in Vienna for the East-West Congress. In August–September, he is back in England for the Oxford Conference on Education. Returning to Dornach, he gives the lectures *Philosophy, Cosmology, and Religion* (CW 215), and gives the third priest's course (CW 344). On September 16, The Christian Community is founded. In October–November, Steiner is in Holland and England. He also speaks to the youth: *The Youth Course* (CW 217). In December, Steiner gives lectures titled *The Origins of Natural Science* (CW 326), and *Humanity and the World of Stars: The Spiritual Communion of Humanity* (CW 219). December 31: Fire at the Goetheanum, which is destroyed.

1923: Despite the fire, Rudolf Steiner continues his work unabated. A very hard year. Internal dispersion, dissension, and apathy abound. There is conflict—between old and new visions—within the society. A wake-up call is needed, and Rudolf Steiner responds with renewed lecturing vitality. His focus: the spiritual context of human life; initiation science; the course of the year; and community building. As a foundation for an artistic school, he creates a series of pastel sketches. Lecture cycles: *The Anthroposophic Movement* (CW 258); *Initiation Science* (CW 227) (in England at the Penmaenmawr Summer School); *The Four Seasons and the Archangels* (CW 229); *Harmony of the Creative Word* (CW 230); *The Supersensible Human* (CW 231), given in Holland for the founding of the Dutch society. On November 10, in response to the failed Hitler-Ludendorf putsch in Munich, Steiner closes his Berlin residence and moves the *Philosophisch-Anthroposophisch Verlag* (Press) to Dornach. On December 9, Steiner begins the serialization of his *Autobiography: The Course of My Life* (CW 28) in *Das Goetheanum*. It will continue to appear weekly, without a break, until his death. Late December-early January: Rudolf Steiner refounds the Anthroposophical Society (about 12,000 members internationally) and takes over its leadership. The new board members are: Marie Steiner, Ita Wegman, Albert Steffen, Elizabeth Vreede, and Guenther Wachsmuth. (See *The Christmas Meeting for the Founding of the General Anthroposophical Society* [CW 260]. Accompanying lectures: *Mystery Knowledge and Mystery Centers* [CW 232]; *World History in the Light of Anthroposophy* [CW 233].) December 25: the Foundation Stone is laid (in the hearts of members) in the form of the "Foundation Stone Meditation."

1924: January 1: having founded the Anthroposophical Society and taken over its leadership, Rudolf Steiner has the task of "reforming" it. The process begins with a weekly newssheet ("What's Happening in the Anthroposophical Society") in which Rudolf Steiner's "Letters to Members" and "Anthroposophical Leading Thoughts" appear (CW 26). The next step is the creation of a new esoteric class, the "first class" of the "School for Spiritual Science" (which was to have been followed, had Rudolf Steiner lived longer, by two more advanced classes). Then comes a new language for anthroposophy—practical, phenomenological, and direct—and Rudolf Steiner creates the model for the second Goetheanum. He begins the series of extensive "karma lectures" (CW 235–40); and finally, responding to needs, he creates two new initiatives: biodynamic agriculture and curative education. After the middle of the year, rumors begin to circulate regarding Steiner's health. Lectures: January–February, *Anthroposophy* (CW 234); February: *Eurythmy as Visible Singing* (CW 278); June: *The Agriculture Course* (CW 327); June–July: *Eurythmy as Visible Speech* (CW 279); *Curative Education* (CW 317); August: (England, "Second International Summer School") *Initiation Consciousness: True and False Paths in Spiritual Investigation* (CW 243); September: *Pastoral Medicine* (CW 318). On September 26, for the first time, Rudolf Steiner cancels a lecture. On September 28, he gives his last lecture. On September 29, he withdraws to his studio in the carpenter's shop; now he is definitively ill. Cared for by Ita Wegman, he continues working, however, and writing the weekly installments of his *Autobiography* and *Letters to the Members/Leading Thoughts* (CW 26).

1925: Rudolf Steiner, while continuing to work, continues to weaken. He finishes *Extending Practical Medicine* (CW 27) with Ita Wegman.

On March 30, around ten in the morning, Rudolf Steiner dies.

INDEX

A

T

U

RUDOLF STEINER'S BLACKBOARD DRAWINGS

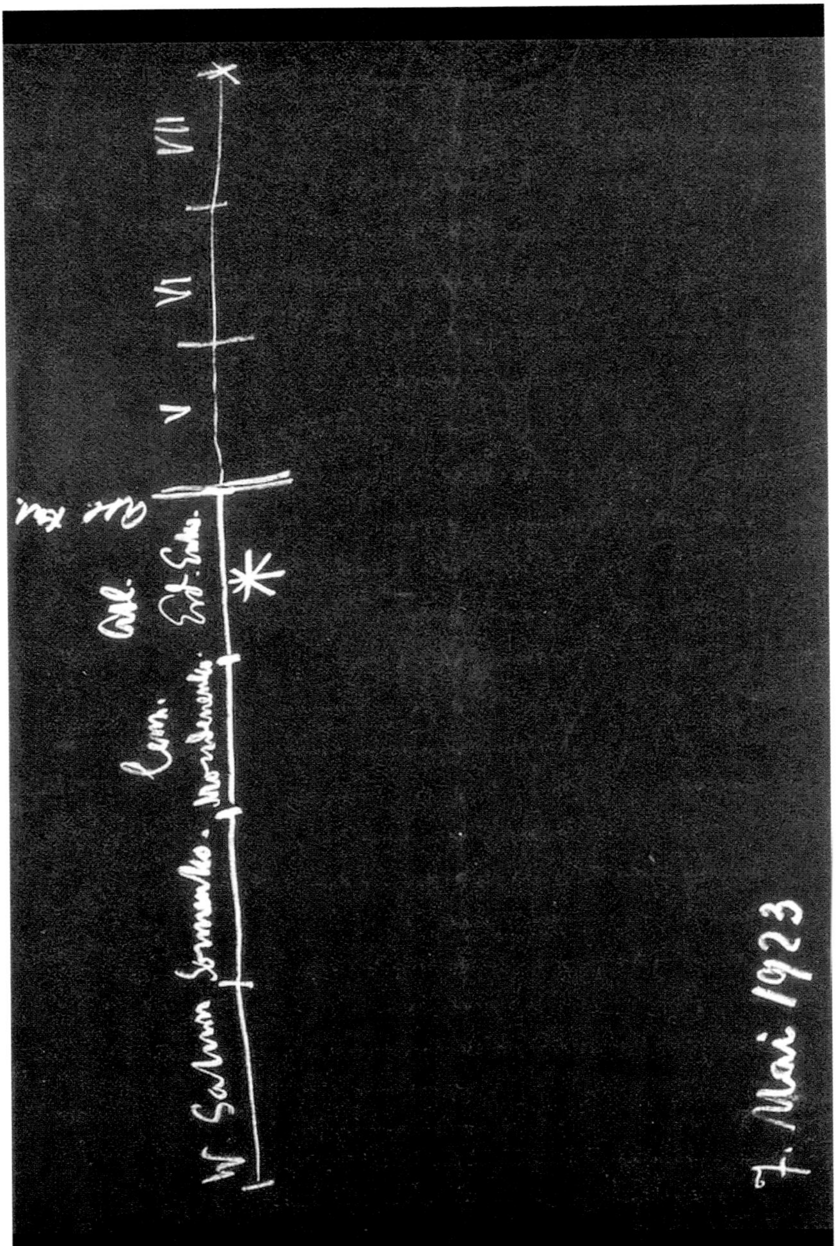

PLATE 1

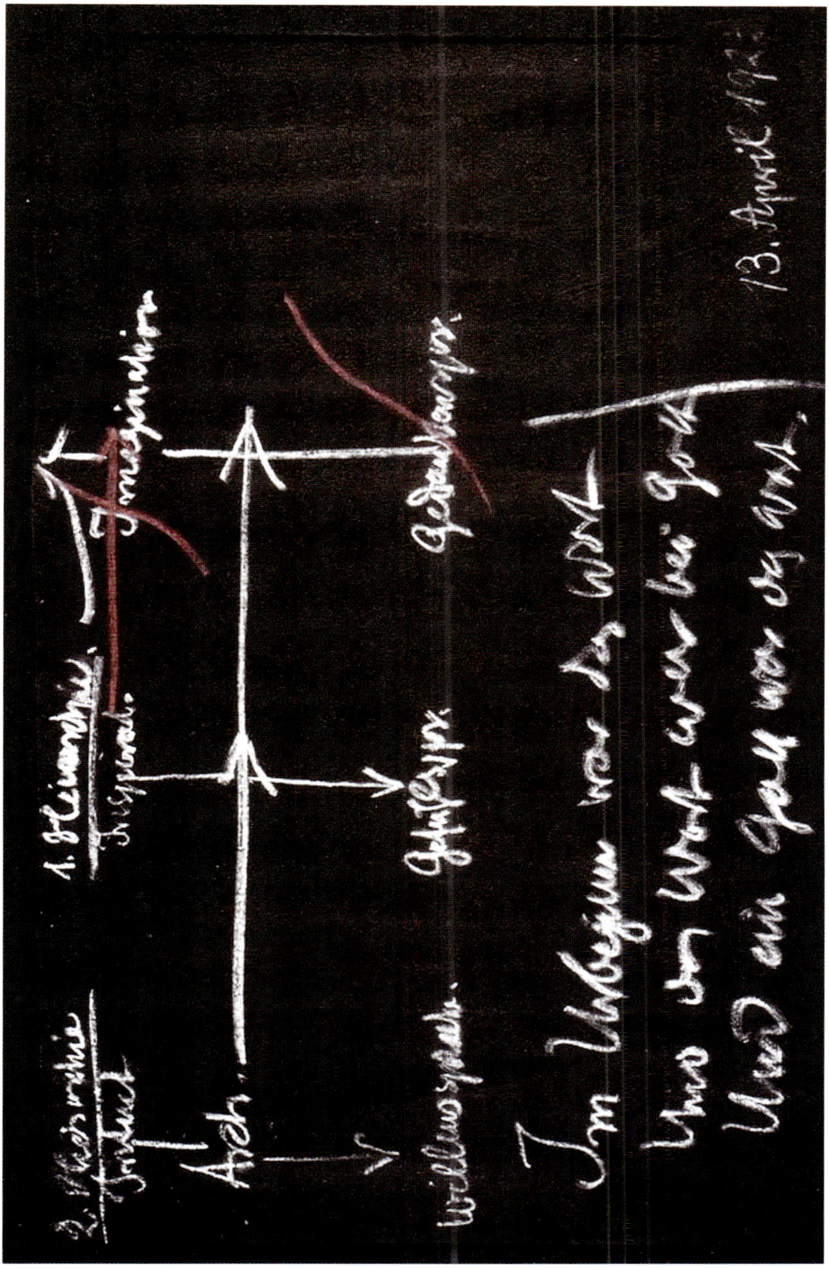
Im Urbeginne war das Wort
Und das Wort war bei Gott
Und ein Gott war das Wort.

PLATE 2